KW-419-180

WITHDRAWN
FROM
UNIVERSITY OF PLYMOUTH
LIBRARY SERVICES

This book is to be returned on
or before the date stamped below

UNIVERSITY OF PLYMOUTH

PLYMOUTH LIBRARY

Tel: (01752) 232323
This book is subject to recall if required by another reader
Books may be renewed by phone
CHARGES WILL BE MADE FOR OVERDUE BOOKS

Butterworths Professional Dictionary Series

DICTIONARY OF
EMPLOYMENT LAW

by

NORMAN SELWYN,
LLM, Dip Econ(Oxon), ACIS

*Barrister. Formerly Lecturer in Law,
University of Aston in Birmingham*

LONDON

BUTTERWORTHS

1985

SOUTH POLYTECHNIC
LIBRARY

Accn.
No.   172642-7

Class.
No.   344.01003 SEL

Contl.   0406207909
No

England	Butterworth & Co (Publishers) Ltd, 88 Kingsway, LONDON WC2B 6AB
Australia	Butterworths Pty Ltd, SYDNEY, MELBOURNE, BRISBANE, ADELAIDE, PERTH, CANBERRA and HOBART
Canada	Butterworth & Co (Canada) Ltd, TORONTO and VANCOUVER
New Zealand	Butterworths of New Zealand Ltd, WELLINGTON and AUCKLAND
Singapore	Butterworth & Co (Asia) Pte Ltd, SINGAPORE
South Africa	Butterworth Publishers (Pty) Ltd, DURBAN and PRETORIA
USA	Butterworth Legal Publishers, ST PAUL, Minnesota, SEATTLE, Washington, BOSTON, Massachusetts, AUSTIN, Texas and D & S Publishers, CLEARWATER, Florida

©Butterworth & Co (Publishers) Ltd 1985

All rights reserved. No part of this publication may be reproduced or transmitted in any form or by any means, including photocopying and recording, without the written permission of the copyright holder, application for which should be addressed to the publisher. Such written permission must also be obtained before any part of this publication is stored in a retrieval system of any nature.

This book is sold subject to the Standard Conditions of Sale of Net Books and may not be re-sold in the UK below the net price fixed by Butterworths for the book in our current catalogue.

British Library Cataloguing in Publication Data
Selwyn, Norman M.
    Butterworths dictionary of employment law.
    1. Labor laws and legislation—Great Britain—
    Dictionaries
    I. Title
    344.104'1125   KD3007.5

ISBN Hard cover 0–406–20790–9
ISBN Soft cover 0–406–20791–7

Printed by Billings Bookplan, Worcester
Typeset by Cotswold Typesetting Limited, Gloucester

Preface

The purpose of this Dictionary is to provide a quick reference to key words and phrases used in modern Employment Law, with special emphasis on how the courts and tribunals interpret the various statutory provisions. I have generally omitted pure statutory definitions, and included some of the more important common law concepts.

Since the proofs of this book were prepared, the Industrial Tribunal (Rules of Procedure) Regulations 1985 came into force, which generally up-date the 1980 Rules, and lay down the procedure for equal value claims. The Government have also announced proposals to restrict claims for unfair dismissal to employees who have been employed continuously for more than two years, although this change will only affect employees who commence employment after the proposed change comes into force.

I hope this book will prove to be of use to practitioners, students, employers and employees generally, particularly when faced with a point of law on which a speedy answer has to be given.

My thanks are due to the staff of Messrs Butterworths for seeing this book through the press with their usual efficiency.

Solihull, West Midlands
March 1985

NORMAN SELWYN

Abbreviations

ACAS   Advisory, Conciliation and Arbitration Service
CRE   Commission for Racial Equality
EA   Employment Act 1980, 1982
EAT   Employment Appeal Tribunal
EDT   Effective date of termination
EMAS   Employment Medical Advisory Service
EPA   Employment Protection Act 1975
EPCA   Employment Protection (Consolidation) Act 1978
EqPA   Equal Pay Act 1970
GOQ   Genuine occupational qualification
HSC   Health and Safety Commission
HSE   Health and Safety Executive
HSWA   Health and Safety at Work etc. Act 1974
LIFO   Last in first out
PHA   Pre-hearing assessment
RRA   Race Relations Act 1976
SDA   Sex Discrimination Act 1975
SJIC   Statutory Joint Industrial Council
TULRA   Trade Union and Labour Relations Act 1974
UMA   Union Membership Agreement

A

A person discriminates (SDA, s. 1 (1) (a); RRA, s. 1 (1) (a)). A
person discriminates on grounds of sex (*Grieg v Community Industry*
[1979] IRLR 158) or race (*R v CRE, ex p Westminster City Council*
[1984] IRLR 230) even though he does so from a worthy motive, and
without an intention to unlawfully discriminate (*Seide v Gillette
Industries Ltd* [1980] IRLR 427). Affirmative evidence of discrimination may consist of inferences drawn from the primary facts
(*Owens & Briggs v James* [1981] IRLR 133).

    See SEX DISCRIMINATION ACT 1975; RACE RELATIONS ACT 1976.

Absent from work (EPCA, Sch. 13, para. 9 (1) (b)). *See* TEMPORARY
CESSATION OF WORK; ARRANGEMENT OR CUSTOM.

Act complained of (RRA, s. 68 (1)). Where a dismissal is alleged to
have been on racial grounds, the act complained of is the termination
of the employment, not the giving of the notice to terminate.
Consequently, the three months' time limit runs from the date the
employment effectively ended (*Lupetti v Wren's Old House Ltd* [1984]
ICR 348).

    See RACE RELATIONS ACT 1976.

Acted reasonably (EPCA, s. 57 (3)). Whether or not a dismissal is fair
or unfair depends on whether, in the circumstances, including the size
and administrative resources of the employer's undertaking, the
employer has acted reasonably or unreasonably in treating the reason
for the dismissal (*qv*) as a sufficient reason, and the question shall be
determined in accordance with equity and the substantial merits (*qv*)
of the case. The test is whether the employer acted reasonably, not
whether the industrial tribunal agreed or disagreed with what the
employer did (*N. C. Walting & Co Ltd v Richardson* [1978] ICR 1049).
In many cases, there will be a number of options available to the
employer, but provided he acts within the band of reasonableness (*qv*)
the fact that not all employers would have taken such action is
irrelevant (*British Leyland (UK) Ltd v Swift* [1981] IRLR 91). The
question to be decided by the industrial tribunal is largely one of fact
(*UCATT v Brain* [1981] IRLR 224), and the EAT will interfere only if
there is a misdirection in law or the decision was so perverse that it
cannot be allowed to stand.

    How, then, does an employer show that he acted reasonably? It is
submitted that the employer must be prepared to show that the

decision to dismiss was made in accordance with procedural fairness and substantive fairness. Procedural fairness requires that there should be a full investigation into the act or incident in question, the employee must be given an opportunity to state his case, to plead mitigating circumstances, to call witnesses, evidence, etc, to have representation by a trade union official or other person of his choice, and an opportunity to appeal to a level of management not previously involved in the decision to dismiss. Problems arise when any of these matters are not complied with, for this may weaken but not necessarily destroy the employer's case. Thus, it may be argued that a full investigation was not possible, or that the result would have been the same had a full investigation been held; a failure to consult with the employee is not necessarily unfair if consultation would have proved fruitless (*Taylorplan Catering (Scotland) Ltd v McInally* [1980] IRLR 53); a failure to allow an employee to state his case or to permit him to have representation, or failure to give him the right of appeal, will not necessarily be unfair if the dismissal would still have been|fair had these procedural defects not taken place (*Sillifant v Powell Duffryn Timber Ltd* [1983] IRLR 91). But the industrial tribunal is not bound to engage in a hypothetical exercise as to what might have happened had the procedural defect not taken place, and they are entitled to say that the procedural unfairness made the dismissal unfair (*Siggs & Chapman (Contractors) Ltd v Knight* [1984] IRLR 83).

More important, however, is the requirement that the dismissal be justified on substantive grounds, in accordance with the equity and substantial merits of the case. Thus an employer should show some consistency (*Post Office v Fennell* [1981] IRLR 221) although the 'tarrif approach' is not necessarily correct (*Hadjioannou v Coral Casinos Ltd* [1981] IRLR 352). The test is 'What would a reasonable employer have done?' (*Iceland Frozen Foods Ltd v Jones* [1983] ICR 17) and in the final analysis this is a question of fact and degree for the industrial tribunal to determine (*Anandarajah v Lord Chancellor's Department* [1984] IRLR 131).

See REASON FOR THE DISMISSAL; EQUITY AND SUBSTANTIAL MERITS.

Action complained of (EPCA, s. 24 (2)). This may include disciplinary hearings, including an appeal against a sanction which itself is action short of dismissal (*British Airways Board v Clark and Havill* [1982] IRLR 238).

See ACTIVITIES OF AN INDEPENDENT TRADE UNION.

Action (short of dismissal) (EPCA, s. 23 (1)). Action includes a refusal to confer a benefit (see s. 153 (1) and *Cheall v Vauxhall Motors Ltd* [1979] IRLR 253) or to subject a person to a disadvantage (*Carlson v Post Office* [1981] IRLR 158). Whether a threat to take action constitutes action is a moot point. The issue was .discussed but left open by the EAT in *Brassington v Cauldron Wholesale Ltd* [1977] IRLR 479 (a threat by the employer that he would close his business if he was forced to recognise a trade union) but in *Grogan v British Railways Board* (unreported, 17 January 1978) the EAT held that a threat to take disciplinary action did constitute action for the purpose of the section (and see the decision of the industrial tribunal in *Carter v Wiltshire County Council* [1979] IRLR 331).

However, there are several examples of situations where a threat to do an act has been held not to be the doing of the act, e.g. see *Conway v Wade* [1909] AC 506, *Midlands Plastics v Till* [1983] IRLR 9).

See ACTIVITIES OF AN INDEPENDENT TRADE UNION.

Activities of an independent trade union (EPCA, ss. 23 (1) (b), 58 (1) (b)). Every employee has the right not to have action taken against him (short of dismissal) and the right not to be dismissed for the purpose of preventing or deterring him from taking part in the activities of an independent trade union (*qv*) at an appropriate time (*qv*), or penalising him for doing so.

The actions of an individual who is a trade union activist do not necessarily constitute the activities of an independent trade union (*Chant v Aquaboats Ltd* [1978] ICR 643). Equally, if a trade union does something on the behalf of employees, this does not mean that the employees are taking part in trade union activities, for the sections are not concerned with the employer's reaction to trade union activities, but with his reaction to an individual employee's activities in a trade union context (*Therm-a-Stor Ltd v Atkins* [1983] IRLR 78).

If an employee alleges that he was dismissed for taking part in the activities of an independent trade union this can only be in respect of his activities within the period of his employment, and does not refer to activities prior to his employment. There is no law which penalises an employer for refusing to employ a trade union activist, or for dismissing him because of his activities in a previous employment (*City of Birmingham v Beyer* [1977] IRLR 211). Similarly, if he is penalised or dismissed for trade union activities, it must be shown that he proposed to carry out those activities at an 'appropriate time' (*qv*). Thus if no such time has been designated, he cannot complain that he has been penalised (*Robb v Leon Motor Services Ltd* [1978] ICR 506).

Unofficial action by shop stewards does not constitute trade union activities (*McQuade v Scotbeef Ltd* [1975] IRLR 332), nor do the sections give any protection to unconstitutional action (*Stokes and Roberts v Wheeler Green Ltd* [1979] IRLR 211).

See ACTION (SHORT OF DISMISSAL); REASON FOR THE DISMISSAL — TRADE UNION MEMBERSHIP/ACTIVITIES.

Additional award (EPCA, s. 71 (3)). If an industrial tribunal makes an order for reinstatement or re-engagement, but the employer fails to comply, then unless the employer shows that it was not practicable for him to comply with the order, the industrial tribunal will make the normal compensatory award, and an additional award (but not in circumstances where a special award is appropriate). The additional award shall be (a) between 26 and 52 weeks pay if the reason for the dismissal was an act of race or sex discrimination, or (b) between 13 and 26 weeks pay in any other case (*George v Beecham Group Ltd* [1977] IRLR 43). The week's pay for this purpose is subject to the statutory limit of (currently) £152 per week.

See COMPENSATORY AWARD; SPECIAL AWARD.

Advertisements (SDA, s. 38 (1)). In determining whether or not an advertisement indicates an intention to discriminate unlawfully, it must be read as a whole, according to what ordinary reasonable person, without any special knowledge, would find to be the natural and ordinary meaning of the words used. It is not permissible to show what meaning was intended by the advertiser (*Equal Opportunities Commission v Robertson* [1980] IRLR 44).

See SEX DISCRIMINATION.

Advisory, Conciliation and Arbitration Service (ACAS) (EPA, s. 1). Formed in 1974 by Royal Warrant, and placed on a statutory basis in 1975, ACAS is an independent organisation which provides advisory, conciliation and arbitration services, which are available, free of charge, to anyone. The Council of ACAS consists of a chairman, three representatives of employers' organisations, three trade union representatives, and three 'independent' members.

Basically, ACAS performs six general functions. First, where a trade dispute is apprehended or exists, it may offer its assistance to bring about a settlement, by way of conciliation or otherwise. Due regard shall be had to the desirability of encouraging the parties to use any appropriate agreed procedure. It should be noted that the definition of 'trade dispute' for the purpose of this function is the old definition found in s. 29 of TULRA (see EPA, s. 126A), not the new definition based on TULRA but amended by the Employment Act 1982. Thus, for conciliation purposes, the old definition of 'trade dispute' is preserved. Second, ACAS has important conciliation services to offer when individual complaints are made to an industrial tribunal. A copy of every such complaint will be sent to ACAS, who have a duty to try to effect a settlement, whether by way of withdrawal, reinstatement or re-engagement, or a financial settlement. However, an ACAS conciliation officer has no power to persuade a party to settle, or to compel him to do so. His duty is to faithfully record any agreement reached, and in doing so, he is not bound to follow any particular formula. If the settlement is one of reinstatement or re-engagement, it shall be on terms appearing to the conciliation officer to be equitable, but he is under no duty to see that a financial settlement is fair, as long as the parties have agreed to it (*Moore v Duport Furniture Products Ltd* [1982] IRLR 131). Any settlement thus reached is legally binding on the parties, whether made verbally or in writing (EPCA, s. 140 (2), and see *Slack v Greenham (Plant Hire) Ltd* [1983] IRLR 271). Third, where a trade dispute exists or is apprehended, ACAS will provide, with the consent of all the parties to the dispute, arbitration facilities, either by the appointment of someone who is not an officer or servant of ACAS, or utilising the Central Arbitration Committee (*qv*). Fourth, ACAS will provide advice, free of charge, on a wide range of employment and industrial relations matters to anyone, and may publish general advice on such matters. Fifth, ACAS may hold an enquiry into industrial relations matters generally, or in a particular industry, or a particular undertaking, which may be published. Sixth, ACAS may issue Codes of Practice containing such practical guidance as it thinks fit for the purpose of improving industrial relations. A failure on the part of any person to observe the provisions of the Codes shall not render him liable to any proceedings, but in any proceedings before an industrial tribunal or the Central Arbitration Committee, any relevant provision of the Codes shall be taken into account in determining the question to be decided.

See AGREED SETTLEMENT; CONCILIATION OFFICER; CODES OF PRACTICE.

Age of retirement. See NORMAL RETIRING AGE.

Agreed procedure (EPCA, s. 59 (b)). If an employee is dismissed for reason of redundancy and he is selected for dismissal contrary to an agreed procedure, then his dismissal will be unfair, unless there were special reasons justifying a departure from that procedure in his case. But this only applies if there is an actual agreement on the procedure to be adopted; a policy statement made by the employer unilaterally, which has no legal implications is not an agreement (*Jackson v General Accident, Fire and Life Assurance Co Ltd* [1976] IRLR 338).

An agreed procedure can be expressed or implied. It will be implied if it has been operated for many years without opposition from a recognised trade union (*Henry v Ellerman City Liners Ltd* [1984] IRLR 409).

Once an agreement has been reached, both parties must agree to any alteration (*Tilgate Pallets Ltd v Barras* [1983] IRLR 231). The procedure can be an ad hoc agreement reached when redundancies have been announced (*Evans & Morgan v AB Electrical Components Ltd* [1981] IRLR 111). Once an employer follows and adheres to the agreed procedure, it is difficult to envisage that a dismissal can be unfair under s. 57 (3) (*Valor Newhome Ltd v Hampson* [1982] ICR 407). But if the agreed procedure is not followed, the industrial tribunal must ascertain whether there were special reasons for departing from it, and if so, consider whether the dismissal was fair under s. 57 (3) (*GEC Machines Ltd v Gilford* [1982] ICR 725). Further, s. 59 (b) is only concerned with unfair selection; if there is a violation of the consultation provisions of an agreed procedure, the fairness again must be tested under s. 57 (3) (*McDowell v Eastern British Road Services Ltd* [1981] IRLR 482).

As long as there is evidence that the employers have followed the agreed procedure, honestly and conscienciously, it is not the function of the EAT to engage in a detailed analysis of the industrial tribunal's findings and decision (*Kearney & Trecker Marwin Ltd v Varndell* [1983] IRLR 335).

See REDUNDANCY: CUSTOMARY ARRANGEMENT.

Agreed settlement (EPCA, s. 134). Once a financial settlement has been agreed under the auspices of the conciliation officer, who has acted impartially, it is binding on the parties. The conciliation officer is under no duty to advise or inform the employee of his rights under the relevant legislation, but only to endeavour to promote a settlement where appropriate. How he performs this function is a matter for his discretion, depending on the circumstances of the case. In the absence of bad faith, or unfair methods, the agreement will bind in accordance with s. 140 (2) (d), (*Slack v Greenham Plant Hire*) *Ltd* [1983] IRLR 271).

See ADVISORY CONCILIATION AND ARBITRATION SERVICE; CONCILIATION OFFICER.

Agreement with the employee (EPCA, s. 94 (2)). The agreement of the employee to the renewal of his contract or his re-engagement under a new contract, when a new owner takes over the business, can be express or implied (*Ubsdell v Paterson* [1973] ICR 86).

Alternative work. If an employee is unable to perform his normal duties because of ill-health or injury, a reasonable employer will at least look around to see if there is any other alternative work the employee can perform rather than dismiss him. The employer is not expected to go to unreasonable lengths in order to accommodate an employee who cannot carry out his normal duties, but he ought to look at the matter in some detail to see if arrangements can be made. What is reasonable is a question of fact and degree for the industrial tribunal to determine (*Garrick (Caterers) Ltd v Nolan* [1980] IRLR 259) bearing in mind the size of the firm (*Bevan Harris Ltd v Gair* [1981] IRLR 520).

See REASON FOR DISMISSAL – ILL-HEALTH.

Alternative work (EPCA, s. 13 (4) (a)). Since the alternative work can be work other than that which the employee contracted to do, and since it will only be a temporary feature, it is suggested that a wide range of work can be offered (*Purdey v Willowbrook International Ltd* [1977] IRLR 388).

See GUARANTEE PAY.

Amendment to the pleadings. Either party may always apply to the industrial tribunal for an amendment to be made to the pleadings where this is necessary in order to give a correct 'label' to a fully established set of facts (*Nelson v BBC* [1979] IRLR 346) but not for the purpose of establishing a completely new set of facts which would materially affect the outcome of the case (*Blue Star Ship Management Ltd v Williams* [1979] IRLR 16). The amendment, at a late stage, cannot be anything other than technical. The industrial tribunal should ask themselves

(1) does the unamended originating application comply with the Industrial Tribunal (Rules of Procedure) Regulations 1980, r. 1, Sch. 1?

(2) if not, there is no power to amend, and a new originating application must be made;

(3) if it did, was the unamended originating application made within the appropriate time limit;

(4) if not, there is no power to allow the amendment;

(5) if it was, the industrial tribunal have discretion to allow the amendment;

(6) in deciding whether or not to allow the amendment to add or substitute a new party, the industrial tribunal should only do so if they are satisfied that the mistake sought to be corrected was a genuine mistake and was not misleading;

(7) in deciding to exercise their discretion, regard should be had to all the circumstances of the case. In particular they should have regard to the injustice or hardship which may be caused to any of the parties if the proposed amendment was allowed or refused (*Cocking v Sandhurst Ltd* [1974] ICR 650).

An act done (TULRA, s. 13 (1)). A threat to do an act is not an act, unless the threat is accompanied by an act (*Conway v Wade* [1909] AC 506).

See TRADE DISPUTE.

Announcement. An announcement of impending redundancies does not constitute a dismissal for reason of redundancy, and hence an employee who leaves before he has been officially selected for dismissal cannot obtain a redundancy payment (*Morton Sundour Fabrics Ltd v Shaw* [1966] 2 ITR 84). This is so even though a date has been given when all production will cease (*Doble v Firestone Tyres Ltd* [1981] IRLR 300).

See REASON FOR THE DISMISSAL − REDUNDANCY.

Annual reports of companies (Companies Act 1985, ss. 235, 261(5),

Sch. 7, Pts 1, IV, V, Sch. 10). Any company which employs on average 250 employees or more throughout the year (excluding overseas employees) must include in its annual report a statement describing the action taken during the financial year to introduce, maintain and develop arrangements aimed at (1) providing employees systematically with with information on matters of concern to them as employees (2) consulting employees or their representatives on a regular basis so that their views may be taken into account in making decisions which are likely to affect their interests (3) encouraging the involvement of employees in the company's performance through schemes or otherwise (4) achieving a common awareness on the part of all employees of the financial and economic factors affecting the performance of the company. It should be noted that there is no requirement that such action be actually taken, only that a statement should be made describing such action as has been taken.

Any company of the size described above must also include in its annual report a statement as to the company's policy during the previous financial year (1) for giving full and fair consideration to applications for employment made by disabled persons having regard to their particular aptitudes and abilities (2) for continuing employment and for making appropriate training arrangements for employees who have become disabled persons during the period when they were employed by the company (3) for the training, career development and promotion of disabled persons employed by the company. Again, the Act does not require a company to have a policy, merely to describe such policy as the company has applied.

Any other benefits, facilities or services (RRA, s. 4 (2) (b)). A refusal to investigate complaints of unfair treatment may amount to a refusal of access to any benefit, facilities or services. However, to be in breach of the Race Relations Act, such refusal to investigate must be based on racial grounds (*Eke v Commrs of Customs and Excise* [1981] IRLR 334).

See RACE RELATIONS ACT 1976.

Appeal (internal). The importance of having an internal appeal machinery as part of a disciplinary procedure is stressed in the ACAS Code of Practice (No. 1), para. 10, though in small firms this might not prove to be practicable. An appeal should be heard by senior management who have not previously been involved in the matter. The fact that the person hearing the appeal knows of the circumstances of the case is not fatal (*Rowe v Radio Rentals* [1982] IRLR 177) but if he has already formed a preliminary view, the employee or his adviser should be informed, and all the circumstances fully investigated in order to ensure that there is a genuine reconsideration of the case (*Johnson Matthey Metals Ltd v Harding* [1978] IRLR 248).

8

If immediate notice of dismissal is given, it will take effect at once, and that date will constitute the effective date of termination for the purposes of (i) calculating the period of continuous employment (*qv*) and (ii) calculating the period of three months within which the claim for unfair dismissal must be brought, even though an appeal is pending (*Crown Agents etc v Lawal* [1978] IRLR 542). However, it is implicit that if the appeal is allowed, the intervening period (i.e. between the dismissal and appeal) is one of suspension, for the ultimate decision of the appeal relates back to the date on which the purported dismissal was effected. Thus, if the appeal is allowed, there is no break in continuity of employment (*Howgate v Fane Accoustics Ltd* [1981] IRLR 161).

A refusal to allow an employee to exercise his contractual right of appeal can render a dismissal unfair (*West Midlands Co-op v Tipton* [1985] IRLR 116).

See DISCIPLINARY PROCEDURE; EFFECTIVE DATE OF TERMINATION.

Appeal to the Employment Appeal Tribunal. An appeal to the EAT must be lodged within 42 days of the date on which the industrial tribunal's decision was sent, although an extension of time may be applied for. Time will run from that date, even though legal aid has been applied for, or an application for review has been made, or the case has been adjourned pending a decision on remedies (see e.g. *Firestone Tyre and Rubber Co Ltd v Challoner* [1977] IRLR 223).

All appeals are initially vetted by the Registrar, who may decide to reject on the ground of lack of jurisdiction, so informing the appellant. No further action will be taken unless a fresh appeal is brought either within the original 42 days' limit or within 28 days from the Registrar's decision, whichever is the later date. If it is felt that no arguable point of law is disclosed in the appeal, the case may be set down on a preliminary point, when the appellant will have to show cause why the appeal should not be dismissed. The respondent does not need to attend at this stage. If cause is shown, the case will be set down for hearing in the usual way.

The appeal must be drawn up on one of the simple forms (home-made copies are permissible) used by the EAT, which should contain sufficient particulars to show the grounds for the appeal (i.e. the point of law must be identified). There is a special procedure if there is an allegation of bias or misconduct on the part of the industrial tribunal (*Practice Direction 1981* ([1981] ICR 287)).

Legal aid is available for appeals to the EAT.

On an appeal, the EAT will hear new evidence, but only if it can be shown that there was a reasonable explanation for the evidence not being produced in the industrial tribunal, that the evidence was credible, and that it might have affected the outcome (*International*

Aviation Services v Jones [1979] IRLR 155). On an appeal, the EAT can exercise all the powers of the industrial tribunal, and may make any decision or award the tribunal could have made. The appeal may also be allowed, dismissed, or remitted to the industrial tribunal for further consideration. Costs may be awarded against a party if there is unreasonable conduct in bringing or pursuing the appeal.

If there is no actual dispute between the parties (e.g. a complainant has been reinstated) an appeal to establish a point of principle will not be entertained (*IMI Yorkshire Imperial Ltd v Olender* [1982] ICR 69).

If an appeal is being made on a point of law, the EAT must accept the findings of fact made by the industrial tribunal, unless it is clear that on the evidence no reasonable tribunal could have reached those findings. If the EAT would have reached a different conclusion on those facts they must resist the temptation to treat those findings of fact as holdings of law, or mixed fact and law, and the decision should not be reversed merely because the EAT would not have reached the same conclusion on the facts (*Martin v MBS Fastenings (Glynwed) Distributions Ltd* [1983] IRLR 198).

The EAT is entitled to interfere with the decision of the industrial tribunal only if the industrial tribunal (1) has misdirected itself in law, or (2) entertained the wrong issue or proceeded under a misapprehension or misconstrued the evidence, or (3) taken into account matters which were irrelevant to its decision, or (4) reached a decision so extravagent that no reasonable tribunal, properly directing itself on the law, could have arrived at (per Lord President Emslie in *Melon v Hector Power Ltd* [1980] IRLR 80).

See EMPLOYMENT APPEAL TRIBUNAL; CHAIRMAN'S NOTES; COMPLAINTS OF BIAS; COSTS.

Applications forms. The fact that an employee makes a false statement when he applies for employment does not render the contract void, or provide *per se* a justification for dismissal, even though the application form contains a statement to this effect (*Johnson v Tesco Stores Ltd* [1976] IRLR 103). *A fortiori*, if the falsity consists of the denial of a 'spent conviction' under the terms of the Rehabilitation of Offenders Act 1974 (*Property Guards Ltd v Taylor and Kershaw* [1982] IRLR 175). But a false statement could amount to 'conduct' (*Torr v British Railways Board* [1977] IRLR 184) or 'some other substantial reason' (*De Baughn v Star Cinemas (London) Ltd*, unreported) which are capable of being fair grounds for dismissal should the statement be in respect of a criminal conviction which is not spent.

There is generally no duty on an employee to volunteer information about himself which is inimical to his potential employer other than in response to a direct question (*Walton v TAC Construction Ltd* [1981] IRLR 357).

See REHABILITATION OF OFFENDERS.

Apprentice. A contract of apprenticeship is a contract whereby the apprentice binds himself to an employer in order to learn a trade and the employer agrees to teach and instruct him. There must be a written agreement, signed by the parties, and the contract cannot be terminated by the employer except for gross misconduct or a refusal by the apprentice to carry out his duties. An apprentice who is wrongfully dismissed may claim by way of damages a sum which represents the loss of his future prospects as a qualified person (*Dunk v George Waller & Son Ltd* [1970] 2 All ER 630). An employer stands *in loco parentis* vis-à-vis an apprentice, and therefore should not dismiss him for an isolated incident, but only for grave misconduct (*Shortland Ltd v Chantrill* [1975] IRLR 208). An apprentice who has been dismissed unfairly should, if possible, be given an opportunity to finish his apprenticeship, and thus the industrial tribunal will give strong consideration to reinstatement or re-engagement as an appropriate remedy (*Stanton v Woolfenden's Cranes Ltd* [1972] IRLR 82). Once an apprenticeship has been completed, this is equivalent to the expiry of a fixed term contract, and if the employer is unable to offer employment as a fully qualified employee, there is no obligation to make a redundancy payment (*North East Coast Ship Repairers Ltd v Secretary of State for Employment* [1978] IRLR 148).

Appropriate time (EPCA, s. 23 (2), s. 58 (2)). An employee has the right not to have action taken against him by his employer (whether by dismissal or action short of dismissal) for the purpose of preventing or deterring him from taking part in trade union activities at an appropriate time, or penalising him for doing so. Appropriate time is defined as being (a) outside his working hours or (b) within his working hours when, in accordance with arrangements agreed with, or consent given by his employer, it is permissible for him to take part in those activities. Working hours is defined as being time when, in accordance with his contract the employee is required to be at work. Thus an employee can take part in trade union activities outside working hours without restriction (*Miller v Rafique* [1975] IRLR 70). This can be when he is still on the employer's premises e.g. a social club (*Post Office v Crouch* [1974] IRLR 22) or in the canteen at tea-break (*Zucker v Astrid Jewels Ltd* [1978] IRLR 385) for these are not working hours.

If the activity is carried on within working hours, there must be an express or implied agreement to this effect (*Robb v Leon Motor Services Ltd* [1978] IRLR 26). The agreement or arrangement need not be a formal one, and permission is not limited to the cases where express consent has been given. Thus, if a shop steward of a recognised trade union takes up a grievance on behalf of a member, this will be a trade union activity at the appropriate time even if the management has not given specific permission for him to do so, for the permission can be inferred from the willingness of the management to work together with the trade union. No such agreement can be implied if the trade union is not recognised (*Marley Tile Ltd v Shaw* [1980] IRLR 25).

The right applies to all trade union members, not just to shop stewards. If there is a union membership agreement (*qv*) in force, the right applies only to the activities of the specified trade union in so far as the activities are carried out on the employer's premises.

See ACTIVITIES OF AN INDEPENDENT TRADE UNION; ACTION (SHORT OF DISMISSAL).

Arrangement or custom (EPCA, Sch. 13, para. 9 (1) (c)). If an employee is absent from work by virtue of an arrangement or custom, the period of absence will not break his continuity of employment. The arrangement or custom must be agreed or be in existence before the absence commences (*Murphy v Birrell & Sons Ltd* [1978] IRLR 458). The burden is on the applicant to show that there was an arrangement or custom (*Brown v Southall and Knight* [1980] IRLR 130), and the circumstances must be such that the employee is regarded as continuing in employment despite his absence (*Southern Electricity Board v Collins* [1969] 2 All ER 1166).

See CONTINUOUS EMPLOYMENT.

Arrangements (SDA, s. 6 (1) (a); RRA, s. 4 (1) (a)). A job advertisement is an arrangement (*Brindley v Tayside Health Authority* [1976] IRLR 364) as is the asking of questions at an interview (*Panesar v Nestle Co Ltd* [1980] IRLR 60) or excluding a person from a short-list of candidates (*Brennan v Dewhurst Butchers Ltd* [1983] IRLR 357), or the restricting of recruitment from certain areas, or excluding recruitment from areas (*Hussein v Saints Complete House Furnishers* [1979] IRLR 337). If the arrangement is designed to be discriminatory, or in practice operates in a discriminatory manner, an aggrieved person may bring a complaint (*Saunders v Richmond London Borough Council* [1977] IRLR 362). It is irrelevant that no contract of employment comes into existence, for at the time of the discriminatory arrangements, no contract of employment can be in existence (*Roadburg v Lothian Regional Council* [1976] IRLR 283).

See SEX DISCRIMINATION ACT 1975; RACE RELATIONS ACT 1976.

Associated employer (EPCA, s. 153 (4); SDA, s. 82 (2)). Two employers are to be treated as being associated if one is a company of which the other (directly or indirectly) has control, or if both are companies of which a third person (directly or indirectly) has control. Since by the Interpretation Act 1978, s. 6 the singular includes the plural, the word 'person' can mean 'persons'. Thus, if two or more persons (whether natural or artificial) own more than 50% of the shares of two separate companies, both companies are associated (*Umar v Pliastar Ltd* [1981] ICR 727). But if the 'third person' who has control of two companies is in fact two or more persons, they must be the same individuals in respect of both companies. Thus if a man, together with his wife, controls company A, and he, together with his sister, controls company B, the two companies are not associated (*Poparm Ltd v Weeks* [1984] IRLR 388). 'Control' is a legal, not a factual test (*Washington Arts Association Ltd v Forster* [1983] ICR 346) to be determined by the number of votes attached to the shares, exercised in the company's general meeting (*Secretary of State for Employment v Newbold* [1981] IRLR 305). The definition of control does not extend to 'negative control' so as to mean that a person who has exactly 50% of the shareholding of a company has control, because he can thwart the wishes of those who hold the remaining 50% (*Hair Colour Consultants Ltd v Mena* [1984] IRLR 386). If a group of persons act as one, in respect of two companies, there is control (*Zarb and Samuels v British and Brazilian Produce Co (Sales) Ltd* [1978] IRLR 78).

Associated employers can only be companies (*Gardiner v London Borough of Merton* [1980] IRLR 472).

See CONTINUOUS EMPLOYMENT: OVERSEAS ASSOCIATED EMPLOYER.

Assumptions. It is dangerous to make sexist assumptions, such as 'women with children make unreliable employees' (*Hurley v Mustoe* [1981] IRLR 208), 'the man will be the breadwinner of the family' (*Skyrail Oceanic v Coleman* [1981] IRLR 398), 'married women will give up their employment to follow their husbands' (*Horsey v Dyfed County Council* [1982] IRLR 395).

See SEX DISCRIMINATION ACT 1975.

At the earliest opportunity (EPA, s. 99 (3)). As soon as the employer decides that redundancies are inevitable, consultation should begin, and should precede any dismissal notices, otherwise there may be serious doubt that the consultations are genuine (*NUT v Avon County Council* [1978] IRLR 55).

See CONSULTATION ON REDUNDANCIES.

Attachment of earnings. A court may make an order directing an employer to deduct a specified sum of money from an employee's wages and send the sum to the court. The court may fix the employee's protected earnings, which is the minimum remuneration which the employee is to receive, although arrears may be deducted subsequently. Once the employee ceases to be employed, the employer must notify the court. The employer is entitled to make a small charge to cover administrative expenses (see the Attachment of Earnings Act 1971).

Attempt to procure (RRA, s. 30). *See* PROCURE OR ATTEMPT TO PROCURE.

Attributable (EPCA, s. 74 (1)). The loss of a tax rebate (which would otherwise be payable) is an aspect of loss of wages, and therefore is a loss attributable to the action of unfair dismissal taken by an employer (*Lucas v Laurence Scott Ltd* [1983] IRLR 61).

See COMPENSATORY AWARD.

Average hourly rate of remuneration (EPCA, Sch. 14, Part II, para. 3). In calculating the average hourly rate of remuneration, regard must be had only to those hours when the employee was working, and only to remuneration apportioned to those hours. Employees are not working if they are not on the employer's premises, even though they are receiving fall back pay (*Adams v John Wright & Sons Ltd* [1972] ICR 463).

See REDUNDANCY PAY.

B

Ballots on employer's premises (EA 1980, s. 2). At the request of the representatives of an independent trade union, an employer, so far as is reasonably practicable, shall permit the use of his premises to give his employees who are members of that union a convenient opportunity of voting in a ballot held by the union. The ballot must be for one of the statutory purposes and must be a secret one. This provision does not apply to employers who employ less than 21 employees. A failure by an employer to permit a trade union to use the premises in accordance with this section may result in a complaint to an industrial tribunal, which may make an award of compensation. *See* PUBLIC FUNDS FOR BALLOTS.

Ban on overtime. *See* OTHER INDUSTRIAL ACTION.

Band of reasonableness. There is a band of reasonableness within which one employer might reasonably dismiss the employee while another employer might reasonably keep him on. It depends entirely on the circumstances of the case. If it is reasonable to dismiss, a dismissal is fair even though another employer may not have taken such a step (*British Leyland (UK) Ltd v Swift* [1981] IRLR 91). The function of the industrial tribunal, acting as an industrial jury, is to determine whether in the particular circumstances of the case the decision to dismiss fell within the band of reasonable responses which a reasonable employer may have adopted. If the decision falls outside that band, it is unfair (*Iceland Frozen Foods v Jones* [1982] IRLR 439). *See* ACTED REASONABLY; EQUITY AND SUBSTANTIAL MERITS.

Bank holidays. Schedule 1 (as amended) of the Banking and Financial Dealings Act 1971 specifies those days which are designated as Bank holidays. In addition, there are certain days which are customary holidays (referred to as Public holidays) and other days which may be specified as Public holidays by Royal Proclamation (e.g. on the day of a Royal Wedding, etc.). The current list is as follows;

15

Basic award

Bank holidays

England and Wales	Scotland	Northern Ireland
1 January	1 January	1 January
Easter Monday	2 January	17 March
1st Monday in May	Good Friday	Easter Monday
Last Monday in May	1st Monday in May	1st Monday in May
Last Monday in August	Last Monday in May	Last Monday in May
26 December	1st Monday in August	12 July
	Christmas Day	Last Monday in August
	26 December	26 December

Public holidays

Good Friday	Good Friday
Christmas Day	Christmas Day

If any of the above days falls on a Saturday or Sunday, the following Monday is a holiday, unless the Monday is already a holiday, in which case the Tuesday becomes the holiday.

There is no automatic entitlement to have a holiday on the above days, for this will depend on the terms of the contract. Thus management may retain the right to transfer a holiday from Bank or Public holiday to another day. However, the Factories Act 1961 requires an employer in England to allow Bank holidays, Christmas Day and Good Friday to women and young persons, although another day may be specified by the employer, on giving three weeks notice posted in the factory. In Scotland, the employer must give six weekdays as holidays to women and young persons, the actual dates being fixed by the employer, except that in burghs, two of these days shall be fixed by the town council.

Wages Councils and the Agricultural Wages Boards may by Order fix specified days (including Bank holidays) as holidays for those persons whose wages are regulated by the Council.

See HOLIDAYS.

Basic award (EPCA, s. 73). The basic award is calculated on the following scale:
 (a) for each year's employment below the age of 22, one half of a week's pay;
 (b) for each year's employment between the ages of 22 and 40, one week's pay;
 (c) for each year's employment between the ages of 41 and 64 (men) or 59 (women), one and a half week's pay.

The week's pay is subject to the statutory maximum of (currently) £152 per week, and not more than 20 weeks are to be counted. The basic award shall be reduced by 1/12th for each month when, at the time of the effective date of termination (*qv*) the employee was over the age of 64 (men) or 59 (women), until it is extinguished entirely at the ages of 65 or 60 respectively.

In two cases, the basic award will be two weeks pay. These are when the employee has been dismissed for reason of redundancy, and either (a) the employer has made an offer under s. 82 (3) to renew his contract of employment, or re-engage him under a new contract, and the employee unreasonably refuses that offer (*qv*) (s. 82 (5)), or (b) if such an offer of a new contract is made, or re-engagement offered, and after the trial period the employee terminates the employment, he will still be treated as having been dismissed, and even though the termination amounts to an unreasonable refusal (s. 82 (6)) he will be regarded as having been dismissed (despite s. 84 (1)) and entitled to two weeks basic award (s. 73 (2)).

If the dismissal is unfair because of s. 58 (on grounds of trade union membership or non-membership, or s. 59 (a) (unfair selection for redundancy on grounds of trade union membership or non-membership) the Basic award shall be a minimum of (currently) £2100.

The Basic award can be reduced (a) if the employee contributed towards the dismissal (b) if he unreasonably refuses an offer for reinstatement (c) because of the employee's conduct before the dismissal (whether or not discovered before or after the dismissal) (d) by any amount awarded by the industrial tribunal, or any payment made by the employer, in respect of redundancy (e) by any compensation made under the Sex Discrimination Act 1975 or the Race Relations Act 1976 in respect of the same matter.

See COMPENSATORY AWARD.

Before the end of the period of six months (EPCA, s. 101). An employee will not be entitled to a redundancy payment unless before the end of the period of six months beginning with the relevant date (*qv*) (a) the payment has been agreed and paid; (b) the employee has made a claim in writing to the employer (but if he gives notice before the relevant date, this does not comply with s. 101 (1) (b), see *Watts v Rubery Owen Conveyancer Ltd* [1977] 2 All ER 1); (c) a question as to the right to a redundancy payment, or the amount, has been referred to an industrial tribunal; (d) a complaint of unfair dismissal has been presented. However, the industrial tribunal has a discretion to allow the redundancy payment if either (b) (c) or (d) above happens within a further six months having regard to the reason shown by the employee for his failure to take any of these steps earlier, and all other relevant circumstances.

See REDUNDANCY.

Benefits, facilities or services (SDA, s. 6 (2) (a); RRA, s. 4 (2) (b)). The maxim '*de minimus non curat lex*' (the law does not concern itself with trifles) applies to complaints that an employer has failed to allow access to any benefits, facilities or services (*Peake v Automotive Products Ltd* [1977] IRLR 365). If there is a denial of a benefit which is of a continuing nature, the effect of past discrimination must be removed (*Steel v Union of Post Office Workers* [1977] IRLR 288). A refusal to investigate a complaint of discrimination may amount to the denial of a benefit, if the reason for the refusal was on grounds of race or sex (*Eke v Customs and Excise Commissioners* [1981] IRLR 334).

See SEX DISCRIMINATION ACT 1975; RACE RELATIONS ACT 1976).

Body corporate (TULRA, s. 2 (1)). A trade union which is not on the special register is not a body corporate, and hence does not have legal personality, save that it can carry out those functions expressly mentioned in the various statutes. But the lack of corporate personality means that (for example) it cannot sue for libel (*EEPTU v Times Newspapers Ltd* [1980] 1 All ER 1097).

See INDEPENDENT TRADE UNION.

Bonus. An obligation to pay a bonus can be contractual or non-contractual (*WPM Retail Ltd v Lang* [1978] IRLR 243), depending on the true construction of the contract (*Bond v CAV Ltd* [1983] IRLR 360). A weekly bonus can also constitute part of the week's pay for the purpose of calculating the amount of redundancy payment (*Donelan v Kerrby Construction Ltd* [1983] IRLR 191).

See REDUNDANCY PAY.

Breach of contract. The fact that an employer is in breach of the contract of employment does not automatically mean that a dismissal is unfair (*Brandon & Gould v Murphy Bros* [1983] IRLR 54); equally, if the employee is in breach of contract a dismissal may still be unfair (*Ladbroke Racing v Arnott* [1983] IRLR 154). If an employee's contract includes the disciplinary procedure, a failure to follow that procedure can lead to an application for an injunction to restrain a breach (*Gunton v London Borough of Richmond* [1980] IRLR 321), although whether or not the court will grant such a remedy is a matter of discretion (*R v BBC, ex p Lavelle* [1982] IRLR 404).

An employer may still seek common law remedies for breach of contract (*Janata Bank v Ahmed* [1981] IRLR 457), as may an employee (*Robertson v British Gas Corpn* [1983] IRLR 302).

Bringing any proceedings (EPCA, s. 140 (1)). There are two stages in the complaints procedure: (a) the presentation of a complaint to the industrial tribunal, and (b) the bringing of any proceedings. The former phrase refers to the initiation of proceedings, the latter to the proceedings which follow thereafter. Consequently, a settlement reached after a complaint has been presented, but before the industrial tribunal has heard the claim, is void under s. 140 (1) unless validated by the provisions of s. 140 (2) (*Naqvi v Stephens Jewellers Ltd* [1978] ICR 631).

See VOID; CONCILIATION OFFICER.

Broadly similar nature (EqPA, s. 1 (4)). To decide whether or not the work is of a broadly similar nature, two questions must be posed. The first is to look at the general considerations of the type of work involved, and the skill and knowledge required to do it. There does not have to be a minute examination of the differences between the work done by a man and a woman. Second, if the work is thus broadly similar, are the differences between the work of practical importance in relation to the terms and conditions of employment, so that it is reasonable to expect that different payments would be made (*Capper Pass Ltd v Lawton* [1976] IRLR 366)? The time at which the work is to be done should be disregarded, as this does not affect basic rates, and can be compensated for by premium or shift payments (*Dugdale v Kraft Foods Ltd* [1976] IRLR 368). If there are differences in the work, the frequency with which they arise should be examined (*Harper v Redlands Roofs Tiles* [1976] IRLR 208) and if there is a contractual obligation to do different duties, these must be performed to a significant extent in practice (*Electrolux Ltd v Hutchinson* [1976] IRLR 410).

See EQUAL PAY ACT 1970; LIKE WORK.

Bumping redundancy. *See* TRANSFERRED REDUNDANCY.

Burden of proof. Section 57 (1) of EPCA places the burden of proof on the employer to show what the reason was for the dismissal (or, if there was more than one reason, the principal reason), and to show that it was one of the five reasons mentioned in the Act. If the employer introduces evidence to show what that reason was, the burden is then passed to the employee to show that there is a real issue about that reason, and that there is another reason. The burden on the employee is somewhat lighter than that on the employer, i.e. it is an evidential burden to cast doubt on the employer's reason. But a mere assertion that there is another reason is not enough. There must be some concrete evidence which casts doubt on the employer's reason. If this evidential burden is discharged, the onus remains on the employer to prove the reason for the dismissal (*Maud v Penwith District Council* [1984] IRLR 24).

C

Can comply (SDA, s. 1 (1) (b); RRA, s. 1 (1) (b)). This does not mean theoretically possible, but whether or not in practice the person can comply with the requirement or condition (*Price v Civil Service Commission* [1977] IRLR 291). 'Can comply' does not necessarily mean 'can physically comply', but rather 'can consistently comply' with the cultural or other conditions of the racial group (*Mandla v Lee* [1983] IRLR 209) or, so far as women are concerned, according to the usual behaviour of women. The point in time when they can comply is the time when the discrimination takes place, and the fact that they could have complied at some earlier moment in time is irrelevant (*Clark and Powell v Eley (IMI) Kynock Ltd* [1982] IRLR 482).

  See SEX DISCRIMINATION ACT 1975; RACE RELATIONS ACT 1976.

Ceased or diminished (EPCA, s. 81 (2) (b)). The test is not whether the work has ceased or diminished, but whether the requirements of the business for employees to carry out the particular kind of work has ceased or diminished. Thus a reorganisation of the workforce, done in the interests of greater efficiency, so that certain shifts are abolished, and overtime is reduced, does not create a redundancy situation (*Lesney Products Ltd v Nolan* [1977] IRLR 77). Even though the diminishing work can be foreseen, this can constitute a redundancy (*Lee v Nottingham County Council* [1980] IRLR 284).

  See REDUNDANCY.

Ceased ... to carry on business (EPCA, s. 81 (2) (a)). It does not matter that the employer is not the owner of the business or does not have an interest of that kind. The words of the section are used in a general sense to describe the person who is in control of the business (*Thomas v Jones* [1978] ICR 274). 'Cease' means either permanently or temporarily, and for whatever cause (s. 81 (3)) but whereas a permanent cessation will automatically terminate the contract of employment, a temporary cessation will not do so, although it may lead to a constructive dismissal claim (*qv*) or a claim under the lay off and short time provisions (*qv*).

  See REDUNDANCY; PLACE WHERE THE EMPLOYEE WAS SO EMPLOYED.

Central Arbitration Committee (EPA 1975, s. 10). The CAC replaced the Industrial Arbitration Board (formerly known as the Industrial Court) in 1975. It consists of a chairman (and deputy chairman) and representatives of each side of industry. Its work consists of making awards under the provisions relating to disclosure of information for collective bargaining purposes (EPA, s. 19), hearing references relating to collective agreements and Wages Councils awards which may contravene the Equal Pay Act (EqPA, ss. 3, 4), and voluntary arbitration.

Certification Officer (EPA 1975, s. 7) The Certification Officer maintains a list of trade unions, and issues certificates of independence to those unions which apply, and which can show that they are not under the domination or control of the employer (*Squibb UK Staff Association v Certification Officer* [1979] IRLR 75). He has also taken over the functions formerly exercised by the Registrar of Friendly Societies arising from the Trade Union Act 1913, Trade Union and Labour Relations Act 1974, functions assigned to him by the Employment Protection Act 1975 and the provision of public funds for trade union ballots under the Employment Act 1980.

See INDEPENDENT TRADE UNION.

Chairman's notes. In Scotland, a copy of the chairman's notes will only be supplied to the parties (for the purpose of making an appeal to the EAT) on cause shown. In England and Wales, they will be supplied if in the view of the EAT they are necessary for the purpose of the appeal or upon cause shown (*PD* [1981] ICR 287). Thus, if there is an allegation that there was no evidence to support a finding of fact, or the industrial tribunal failed to make a specific finding, or they had misunderstood the evidence or their findings were perverse, the notes will be supplied (*Webb v Anglian Water Authority* [1981] IRLR 494).

See APPEAL TO THE EMPLOYMENT APPEAL TRIBUNAL.

Change in the ownership of the business (EPCA, s. 94). There is an inter-relationship between the phrase 'transferred from one person to another' (*qv*) in EPCA, Sch. 13, para. 17 and the phrase 'change in the ownership of the business' in s. 94 of the Act (see *Lloyd v Brassey* [1969] 1 All ER 382, per Lord Denning). The former phrase is concerned with establishing continuity of employment for the purpose of establishing rights and payments (*Lord Advocate v De Rosa* [1974] ICR 480), the latter is concerned with entitlement to redundancy payment on the happening of certain events. But even though the wording is different, they must be read in the same sense (*Newlin Oil Ltd v Trafford* [1974] IRLR 205). Thus if there is a transfer under Sch. 13, para. 17, there is no break in employment and continuity is preserved. If there is a change in the ownership of the business under s. 94, and the transferor terminates the employment and the new owner offers to re-engage the employee, the contract is not brought to an end by the change, but the trial period provisions come into effect (s. 84). Thus s. 94 deals with the situation which exists at the time of the change, whereas para. 17 deals with the situation at the time when the subsequent contract of employment terminates.

The sale of a collection of assets does not constitute a transfer of the business (*Melton v Hector Powe Ltd* [1980] IRLR 477), the test being, does the transfer put the transferee in possession of a going concern? (*Kenmir Ltd v Frizzell* [1968] 1 All ER 414). It is not necessary that the whole of the business is transferred, as long as there is a transfer of a recognisable and identifiable part of the business (*Green v Wavertree Heating & Plumbing Co Ltd* [1978] ICR 928). If there is a proper, deliberate and accepted termination of the contracts of employment at the time of the transfer, then the workforce is not transferred, and all that is transferred is a collection of assets (*Dhami v Top Spot Night Club* [1977] IRLR 231). But the fact that the employees are employed in different capacities by the new employer does not mean that there is no transfer, or that continuity will be broken (*Lord Advocate v De Rosa*, supra).

A business may be transferred by operation of law (*Young v Daniel Thwaites & Co Ltd* [1977] ICR 877) or by the sale of assets, or goodwill (*Ward v Haines Watts* [1983] ICR 231).

See REDUNDANCY PAY; TRANSFER OF UNDERTAKINGS (PROTECTION OF EMPLOYMENT) REGULATIONS 1981.

Change in the partners (EPCA, Sch. 13, para. 17 (5)). A change from a partnership to a sole practitioner (*Harold Feilding Ltd v Mansi* [1974] 1 All ER 1035) or from a sole practitioner to a partnership (*Wynne v Hair Control* [1978] ICR 870) does not preserve continuity by virtue of para. 17 (5) (but see the comments in *Allen & Son v Coventry* [1979] IRLR 399).

Change in the place of work. *See* PLACE WHERE THE EMPLOYEE WAS SO EMPLOYED.

Check off agreement. An agreement made between an employer and a trade union whereby the employer deducts an employee's union subscription from the employee's wages. Such deductions, being made in favour of a third party, do not contravene the Truck Act (*qv*) (*Williams v Butlers Ltd* [1975] ICR 208). If an employee notifies the employer that he is exempt from contributing to the political fund of the trade union, or has notified the trade union of his objection to contributing towards it, the employer shall ensure that no amount representing a contribution towards the political fund shall be deducted from the employee's emoluments (Trade Union Act 1984, s. 18).

Cheque. The Payment of Wages Act 1960 permits payment of wages by cheque, direct transfer to a bank account, or money order or postal order, to workmen who would otherwise be covered by the provisions of the Truck Acts. The employee must make a written request for one of these modes of payment to be used, and the employer must consent to the arrangement. The employee may cancel the arrangement on giving four weeks notice. These modes of payment (except by cheque) may also be used (without the employee's consent) if he is absent from the usual place of payment (e.g. because he is off work sick or employed elsewhere) but in this case the employee can give written notice that he does not wish to receive his wages by these methods.

See TRUCK ACT.

Children. Children are minors below school leaving age (currently 16). If they are aged 13 or over they may do part-time work, provided this does not amount to more than 2 hours per day on school days or on Sundays. They may not work during school hours, or before 7 a.m. or after 7 p.m., on schooldays, and may not work in certain dangerous employments. They may not be required to lift, carry or move anything so heavy as to be likely to cause injury.

Local authorities have certain supervisory powers over the employment of children (Employment of Children Act 1973, s. 2), and they make byelaws restricting their employment (Children and Young Persons Acts 1933–69).

A child may not be employed in an industrial undertaking or on a sea-going boat, unless the undertaking or boat is one in which only members of the child's family is employed (Employment of Women, Young Persons and Children Act 1920, ss. 1–3). A child may not be employed in a factory (Education Act 1918, s. 14), nor employed underground in a mine except for receiving prescribed instruction (Mines & Quarries Act 1954, s. 124). There are special provisions relating to the employment of children in the field of entertainment (Childrens and Young Persons Act 1933, ss. 22–26).

A child who works for an employer is deemed to be employed whether or not he is paid a wage (Young Persons (Employment) Act 1938, s. 9).

Circumstances of the case (SDA, s. 76 (5). An industrial tribunal has power to consider a complaint which is out of time if, in all the circumstances of the case, they consider it is just and equitable to do so. The circumstances of the case refer to the facts which are relevant to the question of extending the time limit, and do not require the industrial tribunal to hear all the facts of the actual case in order to decide whether or not to extend the time limit (*Hutchinson v Westward Television* [1977] IRLR 69).

See PRESENTED TO THE INDUSTRIAL TRIBUNAL.

Claim for payment (EPCA, s. 101 (1) (b)). The written notice to make a claim for redundancy payment is not a technical matter; suffice that the letter indicates to the employer that it is the employee's intention to make a claim, and this indication can be linked with prior oral discussions (*Price v Smithfield Group* [1978] IRLR 80).

See REDUNDANCY PAY; BEFORE THE END OF THE PERIOD OF SIX MONTHS.

Closed shop. *See* UNION MEMBERSHIP AGREEMENT.

Codes of Practice. Various statutory bodies have the power to issue Codes of Practice, e.g. ACAS, HSC, EOC, and CRE. ACAS have issued three such Codes, (1) Disciplinary practices and Procedures, (2) Disclosure of information for collective bargaining purposes, and (3) Time off work for trade union duties and activities. These Codes have no legally binding force, but in any proceedings before an industrial tribunal or court, the provisions of the relevant Code shall be taken into account in determining the issue. However, a failure to follow the Code is not conclusive of the matter (*Lewis Shops Group v Wiggins* [1973] IRLR 205).

A Code of Practice issued by the Health and Safety Commission does not render a person liable to any criminal or civil proceedings, but in any criminal proceedings, the Code may be admissible in evidence, and if the defendant has failed to observe it with regard to a matter which the prosecution need to prove in order to establish a contravention of a statutory requirement or prohibition, the matter shall be taken as proven, unless the defendant can show that he observed the requirement or prohibition in some other equally efficacious manner.

The Commission for Racial Equality has issued a Code of Practice for the elimination of racial discrimination and the promotion of equality of opportunity in employment, which has the like status as an ACAS Code. The Equal Opportunities Commission is in the process of preparing a similar Code. The Secretary of State for Employment has issued Codes of Practice on (a) the Closed Shop and (b) Picketing.

Codes of Practice are thus not binding rules, but powerful guides. They do not necessarily fit every situation which may arise between employer and employee. For example, the Code of Practice on Disciplinary Practices and Procedures may not necessarily apply verbatim to small firms (*McKellar v Bolton* [1979] IRLR 59) where relationships are more intimate.

Collective agreement (TULRA, s. 18). A collective agreement is any agreement or arrangement made by or on behalf of one or more trade unions and one or more employers or an employers' association, which relates to any of the matters contained in s. 29 (1) of TULRA (as amended), which contains the definition of the phrase 'trade dispute'. A collective agreement made before 1 December 1971, or after 16 September 1974 shall be conclusively presumed not to be intended by the parties to be a legally enforceable contract, unless the agreement is in writing, and contains a provision that the parties did intend that it shall be legally enforceable.

A collective agreement can operate on two levels; (a) the normative agreement, which regulates the conduct of the signatories and (b) the contractual aspect, which is relevant only in so far as its provisions are incorporated, expressly (*Camden Exhibition & Display Ltd v Lynott* [1965] 3 All ER 28) or by implication, into the individual contracts of employment (*McLea v Essex Lines* [1933] 45 Ll.R 254). Not all the terms of a collective agreement are suitable for such incorporation (*British Leyland Ltd v McQuilken* [1978] IRLR 245), and there are problems which may arise when a national agreement conflicts with a local agreement (*Gascol Conversions Ltd v Mercer* [1974] IRLR 155).

The terms of a collective agreement cannot be back-dated unless there is a provision to this effect, but in any case this cannot over-ride the statutory provisions (*Leyland Vehicles Ltd v Reston* [1981] IRLR 19), and the terms may only be varied by mutual agreement (*Robertson v British Gas Corpn* [1983] IRLR 302). But although a breach of a collective agreement by an employer may amount to a breach of contract vis-à-vis the employee, it does not necessarily mean that the employer has acted unreasonably within the meaning of s. 57 (3) of EPCA (*Brandon & Gould v Murphy Bros* [1983] IRLR 54).

See BREACH OF CONTRACT.

Commission for Racial Equality (RRA 1976). Created by the Race Relations Act 1976 the CRE consists of a Chairman and between 8 and 15 members. It has the duty of working towards the elimination of racial discrimination, promoting equality of opportunity and good relations between persons of different racial groups, keeping the Act under review and, when required to do so, draw up and submit proposals for amending the Act. The CRE may assist financially any person or organisation, undertake research and education, conduct formal investigations and issue non-discrimination notices (*CRE v Amari Plastics* [1982] IRLR 252). It has issued a Code of Practice (*qv*) on eliminating discrimination in employment.

See RACE RELATIONS ACT 1976; FORMAL INVESTIGATIONS.

Comparison. A woman claiming equal pay may compare herself under the provisions of Art. 119 of the Treaty of Rome (*qv*) with a man who held her job previously, but whether a difference in pay between a man and a woman occupying the same post but at different periods of time may be explained by the operation of factors which are unconnected with any discrimination on grounds of sex is a question of fact for the industrial tribunal to decide (*Macarthys Ltd v Smith* [1980] IRLR 209).

See EQUAL PAY ACT 1970; MAN IN THE SAME EMPLOYMENT.

Compensatory award (EPCA, s. 74). An employee who has been unfairly dismissed is entitled to a compensatory award which shall be such amount as is just and equitable in all the circumstance, having regard to the loss suffered in consequence of the dismissal. There will also be a basic award (*qv*) and, where appropriate, an additional award (*qv*) and a special award (*qv*). The amount of the compensatory award may be reduced on the ground of contributory conduct (*qv*) and the complainant is under a duty to mitigate (*qv*) against his loss.

The industrial tribunal must make a compensatory award in accordance with the basic principles laid down in *Norton Tool Co Ltd v Tewson* [1972] IRLR 86 as interpreted by the EAT in later decisions. The headings to take into account are as follows:

(a) immediate loss of wages and other benefits up to the date of the industrial tribunal decision. This could include loss of notice, net wages, and other benefits (car, BUPA, accommodation, share option schemes, etc.);

(b) future loss of earnings. Here the industrial tribunal must speculate how long it will take for the employee to obtain other employment at a similar wage (based on net pay, not gross (*Tradewinds Airways Ltd v Fletcher* [1981] IRLR 272), and in doing so they may take account of local employment conditions based on their own knowledge (*Coleman v Toleman's Delivery Service Ltd* [1973] IRLR 67). Compensation can be awarded in respect of employment which can be anticipated to last beyond the statutory retiring ages of 65 or 60 (*Barrel Plating and Phosphating Ltd v Danks* [1976] IRLR 262). Generally, the fact that the employee will receive a tax rebate will be ignored, but the loss of a potential tax rebate can be compensated for (*Lucas v Laurance Scott Electromotors Ltd* [1983] IRLR 61). Loss of regular overtime earnings is allowable (*Mullet v Brush Electrical Machines Ltd* [1977] EAT 552/76 unreported), as is the loss due to a period of ill-health following the dismissal (*Fougere v Phoenix Motor Co Ltd* [1976] IRLR 259). Expenses in looking for new employment can also be allowed. On the other hand, the possibility that the employee may have been dismissed shortly afterwards can be taken into account in reducing the award, e.g. if redundancy was in the offing (*Young of Gosport's Ltd v Kendall* [1977] IRLR 433):

(c) the manner of dismissal. This is only allowed if there is a consequent risk of financial loss, e.g. by making the employee less attractive to other employers (*Vaughan v Weighpack Ltd* [1974] IRLR 105);

(d) loss of statutory protection. Since it will take some time for the employee to build up continuous employment sufficient to gain statutory rights, a modest sum may be awarded under this heading;

(e) loss of pension rights. If necessary, the Government's Actuary's Document should be consulted.

Money paid by the employer by way of wages in lieu of notice must be taken into account when the industrial tribunal makes its assessment (*TBA Industrial Products Ltd v Locke* [1984] IRLR 48), as well as any ex gratia payment made. The maximum amount which may be awarded as a compensatory award by the industrial tribunal is (currently) £8000.

Competition. An employer is entitled to defend himself against unfair competition from his employees, and to take reasonable steps to achieve that end (*Davidson & Maillou v Comparisons* [1980] IRLR 360).

See RESTRICTIVE COVENANT; REASON FOR THE DISMISSAL – SOME OTHER SUBSTANTIAL REASON.

Complaints of bias (PD [1981] ICR 287). The EAT will not normally consider complaints of bias unless full particulars are set out in the grounds of appeal. The registrar may then give appropriate directions for the hearing, including the filing of affidavits, and give the chairman of the industrial tribunal an opportunity of commenting.

See APPEAL TO THE EMPLOYMENT APPEAL TRIBUNAL.

Concerned with industrial relations (EPCA, s. 27 (1) (a)). This phrase is not to be narrowly construed, and is wider than 'collective bargaining' (*Sood v GEC Elliot Process Automation Ltd* [1979] IRLR 416). However, the section does not confer *carte blanche* for anything under this heading (*Depledge v Pye Telecommunications Ltd* [1980] IRLR 390). Whether time off is reasonable is for the industrial tribunal to determine (*Thos Scott & Sons (Bakers) Ltd v Allen* [1983] IRLR 329).

See TIME OFF WORK FOR TRADE UNION DUTIES.

Conciliation officer (EPCA, s. 133). Once a complaint has been presented to an industrial tribunal a copy will be sent to the conciliation officer who is under a duty to try to promote a settlement, either at the request of either party, or on his own volition if he thinks he could act with a reasonable prospect of success. He may also act before a complaint has been presented to an industrial tribunal at the request of a party, so that an appropriate settlement can be reached. Anything communicated to the conciliation officer in connection with his functions is confidential, and may not be admitted in industrial tribunal proceedings without the consent of the person who communicated the information. An agreement thus promoted, whether in writing or made verbally (*Slack v Greenham (Plant Hire) Ltd* [1983] IRLR 271) is binding on the parties, and is not rendered void by the provisions of s. 140 (1) of EPCA (see s. 140 (2) (d), (e)).

The conciliation officer shall seek in particular to promote the reinstatement or re-engagement of the complainant, on terms which appear to the conciliation officer to be equitable. But if the settlement is a financial one, it is not his duty to become involved in the merits, but merely to ensure that the parties are fully aware of the issues (*Duport Furniture Products Ltd v Moore* [1982] IRLR 131).

See ADVISORY, CONCILIATION AND ARBITRATION SERVICE; AGREED
SETTLEMENT; VOID.

Confessions. In unfair dismissal cases, the test to be applied is not 'was
the employee guilty of the offence for which he was dismissed' but
'did the employer have reasonable grounds for believing in the guilt of
the employee'. Thus, a confession, whether voluntary or involuntary,
is a relevant consideration for the employer to take into account. The
strict technicalities of criminal law, e.g. as laid down in the Judges'
Rules, are not appropriate in employee/employer relationships
(*Morley's of Brixton Ltd v Minott* [1982] IRLR 270). A confession may
render a full investigation unnecessary (*Royal Society for the Protection
of Birds v Croucher* [1984] ICR 604).

See ACTED REASONABLY.

Confidential information. If an employee obtains, during the course
of his employment, confidential information (prices, names of
customers, etc.), the information only remains confidential as long as
the employment relationship lasts, and if an employee wrongfully
discloses this information to a third party, he may be fairly dismissed
(*Smith v Du Pont (UK) Ltd* [1976] IRLR 107). If the employer wishes
to restrain the employee from disclosing the information after the
employment has terminated, he should do this by a valid restrictive
covenant (*qv*) (*Faccenda Chicken Ltd v Fowler* [1984] IRLR 61).
However, there can be no confidence protected when 'there is a
disclosure of an iniquity' (*Initial Services Ltd v Putterill* [1968]
1 QB 396).

Conflicting evidence. Where an industrial tribunal is faced with a
conflict of evidence on a significant issue of fact, their view of that
evidence must be made plain, so that the parties can know from
reading the decision what conclusions the tribunal came to in spite of
the conflict. A failure to do so is an error of law on the part of the
tribunal (*Levy v Marrable & Co Ltd* [1984] ICR 583).

Congregation. If workers of a particular racial group congregate
together on their own wishes, and the employer does nothing to
prevent this, he is not segregating persons on racial grounds contrary
to s. 1 (2) of the Race Relations Act 1976 (*FTATU v Modgill* [1980]
IRLR 142).

See RACE RELATIONS ACT 1976.

**Conscience or other deeply held personal conviction (EPCA,
s. 58 (4)).** The phrase 'conscience or other deeply held personal
conviction' is disjunctive, so that the conviction does not have to be of
a moral or conscience nature. Thus, if a person strongly believes that
the trade union has let him down (by, e.g. not pursuing a grievance on
his behalf) this can amount to a deeply held personal conviction (*Home
Delivery Services Ltd v Shackcloth* [1984] IRLR 470).

If the conscience or deeply-held personal conviction is a religious one, it is the belief of the individual concerned, not the sect to which he belongs, which is relevant in determining whether or not it is genuine (*Saggers v British Railways Board* [1978] 2 All ER 20).

See REASON FOR THE DISMISSAL – NON-MEMBERSHIP OF A TRADE UNION.

Consensual termination. If there is an agreement between the employer and employee that the contract of employment will automatically come to an end on the occurrence or non-occurrence of a certain event, then the contract is not terminated by dismissal, but by mutual agreement (*British Leyland (UK) Ltd v Ashraf* [1978] IRLR 330). However, very clear words are required to constitute such an agreement (*Midland Electrical Manufacturing Co Ltd v Kanji* [1980] IRLR 185) for there must be clear evidence of the consensual termination (*Tracey v Zest Equipment Co Ltd* [1982] IRLR 268). Thus, a premature retirement scheme whereby employees are invited to retire does not constitute a dismissal on grounds of redundancy or otherwise (*University of Liverpool v Humber* [1984] IRLR 54). However, this situation can be distinguished from those cases where an employee 'volunteers' to be made redundant, which do constitute a dismissal (*Burton Allton & Johnson Ltd v Peck* [1975] IRLR 87).

If an employee is dismissed with notice, but the parties agree to him leaving at an earlier date, the employer's notice has been varied, and there has not been a consensual termination (*McAlwane v Boughton Estates Ltd* [1973] ICR 470). And once a dismissal takes place, it is unlikely that any subsequent agreement to part company will be a consensual termination (*Glencross v Dymoke* [1979] ICR 536). The important thing is that a consensual termination is not a dismissal, and therefore the remedies which flow from a dismissal do not apply. Thus an agreement 'to part company' made with a financial settlement is not a void agreement (*qv*) (*Sheffield v Oxford Controls Ltd* [1979] IRLR 133).

Consistency. The fact that an employer is not dealing with disciplinary matters in a consistent manner is only relevant (a) if there is evidence that certain conduct is being overlooked (b) if it leads to the inference that the reason for the dismissal was not the real reason, or (c) to establish that some lesser penalty was more appropriate. However, it is of great importance that employers are flexible in their decisions, for a tarrif approach to misconduct is not appropriate (*Hadjiouannou v Coral Casinos Ltd* [1981] IRLR 352).

See REASON FOR DISMISSAL – CONDUCT.

Conspiracy and Protection of Property Act 1875. This Act makes it a criminal offence for a person wilfully and maliciously to break a contract of service or of hiring knowing or having reasonable cause to believe that the probable consequences of doing so will be to endanger human life, or cause serious bodily injury, or expose valuable property to destruction or serious injury. The penalty is £50 or three months imprisonment (s. 5). The Act also makes it an offence, if done with a view to compel any other person to abstain from working, to use violence or to intimidate such other person or his wife or children, or to injure his property, or persistently to follow such other person from place to place, or to hide any tools, clothes, or other property owned or used by such other person, or to watch or beset the house or other place where such other person resides or works or happens to be, or to follow with others in a disorderly manner (s. 7, and see *Galt v Philp* [1984] IRLR 156).

See SIT-IN.

Constructive dismissal (EPCA, s. 55 (2) (c)). A dismissal takes place if 'the employee terminates that contract, with or without notice, in circumstances such that he is entitled to terminate it without notice by reason of the employer's conduct'. This is popularly known as 'constructive dismissal' for although the employee resigns, he does so because of the breach of contract by the employer.

The conduct of the employer must be a serious breach, going to the root of the contract (*Western Excavating Co Ltd v Sharp* [1978] IRLR 27), which may be a breach of an express or implied term. The breach must be serious enough to warrant the employee resigning, and the employer's actions must show an intention not to be bound by that term (*Adams v Charles Zub Associates* [1978] IRLR 551). There must be a connection between the conduct and the resignation; thus, if the resignation comes first, then the conduct, there is no constructive dismissal (*Gaelic Oil Co v Hamilton* [1977] IRLR 77). Moreover, if the employee resigns, and does not make it clear that he is doing so because of the employer's conduct, there may well be doubt as to whether that conduct was the reason for the resignation (*Walker v Josiah Wedgewood Ltd* [1978] IRLR 105).

The breach in question may be a breach of an express term. Examples include demotion (*Robson v Cambion Electrical Products* [1976] IRLR 109) changing an employee's job unilaterally (*Coleman v Baldwin* [1977] IRLR 342), reduction in salary (*Industrial Rubber Products Ltd v Gillon* [1977] IRLR 389), or any substantial change in the employee's terms of employment (*Moore v Rowland Winn Ltd* [1975] IRLR 162).

More difficult is the case of a breach of implied terms (*qv*) for the latter are sadly lacking in definition. There is an implied term in every contract that the employer will treat the employee with respect, and conduct contrary to that term can amount to a constructive dismissal. Examples include treating an employee in a demeaning manner

(*Garner v Grange Furnishing Co* [1977] IRLR 206), falsely accusing the employee of theft (*Robinson v Crompton Parkinson Ltd* [1978] IRLR 6), using foul language (*Palmanour Ltd v Cedron* [1978] IRLR 303), victimising the employee (*Fanshaw v Robinson & Sons Ltd* [1975] IRLR 165), a failure to implement a promised salary increase, or to provide a written statement of terms and conditions of employment (*Bariamis v John Stephens of London Ltd* [1975] IRLR 237), a failure to investigate a complaint of lack of safety precautions (*British Aircraft Corpn Ltd v Austin* [1978] IRLR 332) a failure to provide a safe system of work (*Keys v Shoefare Ltd* [1978] IRLR 476) and so on.

It follows, therefore, that a unilateral variation of the contract (or even a breach) which is insignificant in its effect does not warrant an employee resigning and claiming constructive dismissal (*Gillies v Richard Daniels & Co Ltd* [1979] IRLR 457). Thus a change in job content does not constitute constructive dismissal if the work is still within the employee's contractual duties (*London Borough of Camden v Pederson* [1981] IRLR 173). Further, an employee claiming constructive dismissal must resign his employment, for he cannot claim to have been dismissed if he regards the contract as still being in existence (*Hunt v British Railways Board* [1979] IRLR 379).

The conduct alleged to constitute constructive dismissal must emanate from the employer or someone acting on his behalf and with authority to do that act (e.g. a foreman or manager). The employer is not liable for the acts of other employees unless persons in authority have condoned the act or failed to take reasonable steps to prevent it (*McCabe v Chicpack Ltd* [1976] IRLR 38). Once there has been a fundamental breach by the employer, the employee is entitled, as a matter of law, to treat the contract as being at an end, and is not thus obliged to pursue the matter through the firm's grievance procedure (*Seligman & Sons Ltd v McHugh* [1979] IRLR 130).

However, a constructive dismissal is a dismissal; it does not automatically follow that the dismissal is unfair (*Logabax Ltd v Titherley* [1977] IRLR 77), for it is open to the employer to show that he acted reasonably in the circumstances (*Savoia v Chiltern Herb Farms* [1982] IRLR 166). Thus, there may be 'some other substantial reason' for the dismissal, e.g. to conform to the Government's pay policy (*Industrial Rubber Products Ltd v Gillon* [1977] IRLR 389). Also, it may be possible to reduce compensation on the ground that the employee contributed towards the dismissal (*Associated Tyre Specialists Ltd v Waterhouse* [1976] IRLR 386) but this would only be in exceptional cases (*Holroyd v Gravure Cylinders Ltd* [1984] IRLR 259, but see *Garner v Grange Furnishings Ltd* [1977] IRLR 206).

If, in a constructive dismissal claim, the employer denies that there was a dismissal, and the industrial tribunal uphold the claim that there was, the employer will have failed to have established the reason for the dismissal, and the claim will therefore succeed. The employer, therefore, should plead in the alternative that if there was a dismissal, it was fair for whatever reason they wish to establish (*Derby City Council v Marshall* [1979] IRLR).

Whether conduct by the employer amounts to a constructive dismissal is a question of fact to be determined by the industrial tribunal, and not one of law to be decided by the appeal courts (*Woods v WM Car Services (Peterborough) Ltd* [1982] IRLR 413). Finally, an employee must have the requisite period of continuous employment (*qv*) in order to bring his claim (*Russel v John Gill Transport* [1978] IRLR 196).

See DISMISSAL.

Constructive resignation. In a number of decisions it has been held that where an employee's conduct amounts to a repudiation of the contract, this can constitute a termination of the contract, and does not amount to a dismissal by the employer. Consequently, there can be no question as to whether or not the dismissal was fair or unfair. Such decisions can no longer be regarded as being authoritative. The position is that if an employee breaks the contract, the employer can either accept the breach or not. If he accepts the breach, he dismisses the employee, and he must then justify the dismissal as being fair. Thus, the doctrine of constructive resignation has no legal basis (*London Passenger Executive v Clarke* [1981] IRLR 166).

However, there may be conduct which can amount to an implied resignation, e.g. if the employer discovers that the employee is working for another employer, or if the employee 'disappears', and all efforts to contact him prove to be fruitless. In such cases, it would not be difficult to assume the employee has resigned.

Consult (EPA, s. 99 (1)). The obligation on the employer is to consult on how redundancies are to be effected, not on whether they should be effected. Consequently, a redundancy programme is not itself a matter for negotiation (*NALGO v National Travel (Midlands) Ltd* [1978] ICR 598). The obligation is to consult about proposed redundancies, not possible redundancies (*APAC v Kirvin Ltd* [1978] IRLR 318).

See CONSULTATION ON REDUNDANCIES.

Consultant. A person who is retained as a business consultant is not employed as such; his employment only begins if and when he commences work. If his normal working hours are such that he works for the requisite period of continuous employment, he may be regarded as an employee, but this is a question of fact for the industrial tribunal to determine (*Bromsgrove Castings & Machining Ltd v Martin* [1977] ICR 417).

See SELF EMPLOYED; NORMAL WORKING HOURS; CONTINUOUS EMPLOYMENT.

Consultation. There is no rule of law which requires consultation to take place prior to a dismissal on grounds of redundancy, ill-health or some other substantial reason (*Hollister v National Farmers Union* [1979] IRLR 238), but consultation is required by the Code of Practice and it is good industrial relations practice to consult with trade unions (*Williams v Compair Maxam Ltd* [1982] IRLR 83) or the individual concerned (*Freud v Bentalls Ltd* [1982] IRLR 443). However, consultation must be for a specific purpose, and if that purpose cannot be achieved, the need for consultation diminishes or even disappears (*Taylorplan Catering (Scotland) Ltd v McInally* [1980] IRLR 53). There are no immutable principles of what constitutes good industrial relations practice (*Simpson & Son v Reid and Findlater* [1983] IRLR 401). *See* REDUNDANCY; REASON FOR THE DISMISSAL *et seq.*

Consultation on redundancies (EPA, s. 99). Once an employer recognises an independent trade union, he must consult at the earliest opportunity with representatives of that union about any proposal to dismiss on ground of redundancy any employee covered by the recognition agreement, whether he be a member of that trade union or not. In particular, if the employer proposes to dismiss from one establishment more than 100 employees within 90 days, he must consult with the trade union representatives at least 90 days prior to the dismissals taking effect; if he proposes to dismiss more than 10 employees for redundancy from one establishment, he must enter into consultations at least 30 days before the dismissals take effect. If less than 10 are to be made redundant, consultation must begin at the earliest opportunity. Consultation is required even though the employees in question do not have sufficient continuous employment to bring any claim, or even if they work for less than 16 hours per week, but not if they are employed on contracts for less than 12 weeks (*NATFHE v Manchester City Council* [1978] ICR 1190). In such consultations, the employer must disclose (a) the reasons for his proposals (b) the numbers and descriptions of employees whom it is proposed to dismiss (c) the total number of employees of that description employed at that establishment (d) the proposed method of selection, and (e) the proposed method of carrying out the dismissals, with due regard to any agreed procedure, including the period over which the dismissals are to take effect. The employer must consider any representations made by the trade union, and if he rejects them, he must reply, with his reasons. There is no obligation to reach an agreement.

If there are special circumstances (*qv*) which render it not reasonably practicable to comply with the consultation provisions, the employer shall take all such steps as are reasonably practicable in the circumstances. A failure to consult may lead to an application for a protective award (*qv*).

Consultation on transfers. On the transfer of an undertaking, the transferor or transferee (as appropriate) shall inform representatives of any recognised trade union of
(a) the fact that the transfer will take place, the date of the transfer, and the reasons for it,
(b) the legal, economic and social implications of the transfer for employees effected.
(c) the measures (if any) the employer envisages he will take in relation to the effected employees.
(d) the measures which the transferor envisages the transferee will take (if any) in relation to effected employees.

This information shall be given to trade union representatives long enough before the relevant transfer to enable consultations to take place. If either the transferor or transferee will be taking measures effecting the employees, he shall consult with the trade unions, consider any representations made, and reply to them, stating his reasons if he rejects them.

If the employer fails to inform or consult as appropriate, the trade union may make an application to an industrial tribunal, which may make a declaration, and may award appropriate compensation (which in practice amounts to no more than two weeks pay) to the effected employees.

See TRANSFER OF UNDERTAKINGS (PROTECTION OF EMPLOYMENT) REGULATIONS 1981.

Continues to be employed (EPCA, s. 33 (3) (a). A woman can be employed, but not working, prior to the 11th week prior to the expected week of confinement. Thus if she is absent from work during that time, with the knowledge or consent of the employer, she is still employed, and hence qualifies for maternity pay (*Satchwell Sunvic Ltd v Secretary of State for Employment* [1979] IRLR 455).

See MATERNITY PAY.

Continuous employment (EPCA, Sch. 13). Before an employee can obtain any of the various statutory rights, he must be employed for the relevant period of continuous employment. This period is computed by reference to (a) the number of hours normally worked under his contract, and (b) the length of his continuous employment, computed in weeks, months or years, as the case may be.

If an employee works less than 16 hours per week, then he must be employed for 5 years before he qualifies for any statutory right, except in respect of those rights which do not require any qualifying period of continuous employment. If the employee's normal working week is for 16 or more hours per week, then those weeks count towards continuity, except in so far as continuity is lost or broken.

The period of continuous employment begins on the first day the employee is due to start work (see *Salvation Army v Dewsbury* [1984] IRLR 222), except for redundancy payment purposes, when it cannot begin before the employee's 18th birthday. However, if there are days or weeks which are not to count (e.g. because the employee is on strike) the date of commencement is pushed forward for a period equal to the lost period.

There is a presumption that employment is continuous (which may be rebutted by the employer giving evidence to the contrary (*Nicoll v Nocorrode Ltd* [1981] IRLR 163), from the start of the employment until the effective date of termination (*qv*). There are provisions which deal with continuity when there is short-time working, absence from work because of sickness (*qv*), temporary cessation of work (*qv*), absence because of an arrangement or custom (*qv*), absence due to pregnancy or confinement, and maternity leave of absence. Periods when an employee is on strike do not count towards continuity, but do not break continuity. Continuity is deemed to be preserved if an employee is reinstated or re-engaged following an unfair dismissal (Labour Relations (Continuity of Employment) Regulations 1976), and in certain circumstances if there is a change of employer (*qv*) or on the transfer of a business (*qv*), or if the employee goes to work for an associated employer (*qv*).

The periods of continuous employment required for the various statutory rights are as follows:

(a) Not to be dismissed because of trade union membership or non-membership, or trade union activities, not to be discriminated against or penalised for trade union membership or activities, time off work for trade union duties or activities, public duties, ante-natal care, rights in insolvency, itemised pay statements, protective redundancy awards, discrimination on grounds of race or sex; no minimum period of employment is prescribed.

(b) Guarantee pay and medical suspension payments, dismissal for medical suspension, entitlement to minimum periods of notice; one month's continuous employment.

(c) Written statement of terms and conditions of employment; 13 weeks continuous employment (5 years if employed for less than 16 hours per week).

(d) Written reasons for dismissal; six months.

(e) Not to be unfairly dismissed; one year (or two years in respect of an employee who works for an employer who does not employ more than 20 employees).

(f) Redundancy payment, time off work to look for work; 2 years.

(g) Maternity pay, right to return to work after pregnancy; 2 years prior to the 11th week prior to the expected week of confinement.

See STARTS WORK.

35

Contract of employment (EPCA, s. 153). A contract of employment means a contract of service or apprenticeship, whether express or implied, and whether made orally or in writing. It is important to distinguish between a contract of service (which creates a contract of employment) and a contract for services (which creates a self-employed relationship) (*O'Kelly v Trust House Forte* [1983] IRLR 369).

See EMPLOYEE; SELF-EMPLOYED; EMPLOYMENT.

Contracting out. *See* VOID.

Contributory conduct (EPCA, s. 73 (7B), 74 (6)). If any action or conduct of the employee caused or contributed towards his dismissal the industrial tribunal may reduce the amount of the basic award (except if the reason for the dismissal was redundancy) and the compensatory award by such proportion as they think to be just and equitable. When considering such a reduction, the industrial tribunal should have regard to the employee's conduct, not to his state of mind (*Ladbroke Racing Ltd v Mason* [1978] ICR 49), and that conduct should be blameworthy (*Nelson v BBC* (No. 2) [1979] IRLR 346). Contributory fault may also be found in constructive dismissal (*qv*) cases (*Garner v Grange Furnishings Ltd* [1977] IRLR 206), but this would be unusual (*Holroyd v Gravure Cylinders Ltd* [1984] IRLR 259). It has been stated that if an employee is dismissed because he is inherently incapable of doing his job, this does not constitute contributory conduct (*Kraft Food Ltd v Fox* [1977] IRLR 431) but this view has been doubted (*Moncour v International Paint Co Ltd* [1978] IRLR 223). The test is, was there blameworthy conduct on the part of the employee which was causative of the dismissal (*Warrilow v Robert Walker Ltd* [1984] IRLR 304)? But if an employee is dismissed for taking part in industrial action, and he is not re-engaged when others who did so are re-engaged, his conduct in taking part in the industrial action is not ground for reducing compensation because of his contributory conduct (*Cartland/Northern Spinning Ltd v Moosa* [1984] IRLR 43).

The degree of contributory fault is essentially a question of fact for the industrial tribunal to determine, and is not appealable to the EAT as a point of law (*Hollier v Plysu Ltd* [1983] IRLR 260).

See COMPENSATORY AWARD; BASIC AWARD.

Control test. If an employer exercises a sufficient degree of control over another's activities, it may lead to the conclusion that the relationship of employer/employee is created (*D'ambrogio v Hyman Jacobs Ltd* [1978] IRLR 236).

See EMPLOYEE; SELF EMPLOYED.

Copyright. If the maker of a written work is employed under a contract of employment, and the work was written in the course of that employment, the employer is the first owner of the copyright in the absence of any agreement to the contrary (Copyright Act 1956, and see *Stevenson, Jordan and Harrison Ltd v MacDonald & Evans* [1952] 1 TLR 101).

See PATENTS AND INVENTIONS.

Costs (Industrial Relations (Rules of Procedure) Regulations 1980; Employment Appeal Tribunal Rules 1980). If an industrial tribunal considers that a party has, in bringing or conducting the proceedings, acted frivolously, vexatiously, or otherwise unreasonably, they may make an order that that party shall pay all or part of the costs of the other party, either by way of a specific or taxed sum. It is permissible to take into account the ability of the party to pay the costs, but the fact that an employer's case is conducted by an in-house lawyer is not a ground for refusing to award costs (*Wiggins Alloy Ltd v Jenkins* [1981] IRLR 275).

In the EAT, if the Tribunal thinks that proceedings were unnecessary, improper or vexatious or that there has been unreasonable delay or other unreasonable conduct in bringing or conducting the proceedings, a similar order for costs against the offending party may be made. Thus, if an appeal raises no arguable point of law costs may be awarded, and it is therefore advisable to seek counsel's opinion before launching an appeal which stands little chance of success (*Redlands Roof Tiles Ltd v Eveleigh* [1979] IRLR 11).

See FRIVOLOUS; VEXATIOUS OR FRIVOLOUS.

Counter notice (EPCA, s. 55 (4) (a). If an employer gives notice to terminate the contract of employment, but there is an agreement that the employee may leave before that notice expires, the effective date of termination is the date the notice expired, not the earlier agreed date, unless a new notice to terminate is given (*TBA Industrial Products Ltd v Morland* [1982] IRLR 331).

See EFFECTIVE DATE OF TERMINATION.

Crown employees. Strictly speaking, Crown employees are not employed under a contract of employment, although in practice they have considerable advantages over other employees. However, certain parts of the law are expressedly applicable, e.g. continuity of employment is determined by the provisions of Sch. 13 of EPCA (see para. 19). They are also 'employed persons' within the meaning of the Sex Discrimination Act and the Race Relations Act.

Crown employment is defined as employment under or for the purposes of a Government Department or any officer or body exercising statutory functions on behalf of the Crown (s. 138 (2) of EPCA. The position of employees in the National Health Service is slightly different (see ibid., s. 138 (5)).

Crown employees have most of the rights specified in EPCA,

including the right to have itemised pay statements, guaranteed pay, payment during medical suspension, rights of trade union membership or non-membership and activities, time off work for public duties (but this may be excluded by a term in his contract which restricts his right to take part in political activities or activities which conflict with his official functions, see ibid., s. 138 (8)), maternity pay and right to return to work, written reasons for dismissal, and unfair dismissal. Crown employees have no right to written statement of terms and conditions of employment under s. 1 of EPCA, nor to minimum periods of notice, nor to redundancy payments. The statutory sick pay scheme does apply to Crown employees.

Members of the Armed Forces do not acquire any rights under employment law generally.

However, a Minister of the Crown may issue a certificate excluding certain statutory rights for the purpose of securing national security (s. 138 (4), see *R v Secretary of State for Foreign Affairs ex p Council of Civil Service Unions* [1984] IRLR 309).

See HEALTH SERVICE EMPLOYEES.

Custom and practice. To be acceptable before the industrial tribunals, a custom and practice must be (a) certain (b) of long standing (c) reasonable and (d) notorious (*N. C. Watling Ltd* v *Richardson* [1978] IRLR 255). A custom cannot be invoked to negate an express term of the contract (*Gascol Conversions Ltd v Mercer* [1974] IRLR 155 and may thus be raised only if the contract is silent on a subject *Sagar v Ridehalgh Ltd* [1931] ICL 310). A normal practice is not a custom, especially if it is unreasonable (*Hardwick v Leeds Area Health Authority* [1975] IRLR 319), nor is a 'common practice' (*Spencer Jones v Timmins Freeman* [1974] IRLR 325).

Customary arrangement (EPCA, s. 59 (b)). A customary arrangement is an implied agreed procedure which is so well known and certain as to be equivalent to an agreed procedure (*Bessenden Properties Ltd v Corness* [1974] IRLR 338). The fact that discussions are taking place to work out a different procedure does not alter the customary arrangement until the new procedure has been agreed and adopted (*Tilgate Palletts Ltd v Barras* [1983] IRLR 231).

See AGREED PROCEDURE.

D

Death of the employer or employee (EPCA, Sch. 12). Where an employer or employee dies, industrial tribunal proceedings arising out of claims for itemised pay statements, written reasons for dismissal, guarantee pay, medical suspension pay, trade union membership and activity, time off work, maternity pay and leave of absence, redundancy payments, and claims on the employer's insolvency, may be instituted or continued by the personal representatives of the deceased employee, or defended by the personal representatives of the deceased employer, or, if there is no personal representative, by a person appointed by the industrial tribunal.

If an employer gives the employee notice to terminate the contract, and then dies, the provisions relating to unfair dismissal shall apply as if the contract terminated by notice on the date of the employer's death. If an employee presents a claim for unfair dismissal, and then dies, obviously the industrial tribunal cannot order reinstatement or re-engagement as a remedy, but only compensation. However, if the employee dies after an order for reinstatement or re-engagement has been made, and before the death the employer had refused to obey the order, the additional award shall be made unless the employer can show that it was not practicable to comply with the order. If the employer has not refused to comply with the order, and the employee dies, a normal compensation award shall be made.

The death of an employer operates as a dismissal for the purpose of redundancy payments. However, merely because the employee stays on to do the same sort of work he did for the deceased, this cannot be regarded as having his contract renewed or as having been re-engaged by the personal representatives. The length of time and the circumstances of the case may be consistent with an agreement to continue the employment (*Ranger v Brown* [1978] 2 All ER 726).

Death or retirement (SDA, s. 6 (4); EqPA, s. 6 (1A) (b). This phrase applies to provisions which are about death or retirement, and not solely to provisions which are consequent on death or retirement (*Roberts v Cleveland Area Health Authority* [1979] IRLR 244). Thus a redundancy scheme which enables men to retire at the same time as women, thus accelerating their entitlement to a pension, is excluded from the Act, as being a provision about retirement (*Roberts v Tate & Lyle Food and Distribution Ltd* [1983] IRLR 240), though a provision which is contrary to the terms of Art. 119 of the Treaty of Rome cannot be upheld (*Garland v British Rail Engineering Ltd* [1982] IRLR 111). However, Directives of the European Community are not binding on this country, and therefore disciminatory treatment in retiring ages are not unlawful (*Southampton etc Health Authority v Marshall* [1983] IRLR 237). Where rights are linked to national retirement schemes governed by national social security laws, different retirement ages for men and women are not contrary to EC Directive 76/207 (*Burton v British Railways Board* [1982] IRLR 116).

The phrase means the same when used in the Equal Pay Act, s. 6 (1A), (b) (*see Worringham v Lloyds Bank Ltd* [1979] IRLR 440).

See SEX DISCRIMINATION ACT 1976.

Deductions. An employer may only deduct from the wages of manual workers (*qv*) in respect of bad work if the terms of the Truck Act 1896, s. 2 are observed. The terms of the contract must be available to the employee or signed by him, the deduction must not exceed the actual or estimated loss to the employer, and the amount of the deduction must be fair and reasonable having regard to all the circumstances. The employee may recover any unlawful deduction (but there is a six month limitation period). A Wages Inspector may demand to see the contract which purports to allow the deduction, and may inspect the register of deductions which must be kept under the Act. A deduction in favour of a third party (e.g. a trade union) is not unlawful (*Hewlett v Allen* [1894] AC 383). The Truck Act 1896 does not apply to large sections of the cotton industry, and in *Sagar v Ridehalgh & Son Ltd* [1931] 1 Ch 310 it was held that a deduction for negligent work was held to be a method of calculating wages rather than a deduction for negligent work.

In respect of employees who are not covered by the Truck Act there is no power to make deductions except in accordance with the terms of the contract, and if an employee is penalised in this way without contractual authority, he may resign his employment and claim he was constructively dismissed (*qv*) (*Letherby v Horsman Andrew & Knill Ltd* [1975] IRLR 119). Even if there is contractual authority, the deduction must be reasonable.

Certain deductions are authorised by law for all employees. These are income tax, national insurance and under an attachment of earnings order. Deductions must be notified to an employee by virtue of the itemised pay statement (*qv*).

See TRUCK ACT; FINES; CHECK-OFF AGREEMENT; ATTACHMENT OF EARNINGS.

Deeply held personal conviction. *See* CONSCIENCE OR OTHER DEEPLY HELD PERSONAL CONVICTION.

Demotion. A unilaterally imposed change in an employee's job, whether by way of downgrading, or title, or responsibilities or actual work done which constitutes a demotion in his status amounts to a repudiation of the contract by the employer, and is thus capable of being a constructive dismissal (*Bumpus v Standard Life Assurance Co* [1974] IRLR 232). However, if such demotion has come about because the employee, by his conduct, has repudiated the contract (*Phillips v Glendale Cabinets Ltd* [1977] IRLR 307) or because of an agreed disciplinary procedure (*Theedom v BRB* [1976] IRLR 137) there is no dismissal, though if the demotion is out of all proportion to the offence, it will be a dismissal (*BBC v Beckett* [1983] IRLR 43). The test is a strict contractual one, though the reasonableness of the employer's and employee's actions can be relevant for the purpose of determining whether the dismissal was fair or unfair, and for the purpose of assessing compensation.

See CONSTRUCTIVE DISMISSAL.

Detriment (SDA, s. 6 (2) (b); RRA, s. 4 (2) (c)). An instruction can be a detriment, even before it is implemented (*BL Ltd v Brown* [1983] IRLR 193). But rules etc. which are capable of being a detriment are subject to the maxim *de minimus non curat lex* (the law does not take account of trifling matters) (*Peake v Automotive Products Ltd* [1977] IRLR 365). An employer cannot compel an employee to suffer a detriment, even by offering an inducement of higher wages, for he cannot buy the right to discriminate (*Ministry of Defence v Jeremiah* [1979] IRLR 436).

See SEX DISCRIMINATION ACT 1975; RACE RELATIONS ACT 1976.

Differences . . . are not of practical importance (EqPA, s. 1 (4)). Whether the differences are of practical importance may depend on the frequency, as well as the nature and extent of the differences (*Redlands Roof Tiles Ltd v Harper* [1977] ICR 349). The test is, would it be reasonable to expect those differences to be reflected in different wage rates (*Capper Pass Ltd v Lawton* [1976] IRLR 366)? The industrial tribunal should examine the matter in general terms, without going into a minute examination of the differences. The time at which the work is being done should be disregarded (*Dugdale v Kraft Foods Ltd* [1976] IRLR 368).

See EQUAL PAY ACT 1970; EQUAL PAY (AMENDMENT) REGULATIONS 1983.

Diplomatic immunity. By the State Immunity Act 1978 s. 4 a foreign government cannot claim diplomatic immunity from industrial tribunal proceedings relating to a contract of employment if (a) the contract was made in the United Kingdom or (b) the work is wholly or partly to be performed in the United Kingdom. However, this restriction on the sovereign rights does not apply if the applicant is a national of the State concerned, or is not a UK national or habitually resident in the United Kingdom, or, in any event, if the parties to the contract have expressly agreed in writing that the State Immunity Act shall not apply, unless the claim has to be brought before a court or tribunal in the UK (s. 4 (4)).

See FOREIGN EMPLOYEES.

Direct discrimination (SDA, s. 1 (1) (a); RRA, s. 1 (1) (a)). Discrimination occurs if the race or sex of a person is an important factor, though it does not have to be the whole reason for the discriminatory action (*Owens & Biggs v James* [1982] IRLR 502). The fact that there is a laudable motive for the discrimination is irrelevant (*Grieg v Community Industry* [1979] IRLR 158).

See SEX DISCRIMINATION ACT 1975; RACE RELATIONS ACT 1976; INDIRECT DISCRIMINATION.

Directive. A Directive issued by the European Communities Commission or by the Council of Ministers is binding as to the result to be achieved on member states, but leaves to the national authorities the choice of form and methods. Thus a Directive confers no directly enforceable rights on an individual (*O'Brien v Sim Chem Ltd* [1980] 2 All ER 307). Current Directives, which are applicable to employment law, are (1) 75/117 – application of the principle of equal pay: (2) 76/207 – which deals with the equal treatment for men and women regarding access to employment, training, promotion and working conditions: (3) 75/129 – which relates to collective redundancies: (4) 77/187 – which deals with the acquired rights of employees on the transfer of undertakings: (5) 79/7 – equal treatment on social security rights: (6) 80/987 – protection of employees on the employer's insolvency.

See TREATY OF ROME.

Director. A company director may also be an employee, if it can be shown that there is an express or implied contract of service in existence between him and the company. But if he is remunerated solely by way of director's emoluments, pays self-employed national insurance contributions, and no details of his contract of employment are kept in accordance with s. 26 (1) of the Companies Act 1967, his status will be that of a director, not employee. Consequently he cannot bring a claim for any of the employee rights under modern legislation (e.g. the right not to be unfairly dismissed) (*Albert Parsons & Sons Ltd v Parsons* [1979] IRLR 117).

See EMPLOYEE.

Disabled employee. Where a disabled person is employed in an industry for which there is a statutory minimum wage laid down by a Wages Council (*qv*) an employer may wish to pay a disabled person less than that minimum, because his performance does not warrant paying more. If so, it is necessary to obtain a special permit from the Wages Council, authorising the lower wage, which, if granted, will become the statutory minimum wage for that person (Wages Councils Act 1979, s. 16 (1). If there is no statutory wage machinery, the pay of a disabled person is subject to the usual negotiations.

An employer cannot expect the normal standard of work or output from a disabled person (*Kerr v Atkinsons Vehicles Ltd* [1974] IRLR 36) but if it is below that which could be reasonably expected, a dismissal may be fair (*Pascoe v Hallen & Medway* [1975] IRLR 116). The employer is entitled to say 'I cannot employ this Green Card holder any longer' (*Pascoe v Hallen and Medway*, supra). But the employer's conduct in dismissing a disabled person must always be judged by the standard of reasonableness (*Seymour v British Airways Board* [1983] IRLR 55). Technically, it is an offence to dismiss a registered disabled person without reasonable cause, but only when doing so would cause the employer to drop below the quota.

See DISABLED PERSONS (EMPLOYMENT) ACTS 1944 AND 1958.

Disabled Persons (Employment) Acts 1944 and 1958. These Acts are designed to enable disabled persons to obtain employment. A disabled person is one who is substantially handicapped in obtaining or keeping employment, whether by virtue of physical or mental illness, injury or disease, or congenital deformity. Such a person may apply to the Department of Employment for his name to be placed on a register, and he will be given a certificate of registration (known as a 'Green Card'). Registration is voluntary. In prescribed employments (car park attendants and lift operators) an employer must give preference to a registered disabled person, and it is an offence not to do so unless a special permit is obtained from the Department of Employment.

Every employer who employs more than 20 employees should employ the 'quota' of registered disabled persons which, in normal circumstances, is 3% of the workforce (in prescribed cases there may be a special quota) although it is possible to obtain a dispensation for 12 months.

Technically, it is an offence to fill a vacancy with a non-disabled person unless the employer has fulfilled his quota, but in practice it is rare for prosecutions to be brought.

See DISABLED EMPLOYEE; ANNUAL REPORTS OF COMPANIES.

Disciplinary procedure. The ACAS Code of Practice recommends that all save the small employer (*McKellar v Bolton* [1979] IRLR 59) should have a formal disciplinary procedure, so that the employee can be treated fairly and in accordance with natural justice (*Khanum v Mid-Glamorgan Area Health Authority* [1978] IRLR 215). Thus there should be a full investigation as soon as possible after the incident (*Marley Homecare Ltd v Dutton* [1981] IRLR 380) even though the police are also carrying out their enquiries (*Harris (Ipswich) Ltd v Harrison* [1978] IRLR 382). If an employee, on legal advice chooses to remain silent, the employer can still draw conclusions from his investigations

(*Harris & Shepherd v Courage (Eastern) Ltd* [1982] IRLR 509), and also place reliance on any confession made, even though it is later withdrawn (*Morleys of Brixton Ltd v Minott* [1982] IRLR 270). The employer must satisfy the three-fold test laid down in *British Home Stores v Burchill* ([1978] IRLR 379), namely, he must have a genuine belief in the guilt of the employee, he must have reasonable grounds upon which to base that belief, and he must have carried out such investigation into the matter as the circumstances permit. It follows that if there is a failure to investigate thoroughly, the employer cannot argue that he has reasonable grounds for his belief (*Henderson v Granville Tours Ltd* [1982] IRLR 494).

An employee is entitled to know the nature of the charge against him (*Hutchins v BRB* [1974] IRLR 303), to be given a fair opportunity to state his case, and to challenge, if possible, the evidence against him (*Bentley Engineering Ltd v Mistry* [1973] IRLR 436). He is entitled to be represented in accordance with the procedure (*Rank Xerox Ltd v Goodchild* [1979] IRLR 185) but it is not essential that he be present throughout the hearing provided his representatives are present (*Gray Dunn Ltd v Edwards* [1980] IRLR 23). He is entitled to appeal to a level of management not previously involved in the matter (*S. C. Brown Communications Ltd v Walker* (unreported)), though it may be unreal to expect managers not to discuss the case with each other (*Rowe v Radio Rentals Ltd* [1982] IRLR 177).

But disciplinary procedures are matters of substance, not form. In other words, if an employee is dismissed without going through the procedure, or if a defective procedure is adopted, this is still capable of being a fair dismissal, provided it is clear that the same result would have occurred if the procedure had been followed (*Sillifant v Powell Duffryn Timber Ltd* [1983] IRLR 91). But if neither side adduces evidence about what would have happened had the procedure been adopted, it is wrong for the industrial tribunal to speculate as to the likely outcome *Dunn v Pochin Ltd* [1982] IRLR 449).

If the disciplinary procedure is incorporated into the contract of employment, then at common law, an employee may seek an injunction to restrain a breach of contract (*Jones v Lee & Guilding* [1980] IRLR 67) although the remedy is discretionary, and will only be granted in cases where a serious injustice is likely to occur (*R v BBC, ex p Lavelle* [1982] IRLR 404). In appropriate cases, an action for damages may be brought, the measure being the length of time the employee would have been employed had he been dismissed after the full procedure had been followed (*Gunton v London Borough of Richmond* [1980] IRLR 321).

See ACTED REASONABLY; CONFESSIONS.

Disclosure of information (EPA, s. 17). For the purposes of all stages of collective bargaining, an employer shall disclose to the representa-

tives of an independent trade union recognised by him, on request
(a) information without which the trade union representative would
be impeded to a material extent in carrying on such collective
bargaining, and
(b) information which it would be in accordance with good industrial
relations to disclose.
However, the employer need not disclose
(1) information which he could not disclose without breaking an
enactment,
(2) information the disclosure of which would be contrary to the
national interest,
(3) information communicated to the employer in confidence, or
which the employer has obtained in consequence of the confidence
reposed in him by another,
(4) information relating to an individual, unless he has consented to it
being disclosed,
(5) information the disclosure of which would cause substantial
injury to the employer's undertaking for a reason other than its
effect on collective bargaining,
(6) information obtained for the purpose of bringing, prosecuting or
defending any legal proceedings.

The employer is not required to produce or allow the inspection of
any document, or to compile information which would involve work
or expenditure out of reasonable proportion to its value for collective
bargaining purposes.

To determine what would be good industrial relations practice,
regard shall be had to the Code of Practice on this subject issued by
ACAS.

If the employer fails to provide the information, a complaint may
be made to the Central Arbitration Committee, which may require
the employer to produce the information within a certain period,
failing which, an award relating to the terms and conditions of
employment of the affected employees may be made.

See CONSULTATION ON TRANSFERS; CONSULTATION ON REDUNDANCIES.

**Discovery of Documents (Industrial Tribunal (Rules of
Procedure) Regulations 1980).** An industrial tribunal may grant to
a person making an application an order for discovery or inspection of
documents (including the right to make copies). The order can be
made *ex parte* (i.e. in the absence of the person against whom the order
is made) or enable the latter person to raise objections to the proposed
order. Discovery shall not be ordered if the industrial tribunal are of
the opinion that the order is not necessary for the fair disposal of the
proceedings or in order to save costs (*British Library v Palyza* [1984]
IRLR 308).

If the documents in question are confidential, the industrial tribunal should inspect them, and consider whether special measures could be taken, such as covering up certain information, substituting anonymous names, and, if necessary, hearing the case *in camera* (*Science Research Council v Nasse* [1979] IRLR 465).

Legal privilege does not apply to documents unless they were prepared for the purpose of submission to legal advisers with a view to litigation. If the documents were prepared for some other purpose, they are not privileged (*Waugh v British Railways Board* [1980] AC 521).

The prime sanction against a person who fails to carry out the industrial tribunal's order is that his claim or defence may be struck out (see, in general, County Court Rules, Ord. 14, r. 2).

See FURTHER AND BETTER PARTICULARS.

Dismissal (EPCA, s. 55). There are three ways whereby a dismissal takes place; (a) if the employer terminates the contract (with or without notice) (b) if a fixed term contract expires without being renewed and (c) where the employee resigns in circumstances such that he is entitled to resign because of the employer's conduct (n.b. s. 93 of EPCA provides a fourth way, namely on the death of an employer, but this is relevant only for redundancy purposes). See also ss. 86, 116 for certain 'deemed' dismissals.

So far as termination by the employer is concerned, there is no dismissal if the employee agrees to resign, but if he is threatened with dismissal unless he does resign, this will be a dismissal (*East Sussex County Council v Walker* [1972] 7 ITR 280). If he is threatened with dismissal unless he performs his contract, this is not a dismissal. Where an employer utters words or phrases which do not contain an express termination, but which may do so impliedly (e.g. 'Get out', see *Stern v Simpson* [1983] IRLR 52) it is a question of fact as to what a reasonable person would understand by the use of those words in that industry in those circumstances (*Tanner v Keen Ltd* [1978] IRLR 110). Words used in the heat of the moment may lose their significance in the circumstances (*Martin v Yeomans Aggregate Ltd* [1983] IRLR 49).

If the parties agree that the employee will resign on receiving a satisfactory financial settlement, this will be a resignation, not a dismissal (*Sheffield v Oxford Controls Co Ltd* [1979] IRLR 133).

A warning that a contract of employment will be terminated at some future date is not a dismissal (*Morton Sundour Fabrics Ltd v Shaw* [1966] 2 ITR 84), for a dismissal must specify a date, or at least indicate facts from which a date is ascertainable (*Pritchard-Rhodes Ltd v Boon and Milton* [1979] IRLR 19).

See CONSENSUAL TERMINATION, FIXED TERM CONTRACT; FRUSTRATION; CONSTRUCTIVE DISMISSAL; RESIGNATION; PROJECT TERMINATION; LAWFUL DISMISSAL; WRONGFUL DISMISSAL; FAIR DISMISSAL; SUMMARY DISMISSAL.

Does not comply with reasonable requirements (EPCA, s. 13 (4) (b)). Consideration should be given to the state of the employer's mind, and the information communicated to the employee. (*Meadows v Faithful Overalls Ltd* [1977] IRLR 330).

See GUARANTEE PAY.

Domestic servant (EPCA, s. 100). A domestic servant (except one who is a close relative, see below) may claim a redundancy payment like any other employee, for employment in a private household is deemed to be 'a business' like any other. However, the special rules relating to the transfer of a business do not apply, except when the head of the household dies, for here there may be a transfer to the new head of the household for redundancy payment purposes (see Sch. 11, para. 21 of EPCA), and see *Ranger v Brown* [1978] 2 All ER 726).

Neither the Race Relations Act 1976 nor the Sex Discrimination Act 1975 apply to 'employment for the purpose of a private household', which phrase may be wider than domestic servants, although the victimisation provisions of these Acts do apply. However, the exclusion was criticised by the European Court of Justice in *European Community v United Kingdom* [1984] 1 All ER 353 (a ruling concerning sex discrimination) and it is likely that there may be some amending legislation in the near future.

Close relatives are excluded from the redundancy payment provisions, i.e. where the employer is the parent, grandparent, step parent, child, grandchild, step-child, brother or sister (of the whole or half-blood) of the employee.

Duty . . . to mitigate (EPCA, s. 74 (4)). The duty of a claimant is to take all such steps as are reasonable to mitigate against the loss suffered, and this is a question of fact for the industrial tribunal. Thus, to turn down another job because he would receive less than he would get from State benefits would amount to a failure to mitigate (*Daley v A. E. Dorsett (Alma Dolls) Ltd* [1981] IRLR 385). If an employee decides to set up his own business rather than seek other employment, he does not fail to mitigate, but if it could be shown that a claimant would, on the balance of probabilities, have gained employment after a particular length of time, he fails to mitigate (*Gardiner-Hill v Roland Berger Technics Ltd* [1982] IRLR 498). The industrial tribunal should assess how much he would have earned from such employment and reduce compensation accordingly. Account may be taken, however, of the employee's personal characteristics, e.g. poor health (*Fourgere v Phoneix Motor Co Ltd* [1976] ICR 495) physical incapability (*Brittains Arbofield Ltd v Van Uden* [1977] ICR 211) etc.

See COMPENSATORY AWARD.

E

Economic, technical or organisational reason (Transfer of Undertakings (Protection of Employment) Regulations 1981). If an employee is dismissed because of an economic, technical or organisational reason entailing a change in the workforce, this will amount to 'some other substantial reason' (*qv*) for the dismissal, but without prejudice to the rule that the employer must have acted reasonably (*qv*) in treating that reason as a sufficient reason for dismissal. If the dismissal is found to be fair under s. 57 (3) of EPCA, the employee will be able to claim a redundancy payment, for redundancy is the commonest of the economic, technical or organisational reasons for dismissal on a transfer (*Gorictree Ltd v Jenkinson* [1984] IRLR 391). However, the above reasons must be those which entail a change in the workforce; if the transfer results in a change in the pay, a subsequent dismissal or constructive dismissal does not come within the regulation, and hence is automatically unfair (*Berriman v Delabole Slate Ltd* [1984] IRLR 394).

See TRANSFER OF UNDERTAKINGS (PROTECTION OF EMPLOYMENT) REGULATIONS 1981.

Effective date of termination (EPCA, s. 55 (4)) (EDT). In relation to an employee whose contract is terminated by notice (whether given by the employer or employee) the EDT is the date on which the notice expires. If the employment is terminated without notice, the EDT is the date on which the termination takes effect. If an employee is employed on a fixed term contract which is not renewed, the EDT is the date on which the contract expires.

It is important to ascertain correctly the EDT, as it is up to that date that the employee can compute his period of continuous employment (*qv*) for the purpose of the various statutory rights and remedies. Also, it is the date from which time will run for the purpose of presenting a claim (see s. 67 (2)).

There is a distinction between the case where an employee is dismissed with notice, but given his wages in lieu of working that notice, and the case where no notice is given, but a payment is made in lieu of notice. In the former case he is being allowed to leave early, but is receiving his pay as if he had worked. Thus the EDT is when the notice expires (*TBS Industrial Products Ltd v Moreland* [1982] IRLR 331). In the latter case, he has been dismissed in breach of contract, and the payment in lieu of notice constitutes damages for that breach. Consequently, the EDT is the date the employee ceases to work under the contract (*Adams v GKN Sankey Ltd* [1980] IRLR 416).

If an employee is dismissed summarily, the EDT will be the date he receives his summary dismissal (*Brown v Southall & Knight* [1980] IRLR 130). If an employee is already under notice of dismissal, he can still be summarily dismissed during the notice period, and the date of the summary dismissal will be the EDT (*Stapp v Shaftsbury Society* [1982] IRLR 326). But if, by dismissing summarily, the employee is deprived of a statutory right (e.g. a right to claim unfair dismissal) the remedy would be an action at common law, which would include a claim for damages based on the loss of his rights (*Robert Cort Ltd v Charman* [1981] IRLR 437).

If the employer does not give the minimum period of notice as required by s. 49, the EDT is extended by the period of statutory notice (but not the contractual notice, see *Fox Maintenance Ltd v Jackson* [1977] IRLR 306), for the purpose of s. 53 (written reasons for dismissal, s. 64 (1) (a) and s. 64A (qualifying period for unfair dismissal rights) s. 73 (3) (calculation of basic award) and Sch. 13, para. 8 (3) (week's pay). The EDT is not extended for the purpose of computing the time limit within which a complaint must be presented to the industrial tribunal. Nor is the EDT extended if the employee is dismissed for gross misconduct, for he is not then entitled to any statutory notice, *Ahmed v National Car Parks Ltd* (IDS Brief 149).

If an employee is dismissed, and he appeals within the internal appeal machinery, the terms of the contract or disciplinary procedure will govern the situation. If the appeal if heard after his employment has ceased, and is rejected, the EDT is the date of the dismissal, not the date of the appeal (*Sainsburys Ltd v Savage* [1980] IRLR 109).

See CONTINUOUS EMPLOYMENT; PRESENTED TO THE INDUSTRIAL TRIBUNAL.

Emoluments. Emoluments include the monetary value of services and facilities (e.g. accommodation, etc.) provided under the contract of employment. Since an employee would normally have to meet such expenses out of taxed income, any assessment of the amount of emoluments should be grossed up at the basic rate of income tax (*Leeds City Council v Pomfret*, unreported).

Employed (EPCA, s. 81 (2) (a)). A person is employed for the purpose of a contract of employment in doing that which the contract obliges him to do, and not what he is actually doing (*Haden Ltd v Cowan* [1982] IRLR 314).

Employed on like work (EqPA, s. 1 (2)). This must be construed with reference to the contract of employment, although it is possible to compare not only the contractual obligations but also the actual work done. Once the equality clause operates, it will continue even though no claim exists, e.g. if the male comparator leaves the firm (*Sorbie v Trust House Forte Hotels Ltd* [1976] IRLR 371).

See EQUAL PAY ACT 1970; EQUAL PAY (AMENDMENT) REGULATIONS 1983.

Employee. An employee is a person who has entered into or works under a contract of employment, i.e. a contract of service, as opposed to a contract for services.

There are a number of tests used by the courts and industrial tribunals to determine whether or not a person is an employee or is self employed, e.g. the control test (*Yewans v Noakes* [1880] 6 QBD 530) the organisational test (*Stevenson, Jordan & Harrison Ltd v MacDonald & Evans Ltd* [1952] 1 TLR 101) the multiple test (*Ready Mixed Concrete Ltd v Ministry of Pensions* [1968] 1 All ER 433) and the entrepreneurial test (*Market Investigations Ltd v Ministry of Social Security* [1968] 3 All ER 732). Which test will be applied in any particular case may well depend on the issues involved, for different conclusions may be drawn in unfair dismissal cases, as opposed to cases relating to income tax, national insurance payments, or compensation for injuries at work (compare *Ferguson v John Dawson Contractors Ltd* [1976] 3 All ER 817 and *Massey v Crown Life Insurance Co Ltd* [1978] IRLR 31). How the parties themselves view the relationship is not conclusive (*Davis v New England College of Arundel* [1977] ICR 6) for what matters is the substance of the relationship, not the form (*Maurice Graham Ltd v Brunswick* [1974] 16 KIR 158) and must be determined by the evidence adduced on the facts of each case (*O'Kelly v Trusthouse Forte plc* [1983] ICR 728).

Among the factors to be taken into account are included (1) the contractual provisions (*BSM v Secretary of State for Social Services* [1978] ICR 894) (2) the degree of control exercised by the employer (*Global Plant Ltd v Secretary of State for Health and Social Security* [1971] 3 All ER 385) (3) the obligation on the employer to provide work (*Nethermere (St. Neotts) Ltd v Gardiner* [1984] IRLR 240) (4) the obligation on the employee to perform the work (*Ahmet v Trusthouse Forte Catering Ltd*, unreported EAT 13.1. 1983) (5) the duty of personal service (*Ready Mixed Concrete Ltd v Ministry of Pensions* [1968] 1 All ER 433) (6) the provision of tools, equipment, instruments, etc. (*Willy Scheiddegger Swiss Typewriting School Ltd v Ministry of Social Security* [1968] 5 KIR 65) (7) arrangements made for tax, insurance, VAT, Statutory Sick Pay (*Davis v New College of Arundel* [1977] ICR 6) (8) the opportunity to work for other employers (*WHPT Housing Association Ltd v Ministry of Social Security* [1981] ICR 737) (9) other contractual provisions, including holiday pay, sick pay, notice, fees and expenses, etc. (*Hamerton v Tyne and Clyde Warehouses Ltd* [1978] ICR 661) and (10) whether the relationship of being self-employed is a genuine one, or an attempt to avoid modern protective legislation (*Young & Woods Ltd v West* [1980] IRLR 201).

No single factor, by itself, can be conclusive, and all the relevant factors should be taken into account. As long as the industrial tribunal does this, its decision is a question of fact, not law, and its findings (either way) cannot be challenged in the EAT (*O'Kelly v Trusthouse Forte plc* [1983] ICR 728).

See SELF-EMPLOYED.

Employee's conduct (EPCA, s. 82 (2). An employee's act in taking part in a strike is 'employee's conduct' for the purpose of s. 82 (2). This entitles the employer to terminate the contract without notice, and therefore disqualifies the employee from receiving a redundancy payment (*Simmons v Hoover Ltd* [1976] IRLR 226) except as provided by s. 92.

See REDUNDANCY.

Employee terminates that contract (EPCA, s. 55 (1) (c)). *See* CONSTRUCTIVE DISMISSAL.

Employer (EPCA, s. 153 (1)). An employer is the person by whom the employee is or was employed. Rights can only be acquired against the one employer (*Harold Fielding Ltd v Mansi* [1974] IRLR 79) unless the provisions of Sch. 13 apply, or under the Transfer of Undertakings (Protection of Employment) Regulations. A person who exercises sufficient control over employees may be regarded as being the employer for some purposes (*Road Transport Industry Training Board v Ongaro*). Frequently, the actions of those who are responsible to the employer (e.g. management) are treated as the acts of the employer.

Employers' Association (TULRA, s. 28). An employers' association is an organisation (whether permanent or temporary) which consists (a) wholly or mainly of employers and whose principle purposes include the regulation of relations between employers and workers or trade unions, or (b) wholly or mainly of constituent or affiliated organisations (or representatives of such) whose principle objects include the regulation of relations between employers and workers or trade unions, or between the constituent or affiliated organisations. An employers' association, as well as its officials, have the immunities contained in s. 13 of TULRA (as amended) in respect of acts done in furtherance or contemplation of a trade dispute, but unlike a trade union, there is no limit on the amount of damages which can be awarded. It is possible to sue an employers' association under the general law in respect of wrongful acts, e.g. negligence, nuisance, defamation etc.

Employers' Liability (Compulsory Insurance) Act 1969. Every employer must maintain an insurance policy against liability for injury or disease sustained by his employees arising out of and in the course of employment. An annual certificate must be displayed at every place where the employer carries on business so that it can be seen and read by any person employed at that place. The Act only applies to employment in Great Britain.

Employment (SDA, s. 6 (1); RRA, s. 4 (1)). Employment, for the purpose of these Acts, includes a contract of service and a contract for services (see s. 82). Hence, the sections apply to employees and to self-employed persons (*Quinnen v Hovells* [1984] IRLR 227) but not to cases where there is no employment at all (e.g. the appointment of a justice of the peace, see *Knight v A/G* [1979] ICR 194). Trainees sponsored by the Manpower Services Commission under youth training schemes do not have a contract with their 'sponsor' (*Daly v Allied Suppliers Ltd* [1983] IRLR 14), but see Health and Safety (Youth Training Schemes) Regulations 1983, which apply the Health and Safety at Work etc. Act 1974 to youth trainees as if they are employees.

See SEX DISCRIMINATION ACT 1975; RACE RELATIONS ACT 1976; EMPLOYEE.

Employment Act 1980. This Act enables trade unions to obtain Government funds for the purpose of holding certain ballots, amends the law relating to exclusion from trade union membership, enables the Secretary of State to issue Codes of Practice, amends certain provisions in the Employment Protection (Consolidation) Act relating to unfair dismissal, maternity rights, guarentee payments, and trade union membership and non-membership. It also restates in an amended form the right to peaceful picketing, and lays down when certain secondary action is tortious despite the immunity contained in s. 13 of the Trade Union and Labour Relations Act 1974.

Employment Act 1982. This Act further amends the Employment Protection (Consolidation) Act 1978, prohibits trade union membership requirements in contracts, amends the meaning of 'trade dispute', and makes provisions for actions in tort against trade unions, with financial limits on damages which can be awarded. The Act also amended the Companies Act 1967, s. 16 (now replaced by the Companies Act 1985, ss 235, 261 (5), Sch 7, Pts I, IV, V, Sch 10) by requiring certain companies to include a statement in their annual reports relating to employee involvement.

Employment Appeal Tribunal (EPCA, s. 135). The Employment Appeal Tribunal (EAT) consists of a High Court Judge and between two and four lay members who have special knowledge of industrial relations, either as employers' representatives or as representatives of workers. In practice, these lay members are chosen from lists submitted to the Lord Chancellor and Secretary of State for

Employment by the TUC and CBI. The EAT can sit anywhere in the country, but normally hears cases in London and Glasgow.

The EAT hears appeals from industrial tribunals on questions of law under the following statutes and regulations;

Equal Pay Act 1970 (as amended)
Sex Discrimination Act 1975
Employment Protection Act 1975
Race Relations Act 1976
Employment Protection (Consolidation) Act 1978
Employment Act 1980–2
Transfer of Undertakings (Protection of Employment Regulations) 1981.

The EAT hears appeals on questions of law from the decisions of the Certification Officer under the Trade Union Act 1913 and the Trade Union (Amalgamations) Act 1964, and on questions of law and fact under the Trade Union and Labour Relations Act 1974 (s. 8), the Employment Protection Act 1975 (s. 8), the Employment Act 1980 (s. 4), and has original jurisdiction to determine applications for compensation under the Employment Act 1980 (s. 5).

See APPEAL TO THE EMPLOYMENT APPEAL TRIBUNAL.

Employment Appeal Tribunal Rules 1980. These Rules govern the making and defending of an appeal to the Employment Appeal Tribunal. There are provisions for the serving of a notice of appeal, replies and cross-appeals, joinder, interlocutory applications, directions, hearings and orders, including costs. The Schedule to the Rules contains the various Forms which may be used.

See APPEAL TO THE EMPLOYMENT APPEAL TRIBUNAL.

Employment by the one employer (EPCA, Sch. 13, para. 17). If an employee is employed by A and B as partners, and then his employment is continued by A alone, he is not employed by the one (i.e. the same) employer for the purposes of computing continuity (*Harold Fielding Ltd v Mansi* [1973] IRLR 79). However, the employment with the one employer does not need to be under a single contract of employment (*Re Mack Trucks (Britain) Ltd* [1967] 1 All ER 977), but can be under successive contracts (*Wood v York City Council* [1978] IRLR 228).

See CONTINUOUS EMPLOYMENT.

Employment Protection Act 1975 (EPA). This Act placed the Advisory, Conciliation and Arbitration Service (ACAS) (*qv*) on a statutory basis, with power to issue Codes of Practice (*qv*). It also specifies the functions of the Certification Officer in respect of his regulatory control over trade unions. The Central Arbitration Committee is also established. The Act lays down the duty of employers to disclose information for the purposes of collective bargaining, and the procedures for handling redundancies, with the sanction of a protective award, and the provisions for notifying the Department of Employment in respect of collective redundancies. Certain sections of the Act have been repealed altogether; others have been repealed and re-enacted in the Employment Protection (Consolidation) Act 1978.

Employment Protection (Consolidation) Act 1978 (EPCA). This is the major statute relating to modern employment law, and it consolidates the Contracts of Employment Act 1972, Redundancy Payments Act 1965, and relevant provisions from the Employment Protection Act 1975 and other legislation. It has been amended by the Employment Act 1980 and 1982.

The Act contains detailed provisions relating to the following employment rights; written particulars of terms of employment, itemised pay statements, guarantee payments, suspension from work on medical grounds, right to trade union membership, non-membership and trade union activities, time off work for trade union duties and activities, public duties, to look for work, and for ante-natal care, maternity pay and the right to return to work after pregnancy, minimum periods of notice, written statement of the reasons for dismissal, the right not to be unfairly dismissed, redundancy payments, rights on an employer's insolvency, and the appropriate remedies in respect of a breach of any of these rights.

Employment Protection (Offshore Employment) Order 1976. This Order applies most of the provisions of the Employment Protection (Consolidation) Act and other legislation to offshore employment in ships (but not for fishing purposes) and structures (e.g. oil-rigs and off-shore installations) in British territorial waters or areas designated under the Continental Shelf Act 1964.

Enter an appearance (Industrial Tribunal (Rules of Procedure) Regulations 1980). An employer enters an appearance if he sends in a written notice that he intends to resist the application. The requirement that he should state the grounds on which he intends to resist is directory, not mandatory. Therefore, if he fails to state the grounds, he has still entered an appearance (*Seldun Transport Services Ltd v Baker* [1978] ICR 1035).

Equal Pay Act 1970. An Act designed to ensure equal treatment between men and women as regards terms and conditions of employment. Women who are employed on 'like work' or 'broadly similar work' or 'work which has been rated as equivalent' under job evaluation schemes are entitled to equal pay with men, unless there is a genuine material factor which is not the difference of sex. The Act is intended to comply with Article 119 of the Treaty of Rome and Directive 75/117, the former being directly applicable in national courts. The Act was amended by the Sex Discrimination Act 1975 and by the Equal Pay (Amendment) Regulations 1983, which created a right to equal pay for work which is of 'equal value'.

The Act, together with the Sex Discrimination Act 1975, is a reforming statute, and should therefore be construed in accordance with the social objectives to be achieved. Both Acts, although conferring mutually exclusive rights with different remedies, may be construed in a similar way (*Shields v Coombs (Holdings) Ltd* [1978] IRLR 263).

Equal Pay (Amendment) Regulations 1983. These Regulations amend the Equal Pay Act by adding the concept of equal pay for work which is of equal value. An industrial tribunal may require an expert to prepare a report, and an existing job evaluation scheme may be challenged on the ground that it operates in a discriminatory manner (see *Neil v Ford Motor Co Ltd* [1984] IRLR 339; *Hayward v Cammell Laird Shipbuilders Ltd* [1984] IRLR 463).

Equality clause (EqPA, s. 1 (1)). The terms of a woman's contract of employment shall include an equality clause if she is employed on like work (*qv*) or broadly similar work (*qv*) or work which is rated as equivalent (*qv*) under a job evaluation scheme or work which is of equal value (*qv*). Less favourable terms must be modified (*Atkinson v Tress Engineering Co Ltd* [1976] IRLR 245). The equality clause continues to operate even though the reason for it has ceased to exist (e.g. when the comparable male employee leaves) *Sorbie v Trust House Forte Hotels Ltd* [1977] 2 All ER 155).

See LIKE WORK; BROADLY SIMILAR NATURE; JOB EVALUATION STUDY.

Equity and substantial merits (EPCA, s. 57 (3)). The industrial tribunal should use a broad approach of common sense and fairness, avoiding legal technicalities (*Earl v Slater and Wheeler (Airlyne) Ltd* [1972] IRLR 115). Thus equity requires an employer to take into account the employee's past record and length of service (*Taylor v Parsons Peebles Ltd* [1981] IRLR 119) and employees who behave in the same manner should have meted to them much the same punishment (*Post Office v Fennel* [1981] IRLR 221), although a tarrif approach is not appropriate (*Hadjioannou v Coral Casinos Ltd* [1981] IRLR 352). But if previous misconduct merely attracted a warning (*Rigden-Murphy v Securicor Ltd* [1976] IRLR 106), or the employer acted in a lax manner (*Raymond v Sir Lindsay Parkinson & Co Ltd* [1974] IRLR 298) the inconsistency may be relevant to the equity and substantial merits. If a dismissal is considered necessary because of the demands of a third party, equity requires the employer to consider what possible injustice would occur to the employee, and the question then arises, 'What would a reasonable employer have done?' (*Dobie v Burns International Security Services Ltd* [1984] IRLR 329).

See ACTED REASONABLY; CONSISTENCY.

Establishment (EPA, s. 99 (3); SDA, s. 10; RRA, s. 8; EPCA, s. 62 (4) (b) (ii). This term, used in several statutory provisions, is left undefined, and it is thus for the industrial tribunal, functioning as an industrial jury, to decide on the facts of the case whether separate premises can constitute one establishment (*Barratt Developments Ltd v UCATT* [1977] IRLR 403). Cases on Selective Employment Tax (now repealed) were used to define the word in *Barley v Amey Roadstone Co Ltd* [1977] IRLR 299).

See CONSULTATION ON REDUNDANCIES.

Estoppel. The liability of the Secretary of State for Employment to make a redundancy rebate is conditional on there being a liability on the employer under the Act. If the employer makes a payment which is not warranted under the Act, or makes a promise to pay, this may operate as a contractual arrangement, and may be enforceable as such, but it cannot commit the Minister (*Secretary of State for Employment v Globe Elastic Thread Co Ltd* [1979] IRLR 327).

See REDUNDANCY REBATE.

Ethnic origins (RRA, s. 3 (1)). An ethnic group must regard itself, and be regarded by others, as a distinct community by virtue of certain essential characteristics. These include (1) a long shared history, of which the group is conscious as distinguishing it from other groups, and the memory of which keeps it alive and (2) cultural traditions of its own, including family and social customs, often (but not necessarily) associated with religious observance. In addition the following characteristics are relevant, namely (3) a common geographical origin or descent from a small number of common ancestors (4) a common language, not necessarily peculiar to the group (5) a common literature peculiar to the group (6) a common religion different from that of neighbouring groups and (7) being a minority or an oppressed or dominant group within a larger community. This definition would include converts (e.g. persons who marry into the group), but excludes apostates. Provided a person who joins the group feels he is a member, and is accepted as such, then, for the purposes of the Act, he is a member (*Mandla v Lee* [1983] IRLR 209).

See RACE RELATIONS ACT 1976.

European Communities Act 1972. This Act signalled the United Kingdom's accession to the European Community, and enacts that the treaties relating thereto (especially the Treaty of Rome) shall be given legal effect in the United Kingdom without further enactment. The Treaty of Rome (*qv*) has several provisions relevant to British employment law, and there are a number of Directives (*qv*) which have been given legal effect in this country.

European Court of Justice. This court has jurisdiction under Article 177 of the Treaty of Rome to give rulings concerning the interpretation of the Treaty or Regulations made by the Council of Ministers. A British court may, but is not bound to, make a reference to the ECJ if a ruling is necessary to enable a decision to be made. But whereas the ECJ can give rulings on questions of interpretation, their application to the facts of the case is a matter for the national court (*MacMahon v Department of Education*).

See TREATY OF ROME.

Evidence. On a complaint of discrimination on grounds of race or sex, evidence of hostile acts other than the allegedly discriminatory act are admissible if logically probative and show that the applicant was being treated differently from other people. This applies equally to evidence which is subsequent to the discriminatory act, although legal advisers should not introduce such evidence unless they are satisfied that it will affect the outcome (*Chattopadhyay v Holloway School* [1981] IRLR 487).

See SEX DISCRIMINATION ACT 1975; RACE RELATIONS ACT 1976; CONFLICTING EVIDENCE.

Ex gratia payment. If an employer makes a payment to a dismissed employee prior to a claim for unfair dismissal, which is not stated to include liability for the basic award for unfair dismissal, it is a question of fact in each case whether the payment includes any statutory entitlement. Thus, if a sum paid was sufficient to cover any basic or compensatory award, there is no power to make any such awards (*Chelsea Football Club v Heath* [1981] IRLR 73).

See COMPENSATORY AWARD; BASIC AWARD.

Ex-employee. An employee can be restrained from competing with his former employer after leaving his employment, or from disclosing trade secrets, or approaching customers, but only if a valid restrictive covenant is in operation (*Thomas Marshall (Exports) Ltd v Guinle* [1978] IRLR 174) which is reasonable in all the circumstances (*Nordenfelt v Maxim Nordenfelt* [1894] AC 535). In the absence of such a covenant, the ex-employee may not disclose information which has been imparted to him in confidence (*Faccenda Chicken Ltd v Fowler* [1984] IRLR 61), but he cannot be restrained from using his skill and knowledge, or information acquired in his employment (*United Sterling Corporation v Felton* [1974] IRLR 314).

See RESTRICTIVE COVENANT.

F

Factories Act 1961. This Act applies to those premises which are factories, as defined, as well as to electrical stations, docks, ships, works of building and engineering construction etc. Part I deals with health, and includes provisions relating to cleanliness, overcrowding, temperature, ventilation, lighting, drainage, sanitary conveniences, and medical examinations. Part II deals with safety matters, including provisions relating to prime movers, transmission machinery, the fencing of dangerous parts of machinery, dangerous substances, cleaning of machinery by women and young persons, training and supervision of young persons, hoists, lifts, chains, ropes and lifting tackle, cranes, floors, stairs and passages, steam boilers, air receivers, fire escapes, fire prevention etc. Part III deals with welfare provisions, including supply of drinking water, washing facilities, accommodation for clothing, sitting facilities and first aid. There are special provisions for certain dangerous processes, lifting of excessive weights, and prohibitions on the employment of women and young persons. Part VI deals with the employment of women and young persons, with hours of work, overtime, and exceptions. There are a number of regulations made under the Act dealing with specific industrial processes.

A breach of the Act can lead to a prosecution, and may give rise to a claim by an injured employee in respect of the tort of breach of statutory duty.

See HEALTH AND SAFETY AT WORK ETC. ACT.

Fair dismissal (EPCA, s. 57). A dismissal may be fair if it is for one of the five reasons specified in s. 57, namely (1) capability or qualifications (2) conduct (3) redundancy (4) statutory restriction and (5) some other substantial reason. It is for the employer to show the reason for the dismissal, and that it was one of the five statutory reasons; thus, if he shows no reason, or shows a spurious reason, the statutory requirements are not met. If there is more than one reason, it is the principle reason which counts, but the fact that the employer puts a wrong 'label' to the reason is not important, if there are a set of facts which enable the industrial tribunal to find the principle reason (*Abernethy v Mott Hay & Anderson* [1974] IRLR 213). The industrial tribunal will then have to decide if the employer has acted reasonably in treating that reason as a sufficient reason for dismissal.

See REASON FOR THE DISMISSAL; LAWFUL DISMISSAL; WRONGFUL DISMISSAL; SUMMARY DISMISSAL; ACTED REASONABLY.

Fines. In the absence of any agreement or custom (*Sagar v Ridehalgh* [1931] Ch 310), an employer may not impose a fine on an employee for carelessness or misconduct (*Letharby v Horsman Andrew & Knill Ltd* [1979] IRLR 119), the proper remedy is for the employer to sue the employee for negligent work (*Ahmed v Janata Bank* [1981] IRLR 457). If an employee is a manual worker (*qv*) the terms of the Truck Act must be observed (*Riley v Joseph Frisby Ltd* [1982] IRLR 479). There must be a written contract specifying the acts or omissions in respect of which the fines may be imposed, the amount of the fine (or particulars from which the amount be ascertained), and the amount of the fine must be fair and reasonable having regard to all the circumstances of the case. A works rule which provided for fines in respect of misconduct or disobedience was held to be reasonable in *Bird v British Celanese* [1945] KB 336.

See TRUCK ACT 1831; DEDUCTIONS.

Fixed term contract. A contract of employment can be for a fixed term even though it is terminable by notice given by either side within the period stated (*BBC v Dixon* [1979] IRLR 114), and even though the precise date when it will terminate is not immediately ascertainable (*Wilts County Council v NATFHE* [1980] IRLR 198), although this appears to conflict with s. 2 (2) of EPCA which requires that a statement given under s. 1 of the Act should specify the date on which the fixed term contract expires. A contract which specifies a minimum period of employment but no maximum period is not a fixed term contract (*Weston v University College Swansea* [1975] IRLR 102). A fixed term contract which is not renewed is terminated by dismissal, though capable of being fair dismissal in accordance with the usual principles. An employee can, in writing, before the term expires, surrender his rights to bring a claim for unfair dismissal and/or redundancy at the end of the fixed term, and such an agreement is not void by virtue of s. 140 (see s. 142).

Foreign employees. A person who is not a citizen of an EC member state must obtain a work permit to take up employment in Great Britain, except certain Commonwealth citizens, citizens of Gibraltar, and certain professional persons, representatives of overseas newspapers or broadcasting organisations, and self-employed persons. The rules and procedures can be obtained from the Overseas Labour Section of the Department of Employment.

See FREE MOVEMENT OF LABOUR.

Foreign Governments. *See* DIPLOMATIC IMMUNITY.

Formal investigation (RRA, s. 49 (1)). A formal investigation into the activities of a named person can only be undertaken if there is a real belief that the subject of the investigation might have done or might be doing an unlawful discriminatory act (*London Borough of Hillingdon v CRE* [1982] IRLR 424). Before embarking on such investigation, the CRE must hold a preliminary enquiry (s. 49 (4)) and give that person an opportunity to make representations (*Re Prestige Group* [1984] IRLR 166).

See RACE RELATIONS ACT 1976; COMMISSION FOR RACIAL EQUALITY.

Free movement of labour. Articles 48–50 of the Treaty of Rome require all EC member states to ensure the free movement of labour, without discrimination in employment, remuneration or other conditions of work. Consequently, no work permit is required, and there must be equal access to social security benefits, holidays and equal pay. However, a citizen of an EC country (other than Eire) must obtain a residence permit if he wishes to stay for more than 6 months.

See FOREIGN EMPLOYEES.

Frivolous (Industrial Tribunals (Rules of Procedure) Regulations 1980). An application to an industrial tribunal may be struck out under r. 12 (2) (e) as being frivolous if it is so manifestly misconceived as to have no prospect of success. Thus if a case merits careful consideration, even though it may be unlikely to succeed, it should not be struck out (*Mulvaney v LTE* [1981] ICR 351).

See VEXATIOUS.

Frustration. A contract will become frustrated when without default of either party it has become incapable of being performed because the circumstances in which performance are called for would render it a thing radically different from that which was undertaken by the contract (*Davis Contractors Ltd v Fareham UDC* [1956] 2 All ER 145). In employment law terms, the common situations are when the employment is rendered impossible because of the operation of law (e.g. on the outbreak of war (*Morgan v Manser* [1948] 1 KB 184), death of the employer (*Farrow v Wilson* [1869] 4 CP 744, but not so far as redundancy claims are concerned, EPCA, s. 93), long term sickness (*Marshall v Harland & Woolf Ltd* [1972] IRLR 90), and imprisonment (*Hare v Murphy* [1974] IRLR 342).

In deciding whether or not a contract of employment is frustrated on grounds of sickness, regard should be had to (a) the length the employment has lasted (b) how long it is expected to last (c) the nature of the job (d) the nature, length and effect of the illness or disabling event (e) the needs of the employer for the work to be done and the need for a replacement to do it (f) the risk of the employer acquiring obligations in respect of redundancy payments or unfair dismissal compensation (g) whether wages are continued to be paid (h) the acts and statement of the employer, including his dismissal of the employee, or his failure to do so (i) whether in all the circumstances a reasonable employer could be expected to wait any longer (*Egg Stores v Leibovici* [1976] IRLR 376).

There is some doubt about the application of the doctrine of frustration to the imprisonment of the employee, for although this was allowed in some cases (*Hare v Murphy* supra, *Chakki v United Yeast Co* [1982] ICR 140), more recently it has been held that the doctrine only applies to an event over which the parties have no control. Since, if an employee is sent to prison, it is his conduct which renders the contract incapable of being performed, the contract cannot be frustrated, as there is no doctrine of self-induced frustration. Thus, in such circumstances, the employer dismisses the employee (assuming that he is not permitted to resume work), and the question of the fairness of the dismissal must be decided in accordance with the usual principles (*Norris v Southampton City Council* [1982] IRLR 141).

Further and better particulars (Industrial Tribunal (Rules of Procedure) Regulations 1980). An applicant is entitled to apply for, and receive, further and better particulars in order to enable him to prepare in advance for the hearing, rather than to be in the position of having to apply for an adjournment to consider the respondent's evidence (*White v University of Manchester* [1976] IRLR 218). A respondent may also so apply in order to find out what the allegations are, so that he can identify with reasonable clarity the case he has to meet and the range of argument that is likely to occur before the industrial tribunal (*Honeyrose Products Ltd v Joslin* [1980] IRLR 80). Such orders are not made as a matter of course, but as may be necessary for dealing with relevant matters fairly, and should not be made when the only issue is the amount of compensation which is likely to be awarded (*Colonial Mutual Life Assurance Society v Clinch* [1981] ICR 752).

See DISCOVERY OF DOCUMENTS.

G

Genuine material factor (EqPA, s. 1 (3)). An equality clause shall not operate in relation to a variation which exists between a woman's contract and a man's contract if the employer proves (on the balance of probabilities, *National Vulcan Engineering Insurance Group Ltd v Wade* [1978] IRLR 225) that the variation is genuinely due to a material factor between her case and his. If the employer does not raise this defence at the hearing, it is not open to the industrial tribunal to take the point on his behalf. The following have been held to amount to genuine material factors (a) a pay differential related to a system of grading based on experience, especially if it can be shown to have been built into the contract of employment (*ARW Transformers Ltd v Cupples* [1977] IRLR 228) (b) an agreed differential for night workers which applies to all night workers irrespective of sex (*Kerr v Lister & Co Ltd* [1977] IRLR 259) (c) part-time employees who are re-munerated at a lower rate than full-time employees (*Handley v Mono Ltd* [1978] IRLR 534) if it can be shown that the lesser rate was applied for genuine economic reasons, e.g. in order to ensure a greater use of plant, machinery etc., or because the overheads were higher, but not if this is a way of paying women workers less than men (*Jenkins v Kingsgate Clothing Ltd* [1981] IRLR 228) (d) a difference due to the location of the work, e.g. a London allowance (*NAAFI v Varley* [1976] IRLR 408) (e) a grading system applied irrespective of sex (*National Vulcan Engineering Insurance Group v Wade*, supra) (f) 'red circling' (*qv*) arrangements, provided this has nothing to do with the sex of the person affected (*Snoxell v Vauxhall Motors* [1977] IRLR 123) and is not based on some form of past discrimination (*Charles Early & Marriott Ltd v Smith* [1977] IRLR 123), and is not prolonged for such a length of time that there is doubt as to whether or not it is genuine (*Outlook Supplies Ltd v Parry* [1978] IRLR 12) (g) greater responsibi-lities (*Avon Police v Emery* [1981] ICR 229), and so on.

The fact that an employer has to pay more for a male employee in order to attract him to work (i.e. market forces) is not a genuine material difference (*Fletcher v Clay Cross (Quarry Services) Ltd* [1979] IRLR 361) though it may be if the claim is based on equal value (*qv*). If the defence is raised because there are different duties, as well as there being a contractual obligation to perform those duties, they must be performed in practice to some significant extent (*Electrolux Ltd v*

62

Hutchinson [1976] IRLR 410). If a woman is comparing herself with a male predecessor (*McCarthys Ltd v Smith* [1980] IRLR 209), the reduced profitability of the firm since he left which results in her being paid less than him can amount to a genuine material factor (*Albion Shipping Ltd v Arnold* [1981] IRLR 525).

The existence of a genuine material factor is, in the last analysis, a question of fact to be determined by the industrial tribunal (*Outlook Supplies Ltd v Parry*, supra).

See EQUAL PAY ACT 1970; EQUAL PAY (AMENDMENT) REGULATIONS 1983; LIKE WORK; BROADLY SIMILAR NATURE.

Genuine occupational qualification (SDA, s. 7 (2); RRA, s. 5 (2)). It is not unlawful to discriminate when the sex or race of a person is a genuine occupational qualification (GOQ) for the job. The sex of a person is a GOQ if (1) the essential nature of the job calls for a man for reasons of physiology (excluding physical strength or stamina) or, in dramatic performances or other entertainment, for reasons of authenticity (2) the job needs to be held by a man to preserve decency or privacy because (a) it is likely to involve physical contact with men (*Wylie v Dee Co Ltd* [1978] IRLR 103) or (b) persons may object to the presence of the opposite sex because they are in a state of undress (*Sisley v Britannia Security Ltd* [1983] IRLR 404) or using sanitary facilities (3) the job involves living in and there are no separate sleeping or sanitary facilities and it is unreasonable to expect the employer to provide separate facilities ('living in' involves a concept of residence, whether permanent or temporary, and does not refer to remaining on the premises for limited periods of rest, see *Sisley v Britannia Security Ltd*, supra) (4) the work is done in a single sex institution for persons requiring special care, supervision or treatment which employs persons of one sex (disregarding a person of the other sex whose presence is exceptional) and it is reasonable that persons of one sex should be employed (5) the job involves the provision of personal services promoting welfare or education, which is best done by persons of one sex (*Roadburg v Lothian Regional Council* [1976] IRLR 203) (6) there are legal restrictions against the employment of women (*White v British Sugar Corpn Ltd* [1977] IRLR 121), and see Hours of Employment (Convention) Act 1936, Mines and Quarries Act 1954, Factories Act 1961, etc.) (7) the job is to be performed outside Great Britain in a country whose laws and customs do not permit the job to be done effectively by persons of one sex (8) the job is to be held by a married couple. A GOQ is not grounds for a dismissal under s. 6 (2) (b), but can apply to a failure to transfer or deliberately omitting to offer employment under s. 6 (2) (a) (*Timex Co Ltd v Hodgson* [1981] IRLR 530).

The race of a person is a GOQ if (1) the job involves participation in a dramatic performance or other entertainment where a person of that racial group is required for purposes of authenticity (2) the work involves participation as an artist's or photographic model where a person of that racial group is required for purposes of authenticity (3) the job involves working in a place where food or drink is provided and consumed by the public in a particular setting where a person of that racial group is required for purpose of authenticity (4) the holder of the job provides persons of that racial group with personal services promoting their welfare, and those services can be most effectively provided by persons of that racial group.

See SEX DISCRIMINATION ACT 1975; RACE RELATIONS ACT 1976.

Genuinely due to a material factor (EqPA, s. 1 (3)). *See* GENUINE MATERIAL FACTOR.

Golden formula. Since many acts committed by trade unions are likely to be contrary to the civil or criminal law, their legitimate activities would be severely constrained. Hence, Parliament has recognised since 1875 (Conspiracy and Protection of Property Act, s. 3) that there are circumstances when an immunity from legal action must be given. This is done by means of the 'golden formula' i.e. 'an act done in furtherance or contemplation of a trade dispute shall not be actionable . . .' in those circumstances. It should be noted that there must be a trade dispute in existence not a mere possibility of one (*Bents Brewery Ltd v Hogan* [1945] 2 All ER 570), the act must be in contemplation of that dispute, and in furtherance of it (*Conway v Wade* [1909] AC 506). The current immunities are to be found in the Criminal Law Act 1977, s. 1 (3) (immunity from action in respect of criminal conspiracy) and the Trade Union and Labour Relations Act 1974, s. 13 (immunity from action in tort in respect of inducing breach of contract, and in respect of civil conspiracy). The golden formula has been severely restricted in recent years by the Employment Act 1980, s. 17 (secondary action) Employment Act 1982, s. 14 (pressure to impose union membership or recognition requirements) and Trade Union Act 1984 (ballots before strikes).

See IN CONTEMPLATION OR FURTHERANCE; TRADE DISPUTE.

Gross misconduct. An employee who commits an act of gross misconduct is deemed to have broken his contract of employment, and hence he may be dismissed summarily (i.e. without notice). In determining whether or not certain conduct constitutes gross misconduct, account must be taken of changing social conditions (*Wilson v Racher* [1974] IRLR 114) so that many of the earlier decisions must be treated with considerable reserve. However, certain principles remain constant, e.g. theft (*Sinclair v Neighbour* [1966] 3 All ER 998) etc. It is advisable for employers to specify in their works rules (*qv*) those acts which are regarded as constituting gross misconduct, although there are certain acts which are so obviously so that they scarcely require to be mentioned (*Parsons & Co Ltd v McLoughlin* [1978] IRLR 65). However, for the avoidance of doubt, the rules should specify those acts in a general as well as specific form (*Ayub v Vauxhall Motors Ltd* [1978] IRLR 428 and see *Trusthouse Forte (Catering) Ltd v Adonis* [1984] IRLR 382. Whether specific conduct constitutes gross misconduct is a question of fact for the court or industrial tribunal to determine (*Treganowen v Robert Knee & Co Ltd* [1975] IRLR 247). The standards or reasonableness must still be applied.

See SUMMARY DISMISSAL; DISCIPLINARY PROCEDURE; WORKS RULES.

Guarantee pay (EPCA, s. 12 (1)). Provided an employee has been continuously employed for more than one month, he is entitled to receive a minimum statutory guarantee pay for each whole day he is laid off from work because of (a) a diminution of the employer's requirements for the employee to do the work, or (b) any other occurrence affecting the employer's business. The guarantee pay is only payable for a day when the employee would otherwise be required to work (i.e. holidays, sickness absences or overtime days are not included, see *York v Colledge Hosiery Ltd* [1978] IRLR 53). The employee must comply with reasonable requirements to make his services available (*Meadows v Faithful Overalls Ltd* [1977] IRLR 330) and he must not unreasonably refuse suitable alternative work (*Purdy v Willowbrook International Ltd* [1977] IRLR 388). Guarantee pay is not payable if the reason for the lay-off is because of a strike, lock-out or other industrial action involving any employee of the employer or of an associated employer (*Garvey v Maybank (Oldham) Ltd* [1979] IRLR 408). Nor is it payable if the employee is employed under a contract for a fixed term of three months or less, or a contract made in contemplation of the performance of a specific task which is not expected to last for more than three months unless he has actually been employed for more than three months. The fact that the employee signs on for unemployment benefit does not affect the employer's obligation to make the payment (*Robinson v Claxton & Garland Ltd* [1977] IRLR 159), but contractual remuneration can be set off against the guarantee pay.

Guarantee pay (currently £10.50p per day) is payable for five days in any period of three months, but if an employer makes a payment under the contractual arrangement, those days count for the purpose of the statutory scheme, and liability for further payment in respect of those days is discharged (*Cartwright v Clancy Ltd* [1983] IRLR 355).

See ALTERNATIVE WORK; OCCURRENCE; NORMALLY BE REQUIRED TO WORK; WORKLESS DAY.

H

Harassment. An allegation by an employee that he has been subjected to harassment should be investigated by the employer, and dealt with appropriately. Since it can constitute unlawful discrimination on grounds of sex or race (*Porcelli v Strathclyde Regional Council*, [1984] IRLR 467), it should be considered and dealt with in evidence before an industrial tribunal (*Kingston v British Railways Board* [1982] IRLR 274).

> *See* SEX DISCRIMINATION ACT 1975; RACE RELATIONS ACT 1976.

Has not been offered re-engagement (EPCA, s. 62 (2) (b)). A conditional offer can be an offer to re-engage (*Williams v National Theatre Board* [1982] IRLR 377), but the offer must be communicated to the employee so that, for example, if the employee is deaf, communication must be made in a suitable manner (*Tomczynski v K. Millar Ltd* [1976] 11 ITR 127).

> *See* REASON FOR THE DISMISSAL – TAKING PART IN A STRIKE.

Health and Safety at Work etc. Act 1974 (HSWA). This Act is the major statute governing health and safety at work. It differs from previous legislation on this subject in a number of important ways. First, it is essentially a criminal statute, with penalties of fines and (in certain rare cases) imprisonment which may be imposed in respect of breaches of the Act. No civil liability arises from a breach (i.e. arising out of the tort of breach of statutory duty), although Regulations made under the Act may specify the circumstances when a civil action may be brought in addition to the criminal liability. Second, the Act applies to all employees, wherever they work, and is not confined, as previous legislation, to specific places of work (e.g. factories, offices, mines, etc.). Third, the Act applies to people in different capacities, e.g. to an employer in relation to his employees, and to the employer in his capacity as a manufacturer etc. of plant or substances to be used at work by other employees. Finally, the Act contains a number of new provisions relating to enforcement of the law, and other provisions designed to promote a greater awareness of the need to promote safety and health at work.

The employer is under a general duty to ensure, as far as is reasonably practicable (*qv*) the health, safety and welfare at work of all his employees (s. 2 (1)). Particular aspects of that general duty are laid down in s. 2 (2) (a)–(e). Employers must provide to their employees a safety policy (*qv*), recognised trade unions may appoint safety representatives, and the employer may be required to appoint a safety committee. Employers and self-employed persons owe a duty to those who are not in their employment to conduct their undertakings in such a way as to ensure, so far as is reasonably practicable, that persons who are not in their employment are not exposed to risks to their health and safety. There are duties on persons who control non-domestic premises (*qv*) to ensure that the means of access and exit, as well as any plant or substance on the premises are safe, and duties on those who manufacture, import or design plant or substances to ensure that so far as is reasonably practicable, these are safe and without risks to health when used at work. Employees are under a duty to take care of themselves and others, and to co-operate with employers so far as it is necessary to enable the employer to perform or comply with his duties. An employer must not charge for anything done or provided in pursuance of any specific requirement of a relevant statutory provision.

The Act establishes the Health and Safety Commission (HSC) (*qv*) the Health and Safety Executive (HSE) (*qv*) and continues the Employment Medical Advisory Service (*EMAS*). The Secretary of State may issue Regulations (which may repeal existing health and safety laws) and the HSC may give approval to Codes of Practice (*qv*) and issue guidance notes (which, though they have no statutory force, are frequently of greater practical value than the Codes).

Inspectors from HSE have power to issue improvement notices (*qv*) prohibition notices (*qv*), and have power to seize and render harmless any article or substance likely to be a cause of imminent danger of serious personal injury.

See HEALTH AND SAFETY COMMISSION; HEALTH AND SAFETY EXECUTIVE; SAFETY POLICY; SAFETY REPRESENTATIVES; SAFETY COMMITTEE; NON-DOMESTIC PREMISES; CODES OF PRACTICE; IMPROVEMENT NOTICES; PROHIBITION NOTICES; REASONABLY PRACTICABLE.

Health and Safety Commission. The Commission consists of a Chairman, three members representing employers' organisations, three members representing employees' organisations, and three other members appointed after consultation with interested parties. Its duties are to assist and encourage persons to further the duties under Part I of the Health and Safety at Work etc. Act 1974, to arrange for the carrying out of research, publication of results, and the provision of training, to provide an advisory service, and to submit proposals for the making of regulations. The Commission also issues Codes of Practice and Guidance Notes on health and safety matters. The day-to-day enforcement of the Act is the responsibility of the Health and Safety Executive.

See HEALTH AND SAFETY AT WORK ETC. ACT 1974.

Health and Safety Executive (HSE). HSE is responsible for the day-to-day enforcement of the Health and Safety at Work etc. Act and other statutory provisions relating to health and safety, together with other enforcing authorities (e.g. local authorities). The Executive consists of a Director and two Assistant Directors. Enforcing authorities will appoint inspectors, who have wide powers to enter premises, inspect them and the activities carried on, take samples, etc., as well as issue improvement notices (*qv*) and prohibition notices (*qv*), and seize and render harmless plant or substances. They also institute proceedings for offences under the Act and other legislation.

See HEALTH AND SAFETY AT WORK ETC. ACT 1974.

Health Service employees. In respect of employment rights generally, employees of the National Health Service have all the usual legal rights, except the right to a written statement under s. 1 of EPCA, minimum periods of notice, and redundancy payments. In other respects, they are not to be regarded as being Crown employees (s. 138 (5) of EPCA).

See CROWN EMPLOYEES.

Hearsay evidence. Hearsay evidence is evidence which is given by a person (or document) other than a witness in proceedings. Such evidence is frequently admitted in industrial tribunal proceedings, and the fact that it is hearsay goes to credibility, not admissibility.

Hiving down agreements. A hiving down agreement is an arrangement made by a liquidator or receiver, with the object of protecting the creditors' interests. This is done by a sale of the assets of the company to a wholly owned subsidiary, the company retaining the labour force, with an agreement to sub-contract that labour force to the subsidiary. Thus, if and when the company is wound up, it will have no assets with which to meet claims made by employees (certain monies can be paid from the Redundancy Fund under the provisions of ss. 121–127 of EPCA, but not all claims can be met this way). The nature of a hiving down agreement, and its unfortunate consequences were noted by the EAT in *Pambakian v Brentford Nylons Ltd* [1978] ICR 665.

All hiving down agreements are now subject to the provisions of the Transfer of Undertakings (Protection of Employment) Regulations 1981, in particular reg. 4, which provides that where a receiver or liquidator transfers a company's undertaking to a wholly-owned subsidiary, the transfer is not deemed to have been effected until immediately before (a) the transferee company ceases to be a wholly owned subsidiary of the transferor company or (b) the undertaking is transferred by the transferee to another person. In other words, the transfer of the assets to a wholly owned subsidiary will be deemed to have been delayed until some event other than the hiving down operation.

Holidays. There is no general law which requires an employer to give holidays to his employees, and this is usually covered by the express or implied terms of the contract. Holiday entitlement should be stated in the written particulars of employment under s. 1 of EPCA or other contractual document. An implied term, based on custom and usage, may also be resorted to (*Tucker v British Leyland Motor Corpn* [1978] IRLR 493). An EC Recommendation (75/457) recommends four weeks paid holiday each year.

In industries governed by Wages Councils (*qv*) or Statutory Joint Industrial Councils (*qv*) provision may be made for holidays with pay, and it is an offence not to comply. Similar powers can be found in the Agricultural Wages Act 1948.

An employee who wishes to sue in respect of his employer's failure to pay holiday pay must bring the claim before a county court, the industrial tribunal having no jurisdiction to deal with such matters.

See BANK HOLIDAYS.

Homeworker. Whether or not a person who works at home for another is an employee is a question of fact for the industrial tribunal to determine, and the EAT cannot interfere with that finding unless the industrial tribunal misdirected themselves in law or the decision was one which no reasonable industrial tribunal, properly directed, could come to (*Nethermere (St Neotts) Ltd v Taverna* [1984] IRLR 240).

See EMPLOYEE; OUTWORKER.

Hours of work (Factories Act 1961). Women and young persons who work in factories are not allowed to work more than 9 hours in any day (excluding intervals allowed for meals and rest) nor more than 48 hours in any week. The period of employment shall not exceed 11 hours in any day, and shall not begin before 7 a.m. nor end later than 8 p.m. (6 p.m. in the case of young persons under the age of 16), nor later than 1 p.m. on Saturday. The spell of work shall not exceed $4\frac{1}{2}$ hours without an interval of at least $\frac{1}{2}$ hour, although if a break of 10 minutes is allowed, the spell of work may be 5 hours.

There are a number of exceptions to the above rules in the case of women and young persons over the age of 16. These include shift systems (s. 97) certain special exceptions (ss. 95, 96, 99, 106) certain specified trades (ss. 101, 110, 111, 113), certain occupations (s. 116), overtime (s. 89), and special exemption orders or general exemption regulations under s. 117. There are also certain exclusions e.g. s. 125 (docks), s. 127 (building operations), and the provisions do not apply to women cleaners (s. 176 (4)) or to errand boys employed outside the factory.

I

Illegal contract. The statutory rights not to be unfairly dismissed, or to receive redundancy payment, etc., cannot be enforced if the contract of employment is illegal (*Tomlinson v Dick Evans U Drive Ltd* [1978] IRLR 77). Thus if an employee receives payments which are not declared for income tax purposes (*Cole v Fred Stacy Ltd* [1974] IRLR 73) the contract is illegal, as being a contract to defraud the revenue. The test is 'Has the employee knowingly been a party to the deception of the Revenue?' (*Newlands v Simons & Willer (Hairdressers) Ltd* [1981] IRLR 359). If the employee did not know or consent, there is no illegality (*Davidson v Pillay* [1975] IRLR 275), but if he knew or ought to have known, the contract will be illegal (*Corby v Morrison* [1980] IRLR 218). But if the employee commits an unlawful or illegal act during the course of his employment, for the purpose of that employment, the contract will not thereby be rendered illegal, if it is capable of being performed in a legal manner (*Coral Leisure Group Ltd v Barnett* [1981] IRLR 204).

Immediately before (Transfer of Undertakings (Protection of Employment) Regulations 1981, reg. 5 (1)). It depends on the facts of each case whether a dismissal was sufficiently proximate to the transfer for a person to have been employed immediately before the transfer (*Apex Leisure Hire v Barratt* [1984] ICR 452).

See TRANSFER OF UNDERTAKINGS (PROTECTION OF EMPLOYMENT) REGULATIONS 1981.

Implied term. A term may be implied into a contract of employment to give it business efficacy. The common law rule was that it was only possible to imply a term when it was an obvious one, so obvious, in fact, that the parties did not bother to insert it in the contract (*Southern Foundries Ltd v Shirlaw* [1940] 2 All ER 455), but in more recent times it has been stated that the court should ask what was reasonable in the general run of such cases, and then state what the obligation should be (*Shell UK Ltd v Lostock Garage Ltd* [1977] 1 All ER 481). Whether a term can be implied into a contract of employment will depend on all the circumstances of the case, and these may differ in accordance with the size of the employer, the nature of the employment etc. (*Warner v Barber Stores* [1978] IRLR 109). Thus there may be an implied term that the employer will find work for the employee to do (*Breach v Epsylon Industries Ltd* [1976] IRLR 180) but not that the employee will be required only to work in particular premises (*Managers (Holborn) Ltd v Hohne* [1977] IRLR 230).

There is a very important implied term that the employer will treat the employee with respect (*Palmanor Ltd v Cedric* [1978] IRLR 303), and will not arbitrarily or unreasonably discriminate against him in relation to his remuneration (*Gardener Ltd v Beresford* [1978] IRLR 63), will ensure his safety at work (*British Aircraft Corpn v Austin* [1978] IRLR 332), and will not damage the relationship of trust, confidence and faith which must exist between the parties (*Courtland Northern Textiles Ltd v Andrews* [1979] IRLR 84) and so on. However, there is no obvious implied term on sick pay, and the industrial tribunal should examine all the facts and circumstances of the relationship between the employer and employee (*Mears v Safeguard Security Ltd* [1982] IRLR 183). Thus, if there is no agreement on the duration of sick pay, the industrial tribunal should imply a reasonable term, having regard to the usual practice in the industry (*Howman v Blyth* [1983] IRLR 139).

An implied term must not be vague and unpredictable in its effect (*Lake v Essex County Council* [1979] IRLR 241).

See CONSTRUCTIVE DISMISSAL.

Improvement notice (HSWA, s. 21). If an inspector is of the opinion that (a) a person is contravening a statutory provision, or (b) has contravened such provision and it is likely that the contravention will be repeated, he may serve an improvement notice, requiring that person to remedy the contravention within a specified period (but not less than 21 days, which is the period within which an appeal may be made to an industrial tribunal, see Industrial Tribunals (Improvement and Prohibition Notices Appeals) Regulations 1974).

See PROHIBITION NOTICE.

In accordance with instructions (EPCA, s. 141 (4)). An employee who returns from abroad for a period of leave, is not returning to Great Britain 'in accordance with instructions given to him by his employer', even though the employer makes the necessary arrangements (*Costain Civil Engineering Ltd v Draycott* [1977] IRLR 17).

See REDUNDANCY; ORDINARILY WORK OUTSIDE GREAT BRITAIN; OVERSEAS EMPLOYMENT.

In contemplation or furtherance (TULRA, s. 13 (1)). To be in contemplation of a trade dispute, the dispute must be more than a mere possibility, and should be imminent (*Bents Brewery Co Ltd v Hogan* [1947] 1 All ER 570). See also s. 29 (5). An act will be done in furtherance of a trade dispute if the doer of the act honestly but subjectively believes that he is seeking to achieve an objective in connection with a trade dispute (*Express Newspapers Ltd v McShane* [1980] IRLR 35). However, there must be an existing trade dispute, and the act must be done for the purpose of promoting the interests of one of the parties to it (*Beaverbrook Newspapers Ltd v Keys* [1978] IRLR 34).

See TRADE DISPUTE.

In order to comply with a requirement (SDA, s. 51). Discrimination is permissible if it is necessary to comply with an Act passed before the Sex Discrimination Act. Thus, it is permissible to refuse to offer employment to women if by so doing, there would be a contravention of the Health and Safety at Work etc. Act 1974 (*Page v Freight Hire (Tank Haulage) Ltd* [1981] IRLR 13), or a breach of a licence granted under relevant legislation (*Greater London Council v Farrar* [1980] ICR 266).

See SEX DISCRIMINATION ACT 1975.

In the course of his employment (SDA, s 41 (1)). An act is done in the course of a person's employment if it is done in the scope of his employment, and for the purpose of the employer's business (*Conway v George Wimpey Ltd* [1951] 1 All ER 363). The act is still within the course of his employment even if the employer has forbidden the employee to do the act, if the act was done for the purpose of the employer's business (*Rose v Plenty* [1976] 1 All ER 96).

See SEX DISCRIMINATION ACT 1975.

Independent contractor. *See* EMPLOYEE; SELF-EMPLOYED.

Independent trade union (EPA, s. 8). A trade union may obtain a certificate of independence provided the statutory test of not being under the domination or control of the employer can be met. The test is an objective one for the courts to determine, and a trade union will be liable to interference (*qv*) from the employer if it is vulnerable to interference (*Certification Officer v Squibb (UK) Staff Association* [1979] IRLR 75). The Certification Officer may take into account the extent to which the employer provides material support, the history, rules and organisation of the staff association, and other relevant factors in order to assess whether the union is free from the likelihood of interference by the employer (*Blue Circle Staff Association v Certification Officer* [1977] ICR 224).

The advantages of a trade union obtaining a certificate of independence are as follows:

(1) representatives of the trade union are entitled to information for the purposes of collective bargaining (EPA, s. 17);

(2) rights of employees not to have action (short of dismissal) taken against them apply only to members of an independent trade union (EPCA, s. 23);

(3) officials of independent trade unions are entitled to have time off work, with pay, for the purpose of carrying out their duties in connection with industrial relations, or to go on approved training courses (EPCA, s. 27);

(4) employees who are members of independent trade unions are entitled to have time off work (not necessarily with pay) for the purpose of taking part in trade union activities (EPCA, s. 28);

(5) an employer must consult with the representatives of an independent trade union recognised by him in the event of redundancies (EPA, s. 99);

(6) an application for interim relief may be made by an employee who claims he was dismissed because he was or proposed to become a member of an independent trade union (EPCA, s. 77);

(7) it is unfair to dismiss an employee for being a member of an independent trade union, or for taking part in its activities at an appropriate time (EPCA, s. 58);

(8) an independent trade union may enter into a valid union membership agreement;

(9) an independent trade union may obtain public funds for the purpose of holding ballots, and may require the employer to make his premises available for that purpose (EA 1980, ss. 1–2);

(10) an independent trade union is entitled to have information and be consulted under the Transfer of Undertakings (Protection of Employment) Regulations 1981.

Indirect discrimination (RRA, s. 1 (1) (b); SDA, s. 1 (1) (b)). When indirect discrimination is alleged, the applicant has to show that there was a particular requirement or condition which must be complied with. He then has to show that it applied to him, and that a substantially smaller proportion of his racial group (or sex) were able to comply than similar persons in a different racial group (or sex). The comparison must be made between like persons (*Perera v Civil Service Commission* [1980] IRLR 233). The requirement or condition may then be shown to be justifiable irrespective of race or sex.

See RACE RELATIONS ACT 1976; SEX DISCRIMINATION ACT 1975; REQUIREMENT OR CONDITION; JUSTIFIABLE.

Industrial action (EPCA, s. 62). See OTHER INDUSTRIAL ACTION.

Industrial tribunals. The constitutional basis for industrial tribunals can be found in the Industrial Tribunals (England and Wales) Regulations 1965 and the Industrial Tribunal (Scotland) Regulations 1965, made under the Industrial Training Act 1964. A Central Office of Industrial Tribunals (COIT) has been established in London and Glasgow, with 16 Regional Offices (ROIT) in England and Wales, and 3 in Scotland. An industrial tribunal may sit at other locations within the region.

An industrial tribunal consists of a chairman and two lay members. The chairman is either a barrister or solicitor, and can be full-time or part-time. The lay members are selected from a panel drawn up after consultation with representatives of employers' organisations and employed persons. There must always be a representative of each side of industry, although a chairman can sit with one lay member if both parties to the case agree. Each member of the industrial tribunal has an equal vote, although in practice it appears that about 96% of all decisions are unanimous, and in the remainder, the 'wingmen' are just as likely to unite in outvoting the legal chairman as the latter is likely to have the support of one or the other side. In cases of sex discrimination, it is desirable to have one member of either sex, and in race discrimination cases, a member who has special experience of race relations, but there is no legal requirement that this should be so (*Habib v Elkington & Co Ltd* [1981] IRLR 344).

The jurisdiction of industrial tribunals is as follows:

(1) Industrial Training Act 1964, s. 12; appeals against assessment of industrial training levies;

(2) Docks and Harbours Act 1966, s. 51; definition of dock worker;

(3) Equal Pay Act 1970, s. 2; complaints of breach of equality clauses in contracts of employment;

(4) Health and Safety at Work etc. Act 1974, s. 24; appeals against improvement and prohibition notices;

(5) Safety Representatives and Safety Committee Regulations 1977, time off work with pay for safety representatives;

(6) Occupational Pension Schemes (Certification of Employments) Regulations 1975; decisions on whether an independent trade union is recognised for collective bargaining purposes, or whether consultations have been carried out;

(7) Occupational Pension Schemes (Equal Access to Membership) Regulations 1976; decisions on equality clauses which permit equal access to occupational pension schemes;

(8) Employment Protection Act 1975, s. 101 (1) failure to consult with recognised trade unions on redundancies; s. 103 (1) applications for protective awards;

(9) Sex Discrimination Act 1975, s. 63 complaints of discrimination on grounds of sex or marital status; s. 68 appeals against non-discrimination notices; s. 72 (3) (a) applications by the EOC relating to discriminatory advertisements; s. 73 applications by EOC prior to county court action;

(10) Race Relations Act 1976, s. 54 complaints of race discrimination; s. 59 appeals against non-discrimination notices; s. 63 (3) (a) applications by the CRE relating to discriminatory advertisements; s. 64 applications by CRE prior to county court actions;

(11) Employment Protection (Consolidation) Act 1978, s. 11 failure to give written statements under s. 1; failure to give itemised pay statements; s. 17 (1) guarantee payments; s. 22 (1) medical suspension payments; s. 24 (1) taking action short of dismissal on

grounds of trade union membership or non-membership; s. 27 (7) time off work for trade union duties; s. 28 (4) time off work for trade union activities; s. 29 (6) time off work for public duties; s. 31 (6) time off work with pay to look for work or make arrangements for retraining; s. 31A (6) time off work for ante-natal care; s. 36 (1) maternity pay; s. 43 (1) maternity pay rebates; s. 53 (4) failure to give written reasons for dismissal; s. 67 (1) complaints of unfair dismissal; s. 77 (1) interim relief; s. 91 (1) redundancy payments; s. 108 (1) claims for redundancy rebates; s. 112 redundancy payments for civil servants; s. 124 (1) rights on employer's insolvency; s. 130 appeals formerly heard by referees or boards of referees under certain statutory provisions;

(12) Employment Act 1980, s. 2 (4) secret ballots on employers' premises; s. 4 (4) unreasonable exclusion or expulsion from a trade union;

(13) Transfer of Undertakings (Protection of Employment) Regulations 1981, failure to inform or consult with trade unions; failure to pay compensation;

(14) Local Government (Compensation) Regulations 1972, British Transport (Compensation to Employees) Regulations 1970 compensation payments for loss of office on re-organisation;

(15) It would appear that industrial tribunals have jurisdiction to hear claims under Article 119 of the Treaty of Rome, even though there is no statutory basis for such jurisdiction (*Albion Shipping Agency v Arnold* [1982] ICR 22, and see *Garland v British Rail Engineering Ltd* [1982] IRLR 257).

The procedure adopted before industrial tribunals is laid down in the Industrial Tribunal (Rules of Procedure) Regulations 1980, and is generally designed to ensure simplicity, absence of legal formalities, speed, cheapness and flexibility.

See COSTS; VEXATIOUS; FRIVOLOUS; HEARSAY EVIDENCE.

Industrial Tribunals (Rules of Procedure) Regulations 1980. These Regulations govern procedure in industrial tribunals, and make provision for the making of an originating application, appearance by respondents, discovery of documents, further and better particulars, witness attendance orders, pre-hearing assessments, procedure at the hearing, applications for review, award of costs, extensions of time, joiner, and other miscellaneous matters. Similar Regulations have been made in respect of proceedings in Scotland.

Injury to feelings (SDA, ss. 65 (1) (b), 66 (4); RRA, ss. 56 (1) (b), 57 (4)). Once an industrial tribunal has decided to award compensation under s. 65 (1) (b), the amount of compensation is to be computed on the basis of what damages would be recoverable in the county court, and not on what the industrial tribunal considers to be just and equitable. The amount should reflect the measure of damages recoverable for the statutory tort of unlawful discrimination (*Hurley v Mustoe* [1981] IRLR 208). Compensation for injured feelings may be awarded in addition to any other heading of damages.

See SEX DISCRIMINATION ACT 1975; RACE RELATIONS ACT 1976.

Insolvency of employer (EPCA, s. 122). If an employer becomes insolvent, an application may be made to the Secretary of State for the following monies to be paid out of the Redundancy Fund, namely, arrears of pay (up to eight weeks) any statutory notice payable, holiday pay owed for up to six weeks, any basic award for unfair dismissal, and any reasonable sum by way of reimbursement of the whole or part of any fee or premium paid by an apprentice or articled clerk. Arrears of pay include those monies which rank as preferential debts (*qv*) which are not satisfied on insolvency.

The rights of an employee under the insolvency provisions against the Secretary of State are no greater than they are against the employer. Thus if an employee is dismissed without contractual notice, his normal remedy is an action for damages for breach of contract, subject to the rules of mitigation of loss. If he obtains employment during the notice period, the claim against the Secretary of State may be correspondingly reduced (*Wilson v Secretary of State for Employment* [1977] IRLR 483), but there should be no reduction because the employee has received social security payments (*Westwood v Secretary of State for Employment* [1982] IRLR 350). An application for a redundancy payment does not need to name the employer as a party to the proceedings (*Jones v Secretary of State for Employment* [1982] ICR 389).

See PREFERENTIAL DEBTS.

Intention . . . to do any act (SDA, s. 38 (1)). To determine whether an advertisement shows an intention to discriminate unlawfully, the advertisement has to be read as a whole, according to what a reasonable person would understand as the natural and ordinary meaning of the words used. It is not permissible to introduce evidence as to what the advertiser actually did mean (*EOC v Robertson* [1980] IRLR 44).

Interim relief (s. 77, EPCA). If an employee alleged that he was dismissed because he was, or proposed to be, a member of an independent trade union (*qv*) or had taken part in the activities of such trade union, or because he was not a member of a trade union, he may seek an application for interim relief. This is an order that he be reinstated or re-engaged, or suspended on full pay, until the matter is finally determined by the industrial tribunal. The application must be presented within seven days of his dismissal and, in the case of a claim relating to trade union membership or activities, be accompanied by a certificate from an authorised trade union official stating that the complainant was, or proposed to become, a member of the trade union, and that the official had reasonable grounds to believe that the reason for the dismissal was as alleged. The trade union should decide who is an authorised official for the purpose (*Farmeary v Veterinary Drug Co Ltd* [1976] IRLR 322), although authority of an official who signs a certificate will be assumed until it is challenged (*Sulemany v Habib Bank Ltd* [1980] ICR 60). The certificate must comply with the requrements of s. 77 (2), although it need not be technically correct in every respect (*Stone v Charrington & Co Ltd* [1977] ICR 248).

The industrial tribunal will hear the case as soon as practicable, and if they form the view that it is likely that the applicant would succeed at a full hearing, they will ask the employer if he will reinstate or re-engage the employee, on terms no less favourable than those which he previously enjoyed, pending the full hearing. If not, an order for continuation of employment will be made, which in effect means that the employee will be suspended on full pay, until the final outcome of the case.

In forming their preliminary view, the industrial tribunal may take into account all the events which led up to the dismissal (*Forsyth v Fry's Metals Ltd* [1977] IRLR 243).

See LIKELY.

International Labour Organisation. Formed in 1919, and now attached to the United Nations, the ILO acts as a forum for discussions between sovereign states, employers' organisations and trade unions. It may pass Conventions, which individual states may ratify and thus adopt as binding obligations (or having done so, may renounce) and Recommendations, which have no effect other than as a statement of principles.

Inventions. *See* PATENTS AND INVENTIONS.

Issue estoppel. For the plea of issue estoppel to succeed, it is essential that the issue in each set of proceedings should be shown to be identical (*Turner v London Transport Executive* [1977] IRLR 441). The doctrine does not apply if there is a changed situation, but the mere potential for change is not sufficient (*McLoughlin v Gordons (Stockport) Ltd* [1978] IRLR 127. A finding of unfair dismissal does not give rise to an issue of estoppel in a claim for wrongful dismissal (*Janata Bank Ltd v Ahmed* [1981] IRLR 457).

IT 1. The Central Office of Industrial Tribunals has issued Form IT 1 for general use by applicants. It is obtainable from Job Centres, Citizens Advice Bureaux, industrial tribunal offices, etc. However, there is no obligation to use Form IT 1, as long as an application is made to COIT in writing, with the name and address of the applicant, the person against whom relief is sought, and the grounds and particulars of the complaint (*Smith v Automobile Pty Ltd* [1973] ICR 306).

Itemised pay statement (EPCA, s. 8). Every employee is entitled to be given an itemised pay statement, in writing, with particulars of (1) gross pay (2) any variable or fixed deductions (3) net pay (4) details of part-payments (if any). However, the statement does not need to include details of sums payable to the employee from sources other than the employer (*Cofone v Spaghetti House* [1980] ICR 155). A standing statement of fixed deductions may be given, but must be re-issued at least annually. If an employer has failed to give an itemised statement, an application may be made by the employee to an industrial tribunal, who may make a declaration to that effect, and in respect of any unnotified deductions made within the period of 13 weeks prior to the application, may order the employer to pay to the employee an amount not exceeding the aggregate of those deductions. The industrial tribunal has a discretion to award the whole sum, or to restrict the award to the amount to which the employee was contractually entitled (*Scott v Creager* [1979] IRLR 162).

A mere statement which refers to 'miscellaneous deductions' does not give sufficient particulars to meet the requirements of s. 8 (*Milson v Leicestershire County Council* [1978] IRLR 433).

See DEDUCTIONS.

J

Job description. A job description is a document which details the precise nature of the tasks which the employee is required to perform. However, the ambit of the contractual obligations may be wider than the particular duties mentioned in the job description, and it is the contractual obligations which are important. Thus it appears that a job description can be changed, provided the new tasks are within the terms of the contract (*Glitz v Watford Electrical Co Ltd* [1979] IRLR 89).

Job evaluation study (EqPA, s. 1 (5)). If there is a proper job evaluation study, the industrial tribunal is bound to accept its conclusions, and it may only be challenged if there is some fundamental error on the face of the record (*Greene v Broxstone District Council* [1977] IRLR 34) or if it contains a factor which is discriminatory on grounds of sex (Equal Pay (Amendment) Regulations). There can be no completed study unless and until the parties have agreed and accepted its potential validity, but once it has been accepted, it is a valid study, and it is irrelevant that it is then disregarded by the parties (*Arnold v Beecham Group Ltd* [1982] IRLR 307).

See EQUAL PAY ACT 1970; EQUAL PAY (AMENDMENT) REGULATIONS 1983.

Job title (EPCA, s. 1 (3) (f)). The written statement under s. 1 of EPCA should contain the title of the job the employee is employed to do. If no such description is given, or if one is given and it is inaccurate, the employee may apply to the industrial tribunal under s. 11 of the Act. In making a declaration, the industrial tribunal can consider any implied, as well as express terms, and these implied terms can be embodied in the declaration (*Mears v Safecar Security Ltd* [1982] IRLR 183). But one party is not entitled to introduce unilaterally terms which have not been agreed with the other party, and therefore prior consultation with employees or their representatives is desirable before seeking to introduce new conditions affecting employees (*Churcher v Weyside Engineering (1926) Ltd* [1976] IRLR 402).

See WRITTEN STATEMENT.

Justifiable (SDA, s. 1 (1) (b) (ii); RRA, s. 1 (1) (b) (ii)). In order to be justifiable, the requirement or condition does not have to be necessary, in the sense that it is essential. It is sufficient if the party applying it can adduce adequate grounds for it (*Ojutiku v Manpower Services Commission* [1982] IRLR 418) in the sense of being right and proper (*Panesar v Nestle & Co* [1980] IRLR 64). There must be external evidence to justify the requirement or condition, i.e. the mere 'say so' of one party is not sufficient (*Ojutiku v Manpower Services Commission*, supra).

See SEX DISCRIMINATION ACT 1975; RACE RELATIONS ACT 1976; A PERSON DISCRIMINATES; INDIRECT DISCRIMINATION.

L

Last in, first out (LIFO). A selection system for redundancy, generally accepted in industry, in the absence of any other agreed criteria, whereby the last employee to become employed is the first to be considered or selected for dismissal for redundancy. LIFO can only be used in relation to the category or description of the jobs affected, e.g. not for grades of employees (*Gargrave v Hotel and Catering Industry Training Board* [1974] IRLR 85). LIFO is subject to any proper modifications or special circumstances, but it is advantageous if these are spelt out beforehand or agreed upon, e.g. skills, aptitude, mobility, flexibility, previous known conduct, lateness, absenteeism, etc. (*Best v Taylor Woodrow Construction Ltd* [1975] IRLR 177). LIFO must be based on continuous employment, not cumulative employment (*International Paint Co Ltd v Cameron* [1979] IRLR 62).

See REDUNDANCY.

Lawful dismissal. An employer may lawfully terminate the contract of employment at any time by the simple expedient of giving the appropriate notice of termination. The length of notice will, in the first place, depend on the provisions of the contract, or, in the absence of such terms, reasonable notice must be given. This will depend on the nature of the employment, the status of the employee, etc. (*Adams v Union Cinemas Ltd* [1939] 3 All ER 136). However, by s. 49 of EPCA certain minimum periods of notice must be given. Thus, after four week's employment, the employee is entitled to one week's notice; thereafter, he is entitled to a week's notice for each complete year's employment, i.e. two week's notice for two year's employment, three week's notice for three year's employment, etc. until a statutory maximum of twelve week's notice in respect of an employee who has worked for twelve or more years.

The employer may require the employee to work during the notice period, or may wave performance by giving the employee paid leave of absence, or may dispense with his services immediately and give him money in lieu of notice, which strictly speaking, is damage for breach of contract. The employee may also wave his statutory right to receive the full statutory notice (s. 49 (3)).

The employer still retains the right to terminate the contract without notice if an employee has committed an act of gross misconduct (*qv*).

See SUMMARY DISMISSAL; WRONGFUL DISMISSAL; MINIMUM PERIODS OF NOTICE.

Lawful order. It is the duty of an employee to obey all lawful and reasonable orders, which are within the terms of his contract (*Walmsley v Udec Refrigeration Ltd* [1972] IRLR 80). However, if he is dismissed for refusing to obey such an order, the dismissal is capable of being unfair, having regard to the reason for his refusal (*UCATT v Brain* [1981] IRLR 224). Conversely, a refusal to obey an unlawful or unreasonable order may make a dismissal unfair (*Payne v Spook Erection Ltd* [1984] IRLR 219).

See ACTED REASONABLY; REASON FOR THE DISMISSAL – CONDUCT; BREACH OF CONTRACT.

Lay off. Where an employee is employed under the terms of a contract whereby his remuneration depends on work being provided for him, he will be taken as being laid off for any period in respect of which, because the employer does not provide him with work, he is not entitled to remuneration. This usually relates to hourly paid or piece workers (*Hulse v Harry Perry Ltd* [1975] IRLR 181). An employer is only entitled to lay off if the contract gives him the power to do so (*Jewell v Neptune Concrete Ltd* [1975] IRLR 147). If it is argued that there is an implied term (*qv*) giving the right to lay off, this must be proven as part of the custom and practice of the firm or industry. The fact that the employee has accepted lay off in the past is not conclusive, for there may be other reasons why he acquiesced in the arrangement which can be explained by reasons other than the employer having the contractual right (*Waine v Oliver Plant Hire Co Ltd* [1977] IRLR 434). Notice of intention to lay off must be given in accordance with the contract, otherwise this may amount to a breach by the employer, and consequently a dismissal (*Johnson v Cross* [1977] ICR 872). A lay off provision can be laid down in, or subject to, the terms of a relevant collective agreement which is incorporated into the individual's contract of employment (*Burroughs Machine Ltd v Timmoney* [1977] IRLR 404).

Where an employer has a contractual right to lay off without any specified time limit, the only remedy for the employee is to claim in accordance with the strict provisions of s. 88 of EPCA. The argument that the contractual right to lay off is subject to the lay off being for a reasonable length of time (see *Dakri & Co Ltd v Tiffin* [1981] IRLR 57) was disagreed with by the EAT in *Kenneth McRae & Co Ltd v Dawson* [1984] IRLR 5.

See LAY OFF – SHORT TIME; GUARANTEE PAY.

Lay off – short time (EPCA, s. 87). Where the terms of an employee's contract are such that his remuneration is determined by the employer providing him with work, and he is laid off, or put on short time working, he may be able to resign his employment and claim redundancy pay. A lay off occurs when an employee is not provided with work for four weeks or more; short time working occurs when he earns less than half of a week's pay for six or more weeks (of which not more than three were consecutive) within a period of thirteen weeks. He must then give, in writing, a notice of his intention to claim redundancy pay, and thereafter give notice (in accordance with his contract) to terminate his employment. The employer may then give a counter notice within seven days, stating that within four weeks, it is expected that he will be able to provide at least thirteen weeks employment without resorting to lay off or short time working. If the employee does not withdraw the notice of intention to claim, the matter will go to the industrial tribunal, who will determine whether or not there was a reasonable prospect of at least thirteen week's employment without there being a lay off or short-time working. If they find there was no such prospect, the employee will receive his redundancy pay.

See LAY OFF.

Less favourably (SDA, s. 1 (1) (a)). That the discrimination was done with a good motive and in the best interests of the person discriminated against or in the interests of the business is no defence to a finding of less favourable treatment (*Grieg v Community Industry* [1979] IRLR 158), but trivial differences of treatment do not have to be taken into account (*Peake v Automotive Products Ltd* [1977] IRLR 365).

See SEX DISCRIMINATION ACT 1975; A PERSON DISCRIMINATES.

Liable to interference (EPCA, s. 153). This phrase means vulnerable to, or at the risk of interference by the employer. The degree or risk is irrelevant, as long as it is not small or insignificant (*Squibb United Kingdom Staff Association v Certification Officer* [1979] ICR 235). The test is the balance of probabilities (*A. Monk & Co Staff Association v Certification Officer* [1980] IRLR 431).

See INDEPENDENT TRADE UNION.

Liable . . . to pay (EPCA, s. 104 (1) (a)). In order to obtain a rebate from the Redundancy Fund, the employer must show that he was liable to make the redundancy payment under the Act. It follows that if a redundancy payment is made which is not under the provisions of the Act, no rebate is payable (*Secretary of State for Employment v Globe Elastic Thread Co Ltd* [1979] IRLR 327). However, if the employer pays more or less than the statutory amount, he may claim a rebate on that amount which is within the statutory limits (*Secretary of State for Employment v John Woodrow & Sons (Builders) Ltd* [1983] IRLR 11).

See REDUNDANCY REBATE.

Like work (EqPA, s. 1 (4)). A woman is employed on like work if it is

83

the same or broadly similar (*qv*), taking into account the nature of the duties, the skill knowledge and effort required, and whether it could be expected that the differences would not be reflected in different wage rates (*Capper Pass Ltd v Lawton* [1976] IRLR 366). It is necessary to consider the contractual obligations and what happens in practice (*Dance v Dorothy Perkins Ltd* [1978] ICR 760) but contractual obligations are irrelevant unless they result in actual and not infrequent differences in practice (*Shields v Coombs (Holdings) Ltd* [1978] IRLR 263). A fair test to apply is, if all the men were to leave and be replaced by women doing the same work as the applicant, would the firm carry on as usual (*Dorman v Hadrian Plastics Ltd* [1976] IRLR 207).

A woman may select the man with whom she wishes to be compared (*Ainsworth v Glass Tubes Ltd* [1977] IRLR 74), including a former male employee (*McCarthys Ltd v Smith* [1980] IRLR 209), if there is a short interval between his employment and hers, but if she wishes to compare herself with an employee at another establishment, this would only be possible if there are common terms and conditions of employment (*Rice v Scottish Legal Life Assurance Co Ltd* [1976] IRLR 330). To claim that she is employed on like work, regard must be had to the employment as a whole, and not what happens on particular days (*Ford v Weston (Chemists) Ltd* [1977] 12 ITR 369).

See EQUAL PAY ACT 1970; BROADLY SIMILAR WORK; JOB EVALUATION STUDY.

Likely (EPCA, s. 77). To succeed in an application for interim relief, the applicant must be able to establish that he would be likely to succeed at a full hearing. 'Likely' means more than probable (*Taplin v Shippam Ltd* [1978] IRLR 450). In *Dunning v United Liverpool Hospitals* [1973] 2 All ER 454) 'likely' was construed as meaning 'a reasonable prospect'.

See INTERIM RELIEF.

Lock-out (EPCA, s. 62 (1)). A lock-out is a refusal on the part of the employer, or a group of employers acting in concert, to furnish work for his or their employees, except on conditions accepted by the employees collectively (*Brown v William Press & Son Ltd* [1975] IRLR 8).

See STRIKE; OTHER INDUSTRIAL ACTION.

M

Man in the same employment (EqPA, s. 1 (2) (a)). The woman claimant may select the man with whom she wishes to be compared (*Ainsworth v Glass Tubes & Components Ltd* [1977] IRLR 74), but if there is no such male comparator, she cannot succeed in her claim (*Meeks v NUAAW* [1976] IRLR 198). However, there is no requirement that the male comparator shall be employed contemporaneously with the woman, so she can compare herself with a predecessor in office (*McCarthys Ltd v Smith* [1980] IRLR 209), if her claim is made under Article 119 of the Treaty of Rome.

See EQUAL PAY ACT 1970.

Manager. An employer has a greater obligation towards a manager to take steps to bring to his notice that he is dissatisfied with his conduct, and contemplating dismissal. On the other hand, there is a higher standard of awareness expected from a manager, which may lead to a reduction in any compensation awarded in respect of an unfair dismissal (*McPhail v Gibson* [1976] IRLR 254).

See DISCIPLINARY PROCEDURE.

Manual worker. The test is, is the manual work a real and substantial part of the employment, or is it accessory and incidental to that employment (*Bound v Lawrence* [1982] 1 QB 226)?

See TRUCK ACT 1831.

Married person (SDA, s. 3 (1)). Since more married persons (of either sex) have young children than unmarried persons, a requirement that an applicant for employment should not have young children is a requirement or condition, which discriminates on the grounds of marital status (*Hurley v Mustoe* [1981] IRLR 208), and to refuse employment on these grounds can be indirect discrimination (*Thorndyke v Bell Fruit (North Central) Ltd* [1979] IRLR 1).

But the dismissal of a woman because she married a man who worked for a competitor is discrimination on grounds of sex, not marital status (*Coleman v Skyrail Oceanic Ltd* [1981] IRLR 398).

See SEX DISCRIMINATION ACT 1975.

Maternity leave. See RIGHT TO RETURN TO WORK.

Maternity pay (EPCA, s. 33). A woman who is absent from work wholly or partly because of pregnancy may be entitled to maternity pay. She must have worked for her employer for two years prior to the eleventh week prior to the expected week of confinement, she must be employed on that eleventh week (but not necessarily working), she must produce (if requested) a medical certificate stating the expected week of confinement, and she must inform her employer in writing, if he so requests three weeks before her absence begins (or as soon as is reasonably practicable) that she intends to be absent. If she thus qualifies, she will be entitled to six weeks maternity pay, which is 9/10ths of her normal pay less the maternity allowance (whether she qualifies for this or not). Any contractual pay due to her during this period may be set off against the maternity pay.

If a woman leaves work before the eleventh week prior to the expected week of confinement, the question is, has she ceased to work but remained an employee, or has she ceased to be an employee. If the former is the case, she qualifies for maternity pay. Thus, if she is placed on an 'absentee register' or similar list, she is still employed (*Secretary of State for Employment v Doulton Sanitaryware Ltd* [1981] IRLR 365).

An employer who pays maternity pay will be able to recover the whole amount from the Maternity Fund, and there is a discretion to make the refund even though the employer was not legally obliged to make the payment (s. 39 (3)). Disputes as to entitlement to maternity pay, or entitlement to the refund, will be settled by the industrial tribunal.

See MATERNITY PAY REBATE; RIGHT TO RETURN TO WORK.

Maternity Pay Rebate (EPCA, s. 39). An employer who has paid maternity pay is entitled to claim a rebate of the whole of the amount so paid from the Maternity Fund, but only in respect of the amount which he was liable to pay under the statutory provisions (*Williams & Co Ltd v Secretary of State for Employment* [1978] IRLR 235). If the rebate is refused, or if it is of a lesser amount than the employer paid, an application may be made to an industrial tribunal (*Lloyds Bank Ltd v Secretary of State for Employment* [1979] ICR 258).

See MATERNITY PAY.

Medical Certificate. *See* SICK NOTE.

Membership of a trade union. Generally, the rules of a trade union will determine who shall be eligible for membership (*Boulting v ACTAT* [1963] 1 All ER 716) and who is not eligible (*Faramus v Film Artistes' Association* [1964] 1 All ER 25) although the rules cannot operate contrary to the law (e.g. Sex Discrimination Act, s. 12, Rehabilitation of Offenders Act, s. 4). Every member has the right to terminate his membership on giving reasonable notice and complying with reasonable conditions (TULRA, s. 7). Disciplinary action against a member can only be taken in strict accordance with the rules (*Spring v NASDA* [1956] 2 All ER 221) and the rules of natural justice (*Lawlor v Union of Post Office Workers* [1965] 1 All ER 353). A member who is wrongly expelled may recover damages at common law (*Bonsor v Musicians Union* [1955] 3 All ER 518). A person who is in employment, or who is seeking employment, with an employer who operates a closed shop has the right not to have his application for membership unreasonably refused, and the right not to be unreasonably expelled from the union (Employment Act 1980, s. 4), with a remedy by way of an application to an industrial tribunal, which may make a declaration. If the applicant is admitted or re-admitted to the trade union, an award of compensation may be made by the industrial tribunal, but if he is not so admitted or re-admitted, compensation must be awarded by the EAT (Employment Act 1980, s. 5).

See TRADE UNION.

Minimum periods of notice (EPCA, s. 49, Sch. 3). The length of notice which an employee must give and is entitled to receive is primarily a matter for the contract to determine. In the absence of any express term, reasonable notice must be given (*Richardson v Koefod* [1969] 3 All ER 1264), which will depend on the position held by the employee (*Hill v Parsons & Co Ltd* [1971] 3 All ER 1345), the custom of the firm and industry, etc. However, whatever the contract states, the notice cannot be less than the statutory minimum periods of notice laid down in s. 49 (below) unless the parties agree to waive the right to notice, or agree on a payment in lieu of notice (*qv*). It should be remembered that if an employee complains that he has not received the notice to which he believes he is entitled, he must bring his claim in the ordinary courts, not the industrial tribunal (*Treganowan v Robert Knee & Co Ltd* [1975] IRLR 247). However, on an unfair dismissal claim, the failure to give the proper notice is a matter which can be reflected in the compensation award.

The statutory minimum periods of notice are as follows: after four weeks and up to two year's employment, the employee is entitled to one week's notice. Thereafter, he is entitled to a week's notice for each complete year's employment, i.e. two week's notice after two year's employment, three week's notice after three year's employment, etc., up to a statutory maximum of twelve week's notice for an employee who has worked for twelve years or more. Notice does not have to be given if an employee is employed for the purpose of a specific task which is not expected to last for more than three months unless it does last for more than three months. An employer does not have to give notice to an employee who is dismissed for gross misconduct (*qv*). The actual giving of the notice may be done on any day in the week, or on any day in the month, unless the contract specifies otherwise.

If an employee is given money in lieu of notice, so that he finished work immediately, or is given less than the statutory period of notice, the period of statutory notice to which he is entitled can be added to his period of continuous employment (but not any contractual period of notice) for the purpose of determining whether he has sufficient period of employment in order to qualify for a statutory right (*Fox Maintenance Ltd v Jackson* [1977] IRLR 306), see s. 55 (5). But an employee who is dismissed for gross misconduct is not entitled to any notice, and therefore he cannot rely on the provisions of s. 55 (5) to 'pull him past the post' (*Ahmed v National Car Parks Ltd*, IDS Brief 149).

If the employee has normal working hours and he is dismissed with notice, or gives notice to terminate his employment, and during those normal working hours (a) he is ready and willing to work but no work is provided, or (b) he is incapable of work because of sickness or injury, or (c) he is on holiday in accordance with his contract, he is entitled to be paid for his normal working hours at his average rate of remuneration. If there are no normal working hours, he is entitled to be paid his week's pay, subject to his willingness to do work of a reasonable nature and amount to earn a week's pay (except if he is off because of sickness, injury or holiday), see Sch. 3.

Payments do not have to be made under Sch. 3 if the employee is absent from work at his own request, or if the employee gives notice to terminate, and before the contract terminates, he takes part in a strike.

An employee who has been employed for more than one month must give a minimum of one week's notice, or more, depending on the contract. Strictly speaking, an employee who gives notice which is less than the statutory or contractual notice could be sued for damages, but this course of action is rarely pursued in practice.

Minister of Religion. As a general rule it can be said that a Minister of Religion is not an employee of the religious authority in question or the congregation, and is more in the position of an office holder (*Parker v Orr* [1966] 1 ITR 488). The spiritual nature of the work is incompatable with a contract of employment (*President of the Methodist Conference v Parfitt* [1984] ICR 176). However, a stipendiary lay reader can be an employee (*Barthorpe v Exeter Diocesan Board of Finance Ltd* [1979] ICR 900) even though he may also be an office holder.

The Sex Discrimination Act does not apply to employment within the meaning of that Act for purposes of organised religion where the employment is limited to persons of one sex so as to comply with the doctrines of the religion or to avoid the religious susceptibilities of a significant number of its followers (s. 19).

See EMPLOYEE; OFFICE HOLDER.

Misrepresentation. A person (such as an employment agency or recruitment counsellor) who induces another to accept a job which fails to materialise or is totally unsuitable may be liable for negligence and misrepresentation if that other suffers damage or loss as a result of the job not being within his capaicty (*McNally v Welltrade International Ltd* [1978] IRLR 497).

Moonlighting. See SPARE TIME EMPLOYMENT.

N

Non-discrimination notice (RRA, s. 58 (4)). On an appeal to an industrial tribunal against the requirements of a non-discrimination notice, all issues of fact on the basis of which the notice was issued are open to consideration by the industrial tribunal, including finding of fact as to whether in the past the employers have been guilty of unlawful conduct which led the CRE to make requirements for the future. Appeals are not confined to the reasonableness of the requirements as they relate to the implementation of the notice. An industrial tribunal may quash the requirement in the notice if it is based on some incorrect finding of fact (*Commission for Racial Equality v Amari Plastics Ltd* [1981] IRLR 340).

    See RACE RELATIONS ACT 1976; FORMAL INVESTIGATION.

Non-domestic premises (HSWA, s. 4 (1) (b)). Non-domestic premises are any premises which are not in the exclusive occupation of the occupants of a private dwelling (*Westminster City Council v Select Management Ltd* [1984] ICR 488).

Normal retiring age (EPCA, s. 64 (1) (b)). The normal retiring age is the age at which employees may reasonably expect to be retired. Where there is a contractual retiring age, there is a presumption that that is the normal retiring age, but the presumption can be rebutted by evidence that there is in practice some higher age at which those relevant employees are regularly retired and which they have reasonably come to regard as their normal retiring age. If there is no normal retiring age, or if the evidence shows that the contractual retiring age has been abandoned, then the statutory alternatives of 65 for men and 60 for women will apply (*Waite v Government Communications Headquarters* [1983] IRLR 341). The relevant employees are those who hold a position equivalent to that held by the applicant, and the point in time at which the matter is to be considered is the effective date of the termination of his contract (*DHSS v Coy* [1984] IRLR 360). The fact that a woman is contractually obliged to retire at the age of 60, whereas men are permitted to retire at 65, although discriminatory, is permitted by s. 6 (4) of the Sex Discrimination Act. The fact that an employee is permitted to stay on after the retiring age (albeit on a temporary contract) does not extend the normal retiring age as long as the employee cannot insist on staying on (*Smith v Post Office*, unreported). Nor is the normal retiring age the same as the pensionable age (*Ord v Maidstone Hospital Management Committee* [1974] IRLR 80). However, compensation for unfair dismissal can take account of the fact that the employee may have continued to be employed beyond the statutory retiring age (*Barrell Plating & Phosplating Co Ltd v Danks* [1976] IRLR 262).

Normal working hours (EPCA, Sch. 14). It is necessary to ascertain the normal working hours of an employee in order to calculate the week's pay (*qv*) for the following purposes: (1) guarantee pay (2) medical suspension pay (3) time off work for redundant employees (4) time off work for ante-natal care (5) maternity pay (6) rights in periods of notice (7) failure to give written reasons for dismissal (8) unfair dismissal (9) redundancy pay. The phrase may also be relevant in ascertaining whether or not the employee is employed under a contract for more than 16 hours per week (or more than 8 but less than 16 hours for five years) in order to qualify for employment rights generally.

The normal working hours are those which are determined by the contract of employment; these may be expressed or implied, or fixed by a collective agreement (*Gascol Conversions Ltd v Mercer* [1974] IRLR 155). If the contract is silent on the matter, it is necessary to see how the parties acted in practice. Thus, if an employee agrees to work such hours as are necessary to do the job, it should be possible to compute how many hours he normally works (*Dean v Eastbourne etc. Club* [1977] IRLR 143). Normal working hours exist even though there is an emergency which brings about a temporary change in the number of hours worked (*Friend v PMA Holdings Ltd* [1976] ICR 330).

Generally, overtime is not to be included in the computation (*ITT Components Ltd v Kolah* [1977] IRLR 53) unless the employee is contractually obliged to work such overtime (*Redpath Dorman Long Ltd v Sutton* [1972] ICR 477), in which case the hours can only count if they are fixed, not variable (*Tarmac Roadstone Ltd v Peacock* [1973] IRLR 157). Equally, there must be an obligation on the part of the employer to provide the overtime. Thus, it is not enough that overtime is regularly worked. It must be obligatory on the employer to provide it and the employee to do it, the mutual obligation to be founded in the contract of employment (*Lotus Cars Ltd v Sutcliffe* [1982] IRLR 381).

Hours wherein an employee is at home preparing for his work do not count (*Lake v Essex County Council* [1979] IRLR 241). If an employee works more hours in one week, and fewer in following weeks, he cannot average the hours to produce a normal weekly number of hours (*Opie v John Gubbins (Insurance Brokers) Ltd* [1978] IRLR 540).

Normally be required to work (EPCA, s. 12 (1)). Days when an employee is off work sick, or on holiday, are not days when he would normally be required to work, and hence no guarantee pay is payable in respect of them (*York and Reynolds v Colledge Hosiery Ltd* [1978] IRLR 53).

See GUARANTEE PAY.

Normally involves employment (EPCA, Sch. 13, para. 4). In considering this phrase the industrial tribunal should look not merely at the terms of the contract as varied, but also the contract as originally drawn up and the variations made to its terms during the period when the contract was in being (*Secretary of State for Employment v Deary* [1948] ICR 413).

See CONTINUOUS EMPLOYMENT.

Not reasonably practicable (EPCA, s. 67 (2)). Whether it is not reasonably practicable to present the claim within the appropriate time limit is a question of fact for the industrial tribunal to determine, but the burden of proof is on the applicant to show this (*Porter v Bainbridge Ltd* [1978] ICR 943). 'Practicable' means 'feasible', and the question may thus be posed 'Was it reasonably feasible for the applicant to present the claim within the three months?' (*Palmer v Southend-on-sea Borough Council* [1984] IRLR 119). Ignorance of one's legal rights is unlikely to succeed nowadays (*Avon County Council v Haywood Hicks* [1978] IRLR 118) for an employee should make such enquiries as are reasonable in the circumstances. However, ignorance of a basic fact which is relevant to the success of a claim may mean that it is not reasonably practicable to present the claim in time (*Churchill v Yeates & Son Ltd* [1983] IRLR 187).

If an employee consults a skilled adviser, be he solicitor (*Norgett v Luton Co-operative Society* [1976] IRLR 306), trade union official (*Times Newspaper Ltd v O'Regan* [1977] IRLR 101) or Citizens Advice Bureau (*Riley v Tesco Stores Ltd* [1980] IRLR 103) etc., then again he can hardly complain if the complaint is not presented in time, and his remedy, if any, would be an action against that adviser. However, he is entitled to delay presenting his claim in order not to prejudice a settlement, or the prospect of obtaining other employment. It is not reasonably practicable to present the claim in time if the employee is physically incapacitated, but if the employee knows that he has rights, but does not know of the time limit, it may be difficult for him to convince the industrial tribunal that it was not reasonably practicable to present the claim earlier (*Walls Meat Co Ltd v Kahn* [1978] IRLR 499).

An applicant is entitled to expect that the application will reach the Central Office of Industrial Tribunals in the normal course of the post (*Burton v Field Sons Ltd* [1977] ICR 106), but if there is a postal delay, the industrial tribunal can hear evidence as to what the reasonable expectation was as to the delivery of letters (*Beanstalk Shelving Ltd v Horn* [1980] ICR 273).

The industrial tribunal should first decide if it was not reasonably practicable to present the claim in time. They should then decide whether to exercise their discretion to allow the claim to be brought out of time (*Ruff v Smith* [1975] IRLR 275).

See PRESENTED TO THE INDUSTRIAL TRIBUNAL; THREE MONTHS BEGINNING WITH.

Not reasonably practicable . . . to comply (EPA, s. 99 (8)). Even if the employer receives incorrect advice from a Government Department, this does not mean that it is not reasonably practicable to comply (*UCATT v H. Rooke & Son Ltd* [1978] IRLR 204).

See CONSULTATION ON REDUNDANCIES.

Notes of evidence. *See* CHAIRMAN'S NOTES.

Notice to terminate employment. *See* MINIMUM PERIODS OF NOTICE.

Notification of mass redundancies (EPA, s. 100). If an employer is proposing to make redundant more than 100 employees from one establishment within 90 days, or more than 10 within 30 days, he must notify the Department of Employment within 90 or 30 days respectively. If there are special circumstances (*qv*) which render it not reasonably practicable to comply, he shall take all such steps as are reasonably practicable.

If an employer fails to notify as above, the Secretary of State may reduce the rebate by up to 10%, although an appeal against this may be made to the Industrial Tribunal. As an alternative, the employer could be prosecuted in the magistrates courts, and fined.

See CONSULTATION ON REDUNDANCIES.

O

Obligatory period (EPCA, s. 85). If the employer gives notice to terminate the contract, and the notice is equivalent to the lawful notice required to be given by statute or by contract, then the obligatory period of notice corresponds with the notice period given. If the employer gives notice to terminate which is longer than that required by statute or by contract, then the obligatory period is the contractual or statutory notice period which expires when the actual notice period expires. Thus, if an employer is bound to give (whether by contract or statute) four week's notice, and he in practice gives eight week's notice, the last four weeks of that notice will constitute the obligatory period.

See REDUNDANCY.

Occurrence (EPCA, s. 12 (1) (b)). An occurrence is something external to the employer. Thus, if he decides to close the factory for his own reasons (e.g. religious beliefs) this is a voluntary act, not an occurrence which gives rise to a guarantee payment (*North v Pavleigh Ltd* [1977] IRLR 461).

See GUARANTEE PAY.

Offer to renew (EPCA, s. 82 (3)). The employer must prove that the offer to renew the contract, or the offer of re-engagement, was made (*Simpson v Dickinson* [1972] ICR 474). The offer to renew must be on identical terms (*Cartin v Botley Garages Ltd* [1973] ICR 144), but the doctrine of *de minimus non curat lex* may be applied (*Allman v Rowland* [1977] ICR 201).

See REDUNDANCY; SUITABLE ALTERNATIVE EMPLOYMENT.

Offered re-engagement (EPCA, s. 62 (2) (b)). The fact that the striking employee does not receive a formal offer of re-engagement is irrelevant, for the offer does not have to be in writing. It is sufficient if he knows about it, and knows that it refers to him (*Marsden v Fairey Stainless Ltd* [1979] IRLR 102). The offer is still an offer even though certain conditions are attached to it (*Williams v National Theatre Board Ltd* [1982] IRLR 377).

See REASON FOR THE DISMISSAL – TAKING PART IN A STRIKE.

Office holder. An office holder has his rights and duties determined by the office he holds, not by virtue of any contract. Thus a policeman holds the ancient office of the constabulary, and is not an employee (*Ridge v Baldwin* [1963] 2 All ER 66), a clergyman is also not employed under a contract of employment (*President of the Methodist Conference v Parfitt* [1984] ICR 176). A company director, as such, is an office holder, but in addition he may have a contract of employment, express or implied (*Folami v Nigerline (UK) Ltd* [1978] ICR 277), depending on the facts of the case (*Albert Parsons & Sons Ltd v Parsons* [1979] ICR 271). In other circumstances, it is a question of fact and degree (*102 Social Club & Institute v Bickerton* [1977] ICR 911) whether a person (e.g. a club secretary) is an employee or not.

See PRISON OFFICER; POLICE; MINISTER OF RELIGION.

Offices, Shops and Railway Premises Act 1963. This Act applies to employment in offices, shops and railway premises, as defined. There are provisions relating to cleanliness, overcrowding, temperature, ventilation, lighting, sanitary conveniences, washing facilities, drinking water, accommodation for clothing, sitting and eating facilities, floors, stairs and passageways, fencing of machinery, exposing young persons to dangers in cleaning machinery, prohibition of heavy work, first aid provisions etc.

A breach of the Act may lead to a prosecution for an offence, and an injured employee may be able to bring a claim in tort for breach of statutory duty.

See HEALTH AND SAFETY AT WORK ETC. ACT 1974.

Official (TULRA, s. 30). A shop steward is an official of a trade union (*UKAPE v AUEW (Tass)* [1972] ICR 151).

See SHOP STEWARD.

On racial grounds (RRA, s. 1 (1) (a)). A person can be discriminated against on racial grounds even though the discrimination is based upon the race of another person. Thus A can discriminate against B on grounds of C's colour or race (*Showboat Entertainment Centre Ltd v Owens* [1984] IRLR 7).

See RACE RELATIONS ACT 1976.

100 or more (EPA, s. 99 (3)). It is not possible to circumvent the statutory provisions by a series of dismissals, in order to reduce each number below that statutory number of 100 (or, where appropriate, 10), for the industrial tribunal will examine the reality of the situation, and, if necessary, add the numbers together (*T & GWU v Nationwide Haulage Ltd* [1978] IRLR 143).

See CONSULTATION ON REDUNDANCIES.

One of two employees. If an employer is of the opinion that an offence has been committed by one of two employees, but is unable to establish which of those two employees committed the offence, then provided he has made an adequate investigation into the matter, he is entitled to dismiss both of them, having regard to the seriousness of the offence, e.g. suspected dishonesty (*Monie v Coral Racing Ltd* [1980]

IRLR 464) or gross negligence (*McPhie and McDermott v Wimpey Waste Management Ltd* [1981] IRLR 316).

See REASON FOR THE DISMISSAL – CONDUCT.

Onus of proof. *See* BURDEN OF PROOF.

Opportunity to state a case. *See* DISCIPLINARY PROCEDURE.

Oral terms. An oral term can supercede or over-ride a written term of the contract (*Hawker Siddeley Power Engineering Ltd v Rump* [1979] IRLR 425).

See TERMS AND CONDITIONS OF EMPLOYMENT.

Ordinarily works outside Great Britain (EPCA, s. 141 (2)). In order to ascertain whether the employee ordinarily works outside Great Britain, the industrial tribunal must look at the express and implied terms of the contract, and what actually happens over the whole period of employment (and not just the period prior to the termination). Having regard to these factors, it will then be possible to establish where the employee's base is, for, in the absence of special considerations, it is the country where the employee has his base which will be the place where he ordinarily works under his contract (*Wilson v Maynard Shipbuilding Consultants A.B.* [1977] IRLR 491). Thus, the fact that an employee spends most of his time abroad is not conclusive, if his pay, national insurance, income tax, etc. are dealt with in this country (*Hillier v Martintrux Ltd* (unreported)). The burden of proof (*qv*) is on the employee to show that he ordinarily works inside Great Britain (*Claisse v Hosteller, Stewart and Keydril Ltd* [1978] IRLR 205), but the industrial tribunal should take a broad approach (*Janata Bank v Ahmed* [1981] IRLR 457).

See OVERSEAS EMPLOYMENT.

Originating application. *See* IT I.

Other industrial action (EPCA, s. 62 (1). Whether or not an employee is taking part in other industrial action is a question of fact for the industrial tribunal to determine, and the decision cannot be appealed against as a point of law unless the industrial tribunal reached a conclusion which the words of the statute could not reasonably bear (*Naylor v Orton & Smith Ltd* [1983] IRLR 233). Previous decisions have held the following acts to constitute other industrial action; a go-slow (*Drew v St Edmundsbury Borough Council* [1980] IRLR 459) a work-to-rule (*Secretary of State for Employment v ASLEF* [1972] ICR 19) refusal to work overtime (although not contractually bound to do so) as part of a campaign to improve wages and conditions (*Faust v Power Packing Casemakers Ltd* [1983] IRLR 117), imposing sanctions on normal working (*Williams v Western Mail* [1980] IRLR 222), and standing around, thus preventing machinery from working (*Thompson v Eaton Ltd* [1976] IRLR 308). However, the mere threat to take action is not other industrial action (*Midlands Plastics v Till* [1983] IRLR 9).

See REASON FOR THE DISMISSAL – TAKING PART IN A STRIKE.

Outworker. In *Airfix Footwear Ltd v Cope* [1978] IRLR 396 an outworker, who worked at home for about five days each week for seven years was held to be an employee, as on the facts it was not difficult to conclude that a contract of employment had grown up between the parties.

See EMPLOYEE; SELF EMPLOYED; HOMEWORKER.

Overpayment. If an employer, in error, overpays an employee, this is a mistake of fact, not law. Consequently, he can seek to recover the amount overpaid from the employee which has not been spent in reliance on the employer's representations that the employee is entitled to the money (*County Council of Avon v Howlett* [1983] IRLR 171). However, for an estoppel to operate in favour of the employee, it must be shown that (a) the employer made a representation of fact which led the employee to believe that the money was his (b) he subsequently changed his position as a result of that representation, and (c) the payment was made without fault on the defendant's part.

Overseas associated employer. The number of employees employed by a company in a foreign country cannot be added to the number employed in a British company in order to surmount the barrier specified in section 64A of EPCA (two years employment required in order to qualify for unfair dismissal rights in the case of an employer who employs 20 or fewer employees (*Cox v ELG Metals Ltd* [1984] IRLR 3).

See ASSOCIATED EMPLOYER.

Overseas employment (EPCA, s. 141). The provisions of ss. 1–4 (written particulars of terms of employment) and ss. 49–51 (minimum periods of notice) do not apply in relation to employment during any period when the employee is engaged in work wholly or mainly outside Great Britain, unless (a) the employee ordinarily works inside Great Britain, and (b) the work outside Great Britain is for the same employer.

Section 8 (right to itemised pay statement) and s. 53 (written reasons for dismissal) and the provisions of Part II (guarantee pay, suspension from work on medical grounds, trade union membership and activities rights, time off work), and Part III (maternity pay, right to return to work after maternity), and Part V (unfair dismissal) do not apply where under his contract the employee ordinarily works outside Great Britain.

Part VII of the Act (priority of certain debts on the employer's insolvency, payments of unpaid contributions to occupational pension schemes, and 'guaranteed debts' payable out of the Redundancy Fund) does not apply where the employee ordinarily works outside the member states of the European Community.

Part VI of the Act (redundancy payments) does not apply if on the relevant date (see s. 90) he is outside Great Britain, unless under his contract he ordinarily worked in Great Britain. If he ordinarily works outside Great Britain, he will not be entitled to a redundancy payment unless on the relevant date he is in Great Britain in accordance with instructions given to him by his employer.

The Equal Pay Act 1970, the Sex Discrimination Act 1975 and the Race Relations Act 1976 do not apply in respect of overseas employments (although the phrase is not used as such). Thus the Equal Pay Act applies only to establishments within Great Britain (s. 1 (1)), and the Sex Discrimination Act states that a person is employed at an establishment inside Great Britain unless he does his work wholly or mainly outside Great Britain. The Race Relations Act also makes discrimination unlawful in respect of employment at an establishment in Great Britain (s. 8).

The Transfer of Undertakings (Protection of Employment) Regulations 1981 do have limited applicability to overseas employees. Thus a transfer of an undertaking in which the overseas employee is employed will operate to transfer the contract of employment to the new employer. Any collective agreement will be transferred, and an obligation to recognise a particular trade union, but there is no duty to consult with the unions in advance of the transfer, and an employee will not be able to claim unfair dismissal if he is dismissed in consequence of the transfer.

Certain weeks which an employee spends abroad will not count for continuity for redundancy payment purposes, but those weeks do not break continuity (Schedule 13, para. 14). The general rule is that a week does not count for redundancy purposes unless the employee remained an employee for national insurance purposes.

By virtue of the Statutory Sick Pay Regulations 1982 a period of entitlement does not arise if at any time the employee is outside the European Community. Generally, an overseas employee is not entitled to statutory sick pay, for the Act applies only to persons employed in Great Britain.

In respect of many of the above-mentioned matters, there are special provisions relating to seamen, persons working on off-shore installations etc.

See ORDINARILY WORKS OUTSIDE GREAT BRITAIN; IN ACCORDANCE WITH INSTRUCTIONS.

Overtime. It requires clear and unambiguous words in the contract to impose an obligation upon an employee to do overtime which is compulsory (*Pearson v William Jones Ltd* [1967] 2 All ER 1062), and the mere fact that other employees work overtime is consistent with it being voluntary (*Graham v Todd Ltd* [1975] IRLR 45). However, it can be unfair to dismiss an employee who refuses to do compulsory overtime, just as it can be fair to dismiss for a refusal to do overtime which is voluntary. The contractual obligations are an important consideration, but are not a crucial element of the statutory test of reasonableness (*Martin v Solus Schall* [1979] IRLR 7). Thus, a refusal to do overtime motivated by a desire to put improper pressure on the employer (*Pengilly v North Devon Farmers* [1973] IRLR 41), can lead to a fair dismissal, though not if the pressure was perfectly proper, e.g. to improve working conditions (*Davies v Ideal Timber Co Ltd*). However, this refusal could amount to other industrial action (*qv*). If all other employees work overtime, and a failure to do so by one employee would cause considerable burden to the employer, e.g. because of the calculation of bonus payments etc., then although the employee may not be in breach of his contract, it could amount to some other substantial reason (*qv*), which may be fair (*Robinson v Flitwick Frames Ltd* [1975] IRLR 261).

If an employer is not contractually obliged to provide the overtime, a reduction in the amount offered does not constitute a repudiation of the contract so as to enable the employee to resign and claim constructive dismissal (*qv*) (*Elliott v Waldair (Construction) Ltd* [1975] IRLR 104).

Overtime ban. *See* OTHER INDUSTRIAL ACTION.

Overtime pay. Overtime pay should not be included in the computation of a week's pay for the purpose of the basic award (*qv*), but the industrial tribunal can include net overtime pay in their calculation of the compensation award up to the time of the hearing, and for a further period thereafter, as this is an aspect of past and future loss (*Brownson v Hire Service Shops Ltd* [1978] IRLR 33).

See BASIC AWARD; COMPENSATORY AWARD.

P

Part-time workers. Provided an employee works for more than 16 hours per week for more than one year, or between 8–16 hours for more than five years, he has all the rights conferred by the relevant statutory provisions, and the fact that the employment is designated to be part-time is irrelevant. However, it is not permissible to average working hours so as to arrive at a minimum of 16 hours per week (*Mailway (Southern) Ltd v Willsher* [1978] IRLR 322) unless the normal working week is contemplated to be 16 hours or more (*Miller v Harry Thornton (Lollies) Ltd* [1978] IRLR 430).

As long as the contract subsists for more than 12 weeks the employees concerned (via their recognised trade union) are within the consultation provisions of s. 99 of EPA, even though the number of hours they work are less than 16 hours per week (*NATFHE v Manchester City Council* [1978] ICR 1190).

The part-time nature of the employment may amount to a genuine material factor (*qv*) for the purpose of paying lower wages than are paid to full-time employees, provided the reason for doing so is to encourage a more efficient use of plant etc. (*Jenkins v Kingsgate Clothing Ltd* [1981] IRLR 388).

See CONTINUOUS EMPLOYMENT.

Patents and inventions. An invention made by an employee shall belong to his employer if (1) it was made during his normal duties or duties specifically assigned to him, and the circumstances were such that an invention might reasonably be expected to result from those duties, or (2) because of the employee's particular responsibilities he has a special obligation to further the interests of the employer's undertaking. Any other invention made by an employee belongs to him, notwithstanding anything to the contrary in the contract of employment. Even if the invention belongs to the employer, the employee may still apply to the Comptroller of Patents (or Patents Court) for an award of compensation, which may be awarded if the patent is of outstanding benefit to the employer (see Patents Act 1977, s. 39).

Pay. Pay can include the contributions to a retirement benefits scheme made by an employer in the name of an employee by means of an addition to the gross salary (*Worringham v Lloyds Bank Ltd* [1981] IRLR 178).

Pay in lieu of notice. An employer, when dismissing an employee, may require him to cease work immediately, and give him pay in lieu of notice. This is regarded as damages for the failure to give due notice of termination. Hence, it is not taxable (Income & Corporation Taxes Act 1970, s. 187) but treated as a payment for loss of office.

If pay is given in lieu of notice, the effective date of termination is when the employee ceases to work for the employer (*Brindle v Smith (Cabinets) Ltd* [1972] IRLR 125).

See NOTICE TO TERMINATE EMPLOYMENT; EFFECTIVE DATE OF TERMINATION.

Payment of Wages Act 1960. This Act enables employers to pay wages direct into a bank account, or by cheque or money order or postal order, and in so doing, he does not offend against the Truck Act or other similar legislation. However, such method of payment must be agreed to by the employee in writing, and the arrangement can be cancelled by either party on giving four week's notice.

This method of payment (by postal or money order) may also be used if the employee is absent from work because of illness or injury, or is away from his usual place of work, even though there is no agreement to this effect, but the employee can give written notice that he does not wish to be paid in this manner.

See TRUCK ACT 1831; CHEQUE.

Peaceful picketing (TULRA, s. 15). *See* PICKETING.

Penalise (EPCA, s. 23). To penalise a person because of his trade union membership or non-membership means to subject to a disadvantage, and it is irrelevant that this was unintended (*Carlson v Post Office* [1981] IRLR 158).

See ACTIVITIES OF AN INDEPENDENT TRADE UNION.

Pension rights. When assessing the future loss of pension rights the industrial tribunal should assess the period during which the employee is likely to be without pensionable employment, and should apply the appropriate factor to past and future loss (*Manpower Ltd v Hearne* [1983] IRLR 281).

See COMPENSATORY AWARD.

Personality conflicts. Where there has been a breakdown in the relationship between two employees, the employer must take steps to try to improve that relationship, so that a decision to dismiss one or the other should only be taken if the breakdown in the relationship is irremediable (*Turner v Vestric Ltd* [1981] IRLR 23). However, a dismissal may ultimately become necessary in order to restore harmony among the workforce (*Gorfin v Distressed Gentlefolks Aid Association* [1973] IRLR 290).

See REASON FOR THE DISMISSAL – SOME OTHER SUBSTANTIAL REASON.

Perverse. A decision of an industrial tribunal will be perverse if (a) there is an improper direction in law (b) if on the evidence no reasonable tribunal could have come to a certain conclusion, and (c) if there is a failure to appreciate standards of good industrial practice (*Payne v Spook Erection Ltd* [1984] IRLR 219).

See APPEAL TO THE EMPLOYMENT APPEAL TRIBUNAL.

Picketing (TULRA, s. 15). It shall be lawful for a person, in contemplation or furtherance of a trade dispute to attend at or near his place of work or, if he is a trade union official, at or near the place of work of a member of the union whom he is accompanying and whom he represents, for the purpose only of peacefully obtaining or communicating information, or peacefully persuading any person to work or not to work. If a person normally works otherwise than at one place, or at a place the location of which it is impracticable to picket, then he may picket at any premises of his employer where he works or where the work is administered. An ex-employee whose last employment was terminated because of the trade dispute, or whose termination of employment was one of the circumstances which gave rise to the trade dispute may picket at his former place of work.

The section makes no mention of the number of persons who may picket the employer's premises (but see the Code of Practice (*qv*) issued by the Secretary of State for Employment, which recommends that no more than six persons should picket the entrance to a workplace), and the fact that pickets converge on premises in large numbers may give rise to a presumption that the purpose of the picketing is not peaceful (*Broome v DPP* [1974] ICR 84). There is no right under the section to stop traffic on the highway (*Broome v DPP*, supra) nor to prevent traffic from using the highway (*Tynan v Balmer* [1966] 2 All ER 133). Nor is there a right to enter private property (*British Airports Authority v Ashton* [1983] IRLR 287). If picketing has any object other than that of peacefully persuading etc., it is not protected by the section.

Picketing which is not rendered lawful by s. 15 can involve civil and criminal liabilities, e.g. nuisance, trespass, watching and besetting (*qv*), breach of the peace, affray, obstruction of the highway, obstructing a constable, etc. (see, for example, *Messenger Newspapers Group Ltd v National Graphical Association* [1984] IRLR 397).

See TRADE DISPUTE.

Place where the employee was so employed (EPCA, s. 81 (2)). An employee is employed at the place where, under his contract of employment, he is required to work (*Sutcliffe v Hawker Siddeley Aviation Ltd* [1973] IRLR 304). Consequently, if there is no work available at one place, but the employer is entitled to require the employee to work elsewhere, an employee who refuses to transfer is not entitled to a redundancy payment (*U.K. Atomic Energy Authority v*

Claydon [1974] IRLR 6). However, the place does not have to be a specific building, so that an employee who is required to move a short distance to a new place of work is not redundant (*Managers (Holborn) Ltd v Hohne* [1977] IRLR 230), although a transfer to a new place of work some distance away may result in a redundancy (*Rowbotham v Arthur Lee & Sons Ltd* [1974] IRLR 377).

There may be an implied term in a contract of employment that an employer is entitled to transfer an employee to a new place of work which is within reasonable travelling distance of his home (*Jones v Associated Tunnelling Ltd* [1981] IRLR 477), and there may be circumstances, especially with senior staff, where an employee can be required to move a considerable distance, and there is no implied term that the move will be limited to a reasonable commuting distance from the employee's home (*Little v Charterhouse Magna Assurance Co Ltd* [1980] IRLR 19).

See REDUNDANCY; SUITABLE ALTERNATIVE EMPLOYMENT.

Pleading. It is not intended that the somewhat primitive pleadings used before industrial tribunals should be equated with the formal pleadings used in the High Court (*Gorman v London Computer Centre Ltd* [1978] IRLR 22). Thus it is open for a party to present his facts (e.g. which establish a reason for dismissal) and then argue that these facts could constitute alternative legal reasons (e.g. redundancy or some other substantial reason). Such a change in position is perfectly permissible as long as the other party is not prejudiced thereby (*Nelson v BBC* [1979] IRLR 346). This is not the same as raising new facts upon which a different legal reason is sought to be established. However, if an industrial tribunal comes to a conclusion that has not been canvassed or argued before them, the parties should be given an opportunity to make submissions or representations on the point before a final decision is made (*Murphy v Epsom College* [1983] IRLR 395).

See AMENDMENT TO THE PLEADINGS.

Police. A person is employed in the police service if he serves as a member of any constabulary maintained by virtue of an enactment, or in any other capacity by virtue of which he has the powers or privileges of a constable. This includes prison officers (*Home Office v Robinson* [1981] IRLR 524), special constables, etc.

A policeman is not an employee within the meaning of EPCA, nor is he a worker within the meaning of TULRA. He is, however, deemed to be employed by the Chief Constable or the police authority for the purpose of SDA (s. 17) and RRA (s. 16), in respect of any act done by him or the authority in relation to discrimination in employment. Accordingly, a policeman has no right to claim unfair dismissal, even in respect of conduct which occurs when he is not exercising those powers or privileges (*Home Office v Robinson*, supra). He has no right to an itemised pay statement, written reasons for dismissal, right to return to work after confinement, guarantee pay, medical suspension pay, trade union rights, time off work, or maternity pay. He does have the right to written particulars under s. 1 of EPCA, minimum periods of notice, and redundancy pay.

Political fund (Trade Union Act 1913; Trade Union Act 1984). Before it can have a political fund, a trade union must hold a ballot of its members, at least every ten years (Trade Union Act 1984, s. 12). The ballot must be conducted in accordance with the provisions of the 1984 Act, s. 13. If there is a resolution in force establishing the fund, no property shall be added to it other than sums representing contributions made by members or any other person (other than the union itself) and property which accrues to the fund in the course of the administration of its assets. If there is no resolution in force, no union rule may require any member to contribute to the fund, and the assets in an existing fund may be transferred to any other fund of the union. A person who opts out of paying to the political fund cannot be excluded from membership of the union, or placed at any disadvantage except in relation to the control or management of the political fund.

Political objects (Trade Union Act 1913, s. 3 (as amended). The political fund of a trade union may be used for any of the following objects: (a) any contribution to the funds of, or on the payment of any expenses incurred by, a political party, (b) the provision of any service or property for use by or on behalf of a political party, (c) in connection with the registration of electors, the candidate of any person, the selection of any candidate or the holding of any ballot by the union in connection with any election to a political office, (d) the maintenance of any holder of a political office, (e) the holding of any conference or meeting by or on behalf of a political party or any other meeting the main purpose of which is the transaction of business in connection with a political party, (f) the production, publication or distribution of any literature, document, film, sound recording or advertisement the main purpose of which is to persuade people to vote for a political party or candidate or to persuade them not to vote for them or him.

Practicable for the employer to comply (EPCA, s. 69 (5) (b)). *See* REINSTATEMENT OR RE-ENGAGEMENT.

Precedent. Where the wording of the Statute is clear and unambiguous, it is the duty of the industrial tribunal to follow it. If it is unclear or ambiguous, the industrial tribunal may follow the precedents laid down by the courts and the EAT. But where the language of the Statute is quite clear (e.g. s. 57 (3)) the decisions of the EAT are mere guidelines and suggested methods of approach. If the industrial tribunal adopts them, they are unlikely to go wrong, but if they do not adopt them it does not mean that they will go wrong. Not to follow a precedent is not, by itself, a point of law, if that precedent merely establishes a test for guidance. As long as the industrial tribunal sticks to the language of the Statute, it does not misdirect itself (*Earl of Bradford v Jowett* [1978] IRLR 16). Reported cases can be helpful for their clear and concise expression of some concept which often comes up in employment law statutes, but they are no substitute for the clear words of the Act (*Anandarajah v Lord Chancellor's Department* [1984] IRLR 131).

Preferential debts (EPCA, s. 121). If an employer is insolvent, wages owed to employees are a preferential debt in a winding up to the extent of the first £800. Any further amount outstanding ranks as an ordinary debt, along with the rest owed to creditors. In addition, the following monies owed are preferential debts, namely any guarantee pay, medical suspension pay, amount of a protective award, any payment in respect of time off work for trade union duties, payment for time off to look for work or make arrangements for retraining, time off work for ante-natal care.

See INSOLVENCY OF EMPLOYER.

Pre-hearing assessment (PHA) (Industrial Tribunals (Rules of Procedure) Regulations 1980, Sch. 1, para. 6). Once a complaint has been submitted to an industrial tribunal, either party (or the tribunal on its own motion) may apply for a pre-hearing assessment. The industrial tribunal will consider the originating application and reply, any written submission and oral argument. If the industrial tribunal consider that the case or defence is weak, so weak, in fact, that it is unlikely to succeed at a full hearing, it will inform that party that if the case is not withdrawn, and at a subsequent hearing that party loses, costs may be awarded against him.

The EAT will not reverse the decision of an industrial tribunal made at a PHA, for the industrial tribunal does not hear the evidence in full, and does not have to give reasons for its decision. The case may still proceed to be heard on its merits, and the question of costs can then be dealt with (*Mackie v John Holt Vintners Ltd* [1982] IRLR 236).

Presented to the Industrial Tribunal (s. 67 (2)). A claim is presented if it is received by the Regional or Central Office of Industrial Tribunals (*Hammond v Haigh Castle & Co Ltd* [1973] IRLR 91), though it does not have to be in the hands of an official (*Post Office v Moore* [1981] ICR 623). Posting a complaint is not presenting so that if it is delayed in the post, it has not been presented within the time limit (*House v Emerson Electric Industrial Controls Ltd* [1980] ICR 795). The rule that where a statutory time limit expires on a non-working day it is taken to expire on the next working day does not apply to complaints made under s. 67, and thus if a time limit expires on a Sunday, delivery the following day would be outside the limit (*Swainton v Hetton Victory Club* [1983] IRLR 164).

See NOT REASONABLY PRACTICABLE; THREE MONTHS BEGINNING WITH.

Pressure (EPCA, s. 63). If employees or a trade union threaten to call a strike or take other industrial action (*qv*) unless an individual is dismissed, the employer cannot advance that as a reason for the dismissal. Consequently, if no other reason is shown, the dismissal must be unfair (*Hazell Offset Ltd v Luckett* [1977] IRLR 430). It is not necessary that the pressure was specifically designed to obtain that dismissal; suffice if it could be reasonably foreseen that the pressure would result in the dismissal (*Ford Motor Co Ltd v Hudson* [1978] IRLR 66). But if it could be shown that the employee's conduct contributed to the situation which led to the pressure being exercised, that may be a ground for reducing the compensation award (*Colwyn Borough Council v Dutton* [1980] IRLR 420). All that the employer can do is to rely on the overall conduct of the employee, rather than the pressure *Sulemanji v Toughened Glass Ltd* [1979] ICR 799).

Prison officer (EPCA, s. 146 (3)). A prison officer has all the powers, authority, protection and privileges of a constable, and therefore, like the police generally, he has no right to bring a claim for unfair dismissal (*Home Office v Robinson* [1981] IRLR 524).

See OFFICE HOLDER; POLICE.

Probationary employee. There is no legal definition of a probationary employee, although it could be argued that there is a 'statutory' period of probation of one year (two years in the case of a small employer), in that the industrial tribunals will not normally hear cases of unfair dismissal unless that period has elapsed. Probationary periods can be for longer periods than one year (e.g. teaching), but it may be that the test of reasonableness for the dismissal of a probationer is not quite the same as for other employees. A probationer knows he is on trial, and must therefore establish his suitability. The employer, on his part, must give the employee an opportunity to prove himself (*Hamlin v London Borough of Ealing* [1975] IRLR 354). There may be an implied term that the employer will take reasonable steps to maintain an appraisal system during the trial period (*White v London Transport Executive* [1981] IRLR 261) and give such guidance, warnings and advice as is necessary (*Inner London Education Authority v Lloyd* [1981] IRLR 394). It is the experience of large employers of labour that a pattern of conduct begins to appear within the first 12 months of employment (*Bowden v Post Office* [1976] IRLR 169) and therefore a failure to reach the required standards during the probationary period may amount to some other substantial reason for the dismissal (*Flude v*

Post Office [1975] IRLR 330). If an employee is put on probation for a certain period of time, he can nonetheless be dismissed before that time has expired if he proves to be unsuitable (*Dalglaish v Kew House Farm Ltd* [1982] IRLR 251).

See REASON FOR THE DISMISSAL – SOME OTHER SUBSTANTIAL REASON.

Procure or attempt to procure (RRA, s. 30). These words are to be construed widely, and include the use of words which brought about (or attempt to bring about) a certain course of action. However, there must be some relationship between the parties so that one person is accustomed to act in accordance with the wishes of the other (*Commission for Racial Equality v Imperial Society of Teachers of Dancing* [1983] ICR 473).

See RACE RELATIONS ACT 1976; TO INDUCE.

Prohibition notice (HSWA, s. 22). If an inspector considers that any activity involves a risk of serious personal injury, he may serve a prohibition notice on the person in control of that activity, requiring that that activity shall not be carried on unless the matters specified in the notice have been remedied. The prohibition notice may take immediate effect, or may be deferred. An appeal against the prohibition notice may be made to an industrial tribunal, which may affirm or cancel it, or modify it (see Industrial Tribunals (Improvement and Prohibition Notices Appeals) Regulations 1974).

See IMPROVEMENT NOTICE.

Project termination. A contract of employment which is for the duration of a particular job of work is not a fixed term contract, because it is of indeterminate duration. When the work is completed, there is no dismissal in law, and no redundancy situation has been created (*Ryan v Shipboard Maintenance Ltd* [1980] IRLR 16).

See DISMISSAL.

Proposing to dismiss (EPA, s. 99). Proposing to dismiss means the giving of notice of dismissal, not the expiry of that notice. Consequently, consultations under s. 99 must begin before the giving of the individual notices of dismissal (*National Union of Teachers v Avon County Council* [1978] IRLR 55). The proposals can only relate to future dismissals, not existing ones (*T&GW v Nationwide Haulage Ltd* [1978] IRLR 143). A proposal connotes a state of mind directed to a planned course of action. The employers must have formed some view as to how many employees are to be dismissed, when this is to take place, and how it is to be arranged. This goes beyond the mere contemplation of an event (*APAC v Kirvin Ltd* [1978] IRLR 318).

See PROTECTIVE AWARD; CONSULTATION ON REDUNDANCIES.

Protective award (EPA, s. 101). If an employer fails to consult with the representatives of a recognised independent trade union on redundancies, as required by s. 99, the trade union may apply to an industrial tribunal for a protective award, which is remuneration payable to the employees who have been dismissed as being redundant. The award shall be for such period as the industrial tribunal think just and equitable, but not more than 90 days (where the employer proposed to dismiss more than 100 employees) or 30 days (where the employer proposed to dismiss more than 10 employees) or 28 days (where less than 10 employees were proposed to be dismissed).

The purpose of the protective award is not to punish the employers for their failure to consult, but to compensate the employees for their loss in consequence of the default. Thus the seriousness of the default is to be considered in relation to the employees, and not in relation to the trade union representatives who had not been consulted (*Talke Fashions Ltd v ASTWKT* [1977] IRLR 309). The industrial tribunal should consider the loss of days consultation which had occurred, rather than the loss of actual remuneration during the relevant period (*GKN Sankey Ltd v National Society of Metal Mechanics* [1980] IRLR 8). A protective award should not be made if the breach is a technical one (*Amalgamated Society of Boilermakers etc. v George Wimpey Ltd* [1977] IRLR 95) or if the breach has been brought about by the trade union negotiating an earlier date for the dismissals to take effect (*ASTMS v Hawker Siddeley Aviation Ltd* [1977] IRLR 418).

See CONSULTATION ON REDUNDANCIES.

Provision in relation to death or retirement (SDA, s. 6 (4)). This phrase means a provision about death or retirement, and is not restricted to provisions which are consequent on death or retirement. Thus, a rule that female employees must retire at 60 is discriminatory, but is excluded from the Act (*Roberts v Cleveland Area Health Authority* [1979] IRLR 244). However, payments which take effect after retirement may be covered by the equal pay rules (*Garland v British Rail Engineering Ltd* [1982] IRLR 257).

See SEX DISCRIMINATION ACT 1975; EQUAL PAY ACT 1970.

Public funds for ballots (EA 1980, s. 1). The Employment Act 1980, s. 1 (as amended by the Trade Union Act 1984, s. 20) enables the Secretary of State to make regulations for a scheme whereby the Certification Officer (*qv*) is empowered to make payments out of public funds to enable trade unions to hold ballots of their members. The purposes for which ballots are to be held are laid down in the Funds for Trade Union Ballots Regulations 1980 (as amended), and ballots may be held for the following purposes: (a) to obtain a decision or ascertain the views of members of a trade union as to the calling or ending of a strike or other industrial action (b) carrying out an election provided for by the rules of a trade union to the principal executive committee of the union (c) the carrying out of an election provided for by the rules of the union to the positions of president, chairman, secretary or treasurer of the union (d) amending the rules of the union (e) obtaining a decision on a resolution to approve an instrument of transfer or amalgamation, or (f) obtaining a decision or ascertaining the views of members as to the acceptance or rejection of a proposal made by an employer which relates in whole or in part to remuneration, hours of work, level of performance, holidays or pensions.

The scheme lays down the conditions to be observed, the conditions subject to which payments can be made, and the amount of payments.

Purposes of a private household (RRA, s. 4 (3); SDA, S. 6 (3) (a)). This can mean the employer's household or the household of some other person. It is irrelevant how many persons in the household benefit from the employment (*Heron Corpn Ltd v Commis* [1980] ICR 713).

See RACE RELATIONS ACT 1976; SEX DISCRIMINATION ACT 1975.

Q

Qualifications. *See* REASON FOR THE DISMISSAL – QUALIFICATIONS.

R

Race Relations Act 1976. The Race Relations Act makes it unlawful (in certain circumstances) to discriminate directly or indirectly against a person, on grounds of race, colour, nationality, national or ethnic origins, or to victimise him because he has brought proceedings under the Act, given evidence or information, or reported an act of discrimination. In employment, it is unlawful to discriminate (a) in the arrangements for determining who shall be employed (b) in the terms upon which employment is offered (c) refusing to offer employment (d) in the terms of employment which are afforded (e) in the arrangements for promotion or training or other benefits, facilities or services, and (f) by dismissing, or subjecting to any other detriment. There are exceptions where the race of a person is a genuine occupational qualification for the job, and employment for the purpose of a private household.

The Act makes provision for making unlawful discriminatory practices, discriminatory advertisements, instructions or pressure to discriminate, and the liability of employers and principals for the acts of their employees or agents.

The Act also creates the Commission for Racial Equality with various powers and functions, including the right to issue a non-discrimination notice and to seek an injunction in the county court, but the main avenue for individual complaints will be through the machinery of the industrial tribunals, where the remedy for unlawful discrimination is a declaration of rights and/or an order for compensation, and/or a recommendation that action be taken to obviate or reduce the adverse affect of the discrimination.

Reason . . . for the dismissal (EPCA, s. 57 (1)). It is for the employer to show what was the reason for the dismissal (or, if there was more than one reason, the principle reason). If he fails to do so, the dismissal is automatically unfair (*Timex Corpn Ltd v Thomson* [1981] IRLR 522). But provided the employers show a set of facts which are capable of justifying the dismissal, it is irrelevant that they put a wrong legal label on those facts, and the industrial tribunal is entitled to find the principle reason as that established by those facts (*Abernethy v Mott Hay & Anderson* [1974] IRLR 213). In practice, it may well be that there are a number of reasons and sub-reasons, all of which can be considered as being 'the reason' (*Patterson v Messrs Bracketts* [1977] IRLR 137).

Reason for the dismissal – capability (EPCA, s. 57 (2) (a)). Strictly speaking, this heading deals with the employee who is inherently incapable of doing his job, rather than the neglectful employee, which is really an aspect of conduct (*Sutton & Gates Ltd v Boxall* [1978] IRLR 486). The employee who is totally incompetent may be fairly dismissed, for the law on unfair dismissal does not require an employer to retain incompetent employees (*Cook v Thomas Linnell & Sons Ltd* [1977] IRLR 132). However, the employer must show that he has done all he can to ensure the competence of the employee, by providing sufficient training, supervision, support staff, adequate facilities, etc. (*Davison v Kent Meters Ltd* [1975] IRLR 145). Retraining should be considered where necessary (*Coward v John Menzies Ltd* [1977] IRLR 428). The fact that the employer has tolerated the incompetence for a long time is not to be held against him (*Kraft Food Ltd v Fox* [1977] IRLR 431). The incapability may be a series of small incidents, each one of which is insignificant, but which, when added together, lead the employer to lose confidence in the ability of the employee to do the job in question (*Miller v Executors of John Graham* [1978] IRLR 309). Equally, the incompetence may be a single act of grave consequence (*Taylor v Alidair Ltd* [1978] IRLR 82). Whether an employer should warn such an employee that his job is at risk unless there is an improvement depends on whether the warning, if given, would do any good (*Dunning (Shopfitter) Ltd v Jacomb* [1973] IRLR 206). An employer need only consider offering alternative employment if there is a suitable job available (*Gair v Bevan Harris Ltd* [1983] IRLR 368). The employer should be careful not to undermine his assertions of incompetence by e.g. providing a laudatory reference (*Castledine v Rothwell Engineering Ltd* [1973] IRLR 99).

Reason for the dismissal – conduct (EPCA, s. 57 (2) (b)). The types of conduct committed inside the employment which entitle an employer to dismiss an employee are too numerous to mention. Examples include fighting (*Parsons & Co Ltd v McLoughlin* [1978] IRLR 65) swearing (*Pepper v Webb* [1969] 2 All ER 216) private trading (*Rowe v Radio Rentals* [1982] IRLR 177) misuse of alcohol (*Dairy Produce Packers Ltd v Beverstock* [1981] IRLR 265) clocking offences (*Elliot Bros (London) Ltd v Colverd* [1979] IRLR 92) abusive behaviour (*Shortland v Chantrill* [1975] IRLR 208) theft (*Trust House Forte Hotel Ltd v Murphy* [1977] IRLR 186) refusal to obey a lawful order (*Wass Ltd v Binns* [1982] IRLR 283) unauthorised absenteeism (*British Leyland UK Ltd v Ashraf* [1978] IRLR 330) working for a competitor (*Golden Cross Hire Co Ltd v Lovell* [1979] IRLR 267) breach of rules (*Hadjiouannou v Coral Casinos Ltd* [1981] IRLR 352) dress (*Atkin v Enfield Group Hospital Management Committee* [1975] IRLR 217) safety hazard (*Marsh v Judge International*, unreported)

111

health hazard (*Singh v Lyons Maid Ltd* [1975] IRLR 328) breach of safety instructions (*Wilcox v Humphreys & Glasgow Ltd* [1976] ICR 306) and so on.

Conduct outside the employment is a relevant factor if it has a detrimental effect on the employer's business, bearing in mind the position held by the employee (*Richardson v City of Bradford* [1975] IRLR 296) the nature of the employment (*Bradshaw v Rugby Portland Cement Co Ltd* [1972] IRLR 46), and the effect of the incident on customers, fellow employees, the public, etc. (*Gardiner v Newport County Borough Council* [1974] IRLR 262). There must be a breach of faith, or a loss of confidence in the employee as a result of the conduct in question (*Moore v C. & A. Modes* [1981] IRLR 71). The conduct could be a criminal act, or immorality, or other act which brings the employee into disrepute (*Wiseman v Salford City Council* [1981] IRLR 202).

An employer does not have to prove that the employee committed the act in question. Suffice that he genuinely believes the employee to be guilty of the act, that he has reasonable grounds for that belief, and that he has carried out such investigation as the circumstances permit (*British Home Stores v Burchell* [1978] IRLR 379).

Whether a dismissal will be fair will depend on whether in all the circumstances, the employer has acted reasonably (*qv*). This means following the correct disciplinary procedure (*qv*) holding an investigation (*Weddell & Co Ltd v Tepper* [1980] IRLR 96), considering mitigating circumstances (*Taylor v Parsons Peebles Ltd* [1981] IRLR 119) and making a decision that a reasonable employer would make (*British Leyland (UK) Ltd v Swift* [1981] IRLR 91). The 'conduct' in question must have an effect on the relationship between employer and employee before the employer can reasonably take action on it (*Thomson v Alloa Motor Co Ltd* [1983] IRLR 403).

Reason for the dismissal – contravention of a duty or restriction (EPCA, s. 57 (2) (d)). If an employee is disqualified from driving (*Appleyard v Smith (Hull) Ltd* [1972] IRLR 19) he cannot be employed as a driver of a vehicle, by virtue of the Road Traffic Act 1974, s. 84; it is unlawful to employ an employee in a food processing plant if he has a beard (*Gill v Walls Meat Co Ltd* [1977] HSIB 22; Food Hygiene Regulations 1970); to employ an employee with psoriassis could be contrary to the Ionising Radiation (Sealed Sources) Regulations 1969 (*Yarrow v QIS Ltd* [1977] HSIB 20), and so on. A genuine or mistaken belief that the employer cannot continue to employ the employee without contravening a duty or restriction imposed by statute is not sufficient, although this could amount to some other substantial reason for the dismissal (*qv*) (*Bouchala v Trust House Forte* [1980] IRLR 382).

The reasonable employer, faced with making a decision to dismiss on this ground, will always consider any viable alternative which may exist (*Sutcliffe & Eaton Ltd v Pinney* [1977] IRLR 349).

Reason for the dismissal – health (EPCA, s. 57 (2) (a)). The decision to dismiss a long-term sick employee for ill-health has to be made in the light of such medical evidence as is available, either from the employee's own doctor or the employer's medical adviser (*East Lindsay District Council v Daubney* [1977] IRLR 181) and there should be a sensible and meaningful consultation between the employer and employee (*Spencer v Paragon Wallpapers Ltd* [1976] IRLR 373) although if consultation would not make any difference there may be no need to undertake this exercise (*Taylorplan Catering (Scotland) Ltd v McInally* [1980] IRLR 53). Otherwise, an employer who dismisses peremptorily is likely to be acting unfairly (*Owen v Funditor Ltd* [1976] ICR 350). The employer is not bound to evaluate a medical report with medical expertise (*Liverpool Area Health Authority v Edwards* [1977] IRLR 471) and must give due weight to the fact that there may be a breach of the common law duty to ensure the safety of his other employees if he ignores the medical evidence (*Harper v National Coal Board* [1980] IRLR 260). If an employer gives notice of dismissal, and subsequently becomes aware of facts (before the notice has expired) which would make the dismissal unnecessary, that dismissal may well become unfair if the employer fails to do that which he has the power to do, i.e. withdraw the notice with the employee's consent (*Williamson v Alcan (UK) Ltd* [1977] IRLR 303). If an employee has made a recovery, the risk of a recurrence of the illness may be relevant if there is a hazard involved (*Jeffries v BP Tankers Co Ltd* [1974] IRLR 260), but not otherwise (*Converform (Darwen) Ltd v Bell* [1981] IRLR 195). Should a dismissal be contemplated, alternative employment ought to be considered, but there is no rule of law that the employer must create a special job for him (*Merseyside & North Wales Electricity Board v Taylor* [1975] ICR 185). It may be that the absence is that of a key employee, or in some way adversely affects the rest of the workforce (*Ali v Tillotson Containers Ltd* [1975] IRLR 272). Whether or not contractual sick pay has been exhausted is irrelevant to the issue of fairness of the dismissal (*Hardwick v Leeds Area Health Authority* [1975] IRLR 319).

In the case of an employee who is off work persistently with a series of minor ailments, a warning as to his future attendance record (together with whatever assistance the employer can offer) may be appropriate, for it may deter him from taking time off work when not warranted, or encourage him to seek medical help where needed (*Smith v Royal Alfred Merchant Seamen's Society*, unreported). In a large firm, absenteeism may be more tolerable than in a small firm, for in the former there will usually be a float of employees who can cover for the absent employee, whereas this may not be possible in the latter firm (*Wilkes v Fortes (Sussex) Ltd*, unreported). Medical certificates may be given due weight, but a doctor does not run an employer's business, and he is entitled to ignore them if he suspects they are phoney (*Hutchinson v Enfield Rolling Mills Ltd* [1981] IRLR 318). If there is an unwarranted level of intermittent absences, the employer must make a fair review of the situation after having given the appropriate warnings. There is no need for a final medical investigation as this would rarely be fruitful in view of the transient nature of the illnesses (*International Sports Co Ltd v Thompson* [1980] IRLR 340). Once the facts have been established, a dismissal can be within the range of reasonable responses (*Rolls Royce Ltd v Walpole* [1980] IRLR 343) and the employer is entitled to say 'enough is enough' (*International Sports Stores v Thompson*, supra).

Reason for the dismissal – non-membership of a trade union (EPCA, s. 58 (1)–(13)). It is automatically unfair to dismiss an employee because he is not a member of a trade union or has refused to become a member. However, it may be fair to dismiss him if a valid union membership agreement is in force, which has been approved by the appropriate ballot within five years of the dismissal. However, even though there is a valid union membership agreement in force, it will still be unfair to dismiss him if (a) he objects on grounds of conscience or other deeply held personal conviction (*qv*) to being a member of a trade union or of a particular trade union (b) he was in the class covered by the agreement before the agreement came into effect and has not been a member after the agreement came into force (c) at the time of his dismissal there was a declaration in force under s. 4 of the Employment Act 1980 (unreasonable exclusion or expulsion from a trade union) (d) the Union Membership Agreement came into force after 14 August 1980, and a ballot was held in which he was entitled to vote, but since the date of the ballot he has never been a member of the union in accordance with the agreement, and (e) where the employee holds a qualification relevant to the employment, and is subject to a written code governing the conduct of those persons who hold that qualification, and has either (i) been expelled from the trade union for refusing to take part in a strike or other industrial action (*qv*) or (ii) has refused to become or remain a member of the trade union, and the fact that taking part in a strike or other industrial action would be a breach of that code.

Where an employee refuses to make a payment to some body other than a trade union (e.g. a charity), or objects to the employer making a deduction to be paid to some other body as an alternative to joining a trade union, the employee is treated as having refused to be a member of a trade union, and the above provisions apply.

Reason for the dismissal – qualifications (EPCA, s. 57 (2) (a)). This is defined in the Act as meaning any degree, diploma or other academic, technical or other professional qualification relevant to the position which the employee held. The qualification must refer to the person's aptitude or ability, and not be a mere permit or licence (*Blue Star Management Ltd v Williams* [1979] IRLR 16). Nor does the word refer to personal qualities (*Singh v London County Bus Service Ltd* [1976] IRLR 176). It can, however, refer to an in-plant aptitude test (*Blackman v Post Office* [1974] IRLR 46), driving licence (*Tayside Regional Council v McIntosh* [1982] IRLR 272), but there must be a contractual obligation to hold or retain the necessary qualification (*Litster v Thom & Sons Ltd* [1975] IRLR 47). If the employee loses the relevant qualification, a reasonable employer will look round for some alternative way of retaining the employee's services (*Sutcliffe & Eaton Ltd v Pinney* [1977] IRLR 349).

Reason for the dismissal – pregnancy (EPCA, s. 60). If a woman is dismissed because she has had a miscarriage, this is a reason connected with her pregnancy (*George v Beecham Group* [1977] IRLR 43) as is hypertension brought about by pregnancy (*Elegbede v Wellcombe Foundation* [1977] IRLR 383). However, if an employer dismisses a woman but is unaware that she is pregant, the pregnancy is not the reason for the dismissal (*Del Monte Foods Ltd v Mundon* [1980] IRLR 224).

The employer must take suitable steps to ascertain if there is alternative employment available before dismissing a pregnant woman (*Martin v BSC Footwear (Supplies) Ltd* [1978] IRLR 95) though with a small employer, such opportunities will be limited (*Brear v Wright Hudson* [1977] IRLR 287). To be entitled to bring a claim for a right under this section, the woman must have the relevant period of continuous employment (*qv*) of one or two years, as appropriate (*Singer v Millward Ladsky & Co* [1979] IRLR 217), and if she lacks this qualification, she cannot bring a claim of sex discrimination (*Turley v Allders Departmental Stores* [1980] IRLR 4).

Reason for the dismissal – redundancy (EPCA, s. 57 (2) (c)). A dismissal may be fair if it was for reason of redundancy (*qv*). The industrial tribunal will not consider the employer's reasons for making the redundancies (*Moon v Homeworthy Furniture (Northern) Ltd* [1977] ICR 117), but he must be prepared to show that the matter was fully considered (*Ladbroke Courage Holidays Ltd v Asten* [1981] IRLR 59).

There are three matters which should be taken into consideration. First, there should be full consultation, with the trade union (if any) (*Williams v Compair Maxam Ltd* [1982] IRLR 83), and with the individual concerned (*Freud v Bentalls Ltd* [1983] ICR 77). Second, alternatives should be considered, either by way of an offer of work with the same employer, or an associated employer (*Vokes Ltd v Bear* [1973] IRLR 363), or even a demotion, leaving it to the employee to decide if he wishes to accept (*Avonmouth Construction Co Ltd v Shipway* [1979] IRLR 14). Third, there must be a proper and fair system of selection, either by way of last in first out (*qv*) or other agreed procedure (*qv*) or customary arrangement (*qv*). However, it is possible to vary the criteria in order to produce a balanced workforce, or other justification (*Abbotts v Wesson Glynwed Steels Ltd* [1982] IRLR 51).

The mere fact that a genuine redundancy does exist does not *per se* lead to the conclusion that the dismissal was fair, for the determining factor is whether the employer acted reasonably in handling the situation (*Redlands Roof Tiles Ltd v Eveleigh* [1979] IRLR 11). However, a redundancy does not become unfair merely because the employer has not given to the employee a larger sum by way of severance pay than the one to which he is entitled by contract or by statute (*Hinkley & Bosworth Borough Council v Ainscough* [1979] IRLR 224).

See SELECTION FOR REDUNDANCY.

Reason for the dismissal – some other substantial reason (EPCA, s. 57 (1) (b)). A wide variety of reasons have been held to come within this provision, e.g. re-organisation (*Hollister v National Farmers Union* [1979] IRLR 238) change in contractual terms (*R.S. Components v Irwin* [1974] 1 All ER 41) refusal to work overtime (*Robinson v Flitwick Frames Ltd* [1975] IRLR 261) reduction in wage rates (*Wilson v Underhouse School* [1977] IRLR 475) personality conflicts between members of staff (*Turner v Vestric Ltd* [1980] ICR 528) misleading job application forms (*O'Brien v Prudential Assurance Co Ltd* [1979] IRLR 40), complaints from third parties (*Dobie v Burns International Security Services (UK) Ltd* [1983] ICR 478) and so on. It is for the industrial tribunal to decide whether or not the reason is a substantial one (*Priddle v Dibble* [1978] 1 All ER 1058), and not every reason advanced will necessarily be so regarded (*Hedger v Davy & Co Ltd* [1974] IRLR 138). Commercial considerations generally will amount to some other substantial reason (e.g. *Robinson v Flitwick Frames Ltd*, supra).

The industrial tribunal must then decide whether the employer has acted reasonably (*qv*) in treating that reason as a sufficient reason for the dismissal. Factors to be considered are the degree of consultation, though this is not an absolute requirement (*Hollister v NFU*, supra), and whether it was reasonable for the employer to seek the change (*Chubb Fire Security Ltd v Harper* [1983] IRLR 310).

Unless the employer pleads some other substantial reason in his defence, it cannot be raised at a later stage of the proceedings (*Nelson v BBC* [1977] ICR 649), unless both parties are given the opportunity to comment on the matter (*Murphy v Epson College* [1983] IRLR 395).

Reason for the dismissal – taking part in a strike or other industrial action (EPCA, s. 62 (1) (b). If an employee is dismissed for taking part in a strike or other industrial action (*qv*) the industrial tribunal has no jurisdiction to hear a claim for unfair dismissal (*Wilkins v Cantrell & Cochrane (GB) Ltd* [1978] IRLR 483) unless others who took part in the strike or other industrial action were not dismissed, or, if they were dismissed they were offered re-engagement and the applicant was not so offered. This is to preserve the neutrality of the law in industrial disputes (*Gallagher v Wragg* [1977] ICR 174), for otherwise the employer would have to give in to the strikers, or face a claim for unfair dismissal. To gain protection from s. 62 (2) the employer cannot dismiss before a strike etc. commences, for a threat to go on strike does not by itself constitute taking part in a strike or other industrial action (*Midlands Plastics v Till* [1983] IRLR 9). Nor can the employer dismiss when the strike etc. is over (*Heath v Longman (Meat Salesman) Ltd* [1973] IRLR 214). If employees stay away from work while a strike is on, for whatever reason, and without protest, they will be regarded as taking part in the strike. Their motives for staying out are irrelevant (*Coates v Modern Methods & Materials Ltd* [1982] IRLR 318). However, an employer may re-engage a person who has been on strike three months after the strikers have been dismissed without enabling those who were dismissed and not re-engaged to bring a claim under s. 62.

Reason for the dismissal – trade union membership/activities (EPCA, s. 58 (1). It is automatically unfair to dismiss a person because he was, or proposed to become, a member of an independent trade union, or had taken part in trade union activities at an appropriate time (*qv*).

To gain the protection of this section, the activities must be those of an individual, not the trade union (*Carrington v Therm-a-Stor Ltd* [1983] 1 All ER 796). Merely because an individual is a member of a trade union this does not make his activities trade union activities (*Drew v St. Edmundsbury Borough Council* [1980] IRLR 459). There must be some nexus between the individual's activities and a trade union (*Gardner v Peeks Retail Ltd* [1975] IRLR 244). Nor is the section designed to safeguard an individual who is caught up in an inter-union dispute (*Rath v Cruden Construction Ltd* [1982] IRLR 9).

If the employer wishes to advance another reason for the dismissal as being the principle reason, the industrial tribunal must look at the co-incidence between the activities in question and the fact of dismissal (*Taylor v Butler Machine Co Ltd* [1976] IRLR 113).

Reason for the dismissal – unfair selection for redundancy (EPCA, s. 59). It is unfair to select a person for redundancy (a) on grounds of his trade union membership or non-membership, or (b) in contravention of a customary arrangement (*qv*) or agreed procedure (*qv*) and there are no special reasons to justify the departure from the arrangement or procedure. However, the circumstances which constitute the redundancy must be applicable to other employees in the same undertaking (*Kapur v Shields* [1976] ICR 26), who held positions similar to the employee declared redundant (*Simpson v Roneo Ltd* [1972] IRLR 5), and who were not declared redundant. Thus, to select a person because he is a trade union activist would be unfair (*Taylor v Butler Machine Tool Co Ltd* [1976] IRLR 113), although the fact that the person selected is a shop steward is irrelevant if the general selection procedure is fair (*Selby v Plessey Co Ltd* [1972] IRLR 36).

See SELECTION FOR REDUNDANCY.

Reason shown by the employer (EPCA, s. 57 (3)). The reason for the dismissal can only be based on facts known to the employer at the time of the dismissal, or other facts discovered subsequent to the dismissal which confirm that reason. Facts which are subsequently discovered which could lead to a different but sufficient reason for dismissal are not relevant to the fairness of the dismissal. However, they may be relevant to the issues of reinstatement/re-engagement or compensation (*Devis & Sons Ltd v Atkins* [1977] IRLR 314).

Reasonable notice. At common law, an employee is entitled to reasonable notice of termination of his contract of employment. The length of that notice will depend on his position, the trade or industry, his duties, salary, responsibilities, length of service and other relevant factors (*Cuthbertson v AML Distributors Ltd* [1975] IRLR 228).

See LAWFUL DISMISSAL; MINIMUM PERIODS OF NOTICE.

Reasonably practicable (EPCA, s. 67 (2)). *See* NOT REASONABLY PRACTICABLE.

Reasonably practicable (HSWA, ss. 2–9). There is a presumption that if it is practicable to do something, the court will not lightly hold that it was not reasonably practicable to do it (*Marshall v Gotham & Co* [1954] AC 360). It is, however, proper to take into consideration the time, trouble and expense involved, and whether these are disproportionate to the risks (*Associated Dairies Ltd v Hartley* [1979] IRLR 171). The burden is on the accused to show that it was not reasonably practicable to do more than was in fact done (s. 40, HSWA), and the mere existence of a universal practice does not, *per se*, discharge that burden, for it still may be reasonably practicable to comply with the obligation in some other way (*Martin v Boulton & Paul Ltd* [1982] ICR 366). In the final analysis, whether it is reasonably practicable to do something is a question of fact for the court to decide, based on the evidence adduced.

See HEALTH AND SAFETY AT WORK ETC. ACT 1974.

Reasonably practicable to consult (EPA, s. 99 (8)). Where the law lays down a binding provision, which imposes a substantive legal obligation in favour of a third party, ignorance of the obligation is never an excuse for non-compliance. Thus, the fact that an employer received incorrect advice from a Government Department does not make it not reasonably practicable to consult within the appropriate period (*UCATT v Rooke & Son Ltd* [1978] IRLR 204), although it may amount to a mitigating circumstance.

See SPECIAL CIRCUMSTANCES; CONSULTATION ON REDUNDANCIES.

Rebate (EPCA, s. 104). *See* REDUNDANCY REBATE.

Recognised trade union (EPA, s. 99). Whether the employer 'recognises' a trade union is a question of fact, to be determined on the evidence (*NUTGW v Charles Ingram Ltd* [1977] ICR 530). Recognition need not be a formal agreement, as long as there is some negotiation taking place on matters contained in s. 29 (1) of the Trade Union and Labour Relations Act 1974. But recognition for representation purposes is not the same as recognition for negotiating purposes (*USDAW v Sketchley Ltd* [1981] IRLR 291) and to be recognised, there must be some person authorised to carry on collective bargaining on behalf of the trade union. Thus, merely because there are shop floor representatives who are members of a trade union, does not mean that the union is recognised, if the shop representatives are not accredited (*T&GW v Sefton Engineering Co Ltd* [1976] IRLR 318).

A single act of negotiation with the union does not constitute recognition for collective bargaining purposes (*T&GW v Andrew Dyer Ltd* [1977] IRLR 93), nor does representation in disciplinary proceedings (*T&GW v Courtenham Products Ltd* [1977] IRLR 8). Equally, the fact that the employers are members of an employers' association which negotiates with the union is insufficient to establish that the employers recognise the union (*NUSGAT v Albury Bros Ltd* [1979] ICR 84). Recognition of a trade union by an employer does not necessarily bind the employer's successor to the business (*UCATT v Burrage* [1978] ICR 314), except where the Transfer of Undertakings (Protection of Employment) Regulations 1981 apply.

See CONSULTATION ON REDUNDANCIES.

Recommendation (SDA, s. 65 (1) (c)). If a person fails to comply with a recommendation, without reasonable justification (*Nelson v Tyne & Wear Passenger Transport Executive* [1978] ICR 1183), an application may be made for an increase in the compensation awarded. However, a recommendation should not be made relating to monetary awards, nor should it be open-ended so far as the period of compliance is concerned (*Irvine v Prestcold Ltd* [1981] IRLR 281).

See SEX DISCRIMINATION ACT 1975.

Red circle. A practice whereby an employer agrees to protect the existing wage rates of an employee who for one reason or another (e.g. transfer to lower paid work) should otherwise be paid at a lower rate. The name derives from the practice of putting a 'red circle' around the employee's name in the wage book to signify preferential treatment. Because the practice perpetuates an anomoly, it can cause problems in relation to the operation of the Equal Pay Act, for the issue will frequently arise as to whether or not the difference in pay between a woman and a man who has been red circled is a genuine material factor (*qv*) other than sex.

The term is a useful shorthand phrase, but should not be used as a substitute for a full analysis of what has happened (*NCB v Sherwin* [1978] ICR 700). A red circle defence can only be raised in respect of each individual employee who, it is claimed, is within the scope, and at the time he was so admitted to this protected grade, the reason must be one which operated irrespective of sex (*United Biscuits Ltd v Young* [1978] IRLR 15). It must also be based on personal consideration (*Farthing v Ministry of Defence* [1980] IRLR 402). Thus if an employee, or a group of employees, have their wages protected for reasons which are neither directly nor indirectly due to a difference in sex, the employer may then be able to assert justifiably that the difference between their pay and that of a woman is genuinely due to a material factor other than sex. But the industrial tribunal must consider the origin of the red circle and the circumstances which gave rise to it (*Charles Early & Marriott (Whitney) Ltd v Smith* [1977] ICR 700). Thus, if the red circle was the product of past discrimination the employers cannot raise the defence (*Snoxell v Vauxhall Motors Ltd* [1977] ICR 700). The fact that a man's salary has been protected for a long time does not deprive the employer of raising the defence, but a prolonged maintenance of a red circle may well lead to doubts as to whether or not it is genuine (*Outlook Supplies Ltd v Parry* [1978] ICR 388). A red circle arrangement which gives protection to employees who are too old or too sick to carry out their former work is acceptable, as long as it operates irrespective of the sex of the persons concerned (*Methven v Cow Industrial Polymers Ltd* [1980] IRLR 289).

See EQUAL PAY ACT 1970; GENUINE MATERIAL FACTOR.

Redundancy (EPCA, s. 81 (2)). A dismissal is for reason of redundancy when it is due wholly or mainly to (a) the fact that the employer has ceased, or intends to cease, to carry on business for the purpose of which the employee was employed, or in the place where he was employed, or (b) the requirements of that business for employees to carry out work of a particular kind have ceased or diminished or are expected to cease or diminish.

The definition of redundancy is contained in s. 81 (2) (a) and (b) is exhaustive and it is important to ensure that the words of the section are satisfied (*Lesney Products Ltd v Nolan* [1977] IRLR 77). Thus a re-organisation which results in a reduced workforce is a redundancy (*Carry On Motors Ltd v Pennington* [1980] IRLR 455) but not if the same numbers are required, and the re-organisation merely results in greater efficiency (*Johnson v Nottingham Police Authority* [1974] IRLR 20). If an employee is taken on for a limited period with the knowledge that at the end of that period the work in which he was engaged would no longer be available, there is a redundancy at the end of that period, and consequently he is entitled to a redundancy payment (*Notts County Council v Lee* [1980] ICR 635). The industrial tribunal should investigate the real reason for the dismissal (*O'Hare v Rotaprint* [1980] IRLR 47), which may sometimes displace the statutory presumption and/or the employer's explanation (*Hindle v Percival Boats Ltd* [1969] 1 All ER 836).

See CEASED OR DIMINISHED; PLACE WHERE THE EMPLOYEE WAS SO EMPLOYED; WORK OF A PARTICULAR KIND; REASON FOR THE DISMISSAL-REDUNDANCY; LAY OFF; LAY-OFF — SHORT TIME; TRANSFERRED REDUNDANCY; REDUNDANCY PAY.

Redundancy pay (EPCA, s. 81 (1)). An employee is entitled to a redundancy payment if (a) he is dismissed by his employer by reason of redundancy or (b) he is laid off or kept on short time within the meaning of s. 88 (1) and complies with the requirement of that section (*Kenneth MacCrae & Co Ltd v Dawson* [1984] IRLR 5). The payment need not be made if the employee is over the age of 65 (men) or 60 (women), or where the employer dismisses because of gross misconduct (except if s. 92 applies), or where an offer of suitable alternative employment is made which the employee unreasonably refuses (s. 82 (5)), or there is an exemption order in force (s. 96). The amount of the payment is dependent on the employee's age, length of service, and week's pay, calculated in accordance with Schs. 4, 13 and 14.

For employment between the ages of 18 and 21, he is entitled to one half of a week's pay; between the ages of 22 and 40, he is entitled to one week's pay for each year's continuous employment; between the ages of 41 and 64 (men) or 59 (women) he is entitled to one and a half week's pay for each year's continuous employment. In respect of an employee who is over the age of 64 (men) or 59 (women) the redundancy payment is reduced by 1/12th for each month over that age, so that it is extinguished altogether at the age of 65 or 60 respectively. Not more than 20 years employment can be counted, and the week's pay is subject to the statutory maximum of (currently) £152 per week.

See REDUNDANCY; WEEK'S PAY.

Redundancy rebate (EPCA, s. 104. Sch. 6). The employer is entitled to a rebate from the Redundancy Fund of 35% of the amount payable by the employer. The Secretary of State for Employment, as guardian of the Fund, is not obliged to pay the rebate in respect of a sum paid by the employer which is in excess of the statutory entitlement, but he can make the rebate if the employer has, in error, paid less than the statutory entitlement (*Secretary of State for Employment v John Woodrow (Builders) Ltd* [1983] IRLR 11).

See REDUNDANCY.

Re-engagement (EPCA, s. 69). See REINSTATEMENT OR RE-ENGAGEMENT.

References. There is no legal obligation on an employer to provide a reference for an employee who is leaving his employment (*Gallear v Watson & Son Ltd* [1979] IRLR 306). If he does, and it is defamatory, he may be able to plead qualified privilege, but this defence will fail if malice is shown to exist. If the employer gives a laudatory reference which is acted upon by a subsequent employer to his detriment, the latter may be able to bring an action for deceit or negligent misrepresentation (*Hedley Byrne & Co v Heller & Parners* [1964] AC 465). Further, if an employer gives a laudatory reference, he may be estopped from denying its truth in subsequent industrial tribunal proceedings (*Hespell v Roston & Johnson Ltd* [1976] IRLR 50).

Referred (EPCA, s. 101 (1) (a)). An application for a redundancy payment is referred to an industrial tribunal when it is received by the office of the industrial tribunal, and not on the date it was sent by the employee. Accordingly, if an employee posts the application within the time limit, but it arrives outside that time limit, it is out of time (*Secretary of State for Employment v Banks* [1983] ICR 48).

See REDUNDANCY.

Refusing ... to offer employment (SDA, s. 6 (1) (1). RRA, s. 4 (1) (c)). To refuse to offer a woman work because 'it is a man's job' (*Batisha v Say* [1977] IRLIB), or to fail to permit a man to start work because women will not work alongside him (*Munro v Allied Suppliers* [1977] IRLIB) constitute a breach of this section.

See SEX DISCRIMINATION ACT 1975.

Rehabilitation of Offenders Act 1974. This Act is designed to enable people who have been convicted of a criminal offence and who, during the relevant rehabilitation period, have not offended again, to be treated as having paid their debt to society, and be entitled not to have their convictions raised against them. Consequently, they are entitled to deny their previous convictions, and a failure to disclose them shall not be a ground for dismissing a person from employment, or prejudicing him in any way. However, the Act itself does not provide any sanction as such; thus, to refuse to employ a person who has become rehabilitated does not *per se* give rise to any legal sanction; *quare* whether a refusal to promote a rehabilitated person would lead to a successful claim for constructive dismissal. To dismiss a person because of the discovery of a spent conviction would be unfair (*Hendry v Scottish Liberal Club* [1977] IRLT 5).

The main rehabilitation periods are as follows:

Sentence	Rehabilitation period
Imprisonment of more than 6 months but less than 2½ years	10 years
Imprisonment of 6 months or less	7 years
Youth custody	7 years
Fine or community service order	5 years
Detention centre	3 years
Probation order, conditional discharge, bind over, care order, or supervision order	One year, or until the order expires, whichever is the longer

Other sentences which come within the Act include an approved school order, attendance centre order, and a hospital order. There are certain reductions in the rehabilitation periods in the case of offenders who were under the age of 17. In the case of imprisonment, it is the actual period imposed by the court which counts (including a suspended sentence), not the time spent in prison. The rehabilitation period runs from the date of conviction, not from the expiry of the sentence.

The Act does not apply to questions which are asked to ascertain the suitability of a person for the admission to certain professions, nor for the purpose of certain employments, including employment connected with the punishment of offenders, constables, traffic wardens, probation officers, further education teachers, certain local government social workers, hospital workers, youth club leaders, and employment with cadet forces. The Act also does not apply to certain judicial appointments and certain other regulated occupations.

See SPENT CONVICTIONS.

Rehabilitation of Offenders Act 1974 (Exceptions) Order 1975. This Order excludes certain professions, offices, employment and occupations from the provisions of the Rehabilitation of Offenders Act. A person cannot claim that his conviction was spent if questions are asked for the purpose of assessing his suitability for admission to the following professions, namely medical practitioner, barrister, advocate or solicitor, chartered or certified accountant, dentist, dental hygienist, dental auxilliary, veterinary surgeon, nurse, midwife, ophthalmic or dispensing optician, pharmaceutical chemist, registered teacher in Scotland, and any profession to which the Professions

Supplementary to Medicine Act 1960 applies, i.e. chiropodists, dieticians, medical laboratory technicians, occupational therapists, physiotherapists, radiographers, and remedial gymnasts. Nor does the Act apply to questions relating to the following offices or employment, namely, judicial appointments, the Director of Public Prosecutions and anyone employed in his office, procurator fiscals, district court prosecutors, and any employment in their office or the Crown Office, justices clerks or their assistants, clerks, deputy or assistant clerks, and officers of the High Court, the Court of Session, and district court, sheriffs' clerks and assistants, constables, police cadets, employment concerned with the administration or carried out within the precincts of a prison, remand centre, detention centre, youth custody centre, or other young offenders institution, and a member of the board of visitors, traffic wardens, probation officers, teacher in a school or establishment for further education, other employment carried out within the precincts of a school or further education establishment where the holder has access to persons under the age of 18 in the normal course of his duties, proprietors of independent schools, employment by a local authority in connection with social services where the holder has access to persons under the age of 18 or over the age of 65 or persons suffering from serious illness or mental disorder or alcohol or drug addiction, or who are deaf, blind or dumb, or who are substantially and permanently handicapped, employment concerned with the provision of health services, employment concerned with the provision of leisure or recreational services for persons under the age of 18, and employment with a cadet force.

Nor does the Act apply to certain regulated occupations, i.e. firearms dealer, director, controller or manager of an insurance company operating under the Insurance Companies Act 1974, dealer in securities, manager or trustee of a unit trust scheme, any occupation concerned with the management of an abortion clinic, registered nursing home, registered residential home, and occupier of premises on which explosives are kept where there is a certificate of fitness to keep them is obtained.

Reinstatement or re-engagement (EPCA, s. 69). An order for reinstatement or re-engagement should not be refused merely because it is inexpedient to do so (*Qualcast (Wolverhampton) Ltd v Ross* [1979] IRLR 98), but the industrial tribunal is entitled to consider the consequences which may flow (*Bateman v British Leyland (UK) Ltd* [1974] ICR 403), for merely because reinstatement is possible, this does not necessarily mean it is practicable (*Coleman v Magnet Joinery Ltd* [1974] IRLR 343). However, it may not be practicable to make the order if the firm is a small one, with close personal relationships between the staff (*Enessy Co SA v Minoprio* [1978] IRLR 489), where an unpleasant atmosphere has been created (*Schembri v Scott Bowyers Ltd* [1973] IRLR 10), where there is redundancy (*Tayside Regional Council v McIntosh* [1982] IRLR 272), or where there is mistrust between the parties (*Nothman v London Borough of Barnett* [1980] IRLR 65). The industrial tribunal should take a broad common sense view on what is practicable, for the word must be considered in an industrial context (*Meridian Ltd v Gomersall* [1977] IRLR 425).

Relevant circumstances (SDA, s. 5 (3)). If the relevant circumstances when dealing with a man and woman are not the same, or are materially different, then no act of discrimination occurs. Thus, if a woman is refused a job because she is not tall enough, or not strong enough, there is no discrimination on grounds of sex (*Thorn v Meggitt Engineering Ltd* [1976] IRLR 241).

See SEX DISCRIMINATION ACT 1975.

Relevant date (EPCA, s. 90). The definition of relevant date contained in s. 90 (3) applies only to para. 1 of Sch. 4, not to other paragraphs in that Schedule. Thus, if an employee is dismissed with pay in lieu of notice some time after his 64th birthday, the relevant date is the date he ceased to be employed (s. 90 (1) (b)), and is not to be extended to the date when his notice would have terminated in accordance with the provisions of s. 90 (3) (*Slater v John Swain & Son Ltd* [1981] ICR 554).

See REDUNDANCY.

Relevant employees (EPCA, s. 62 (4) (b)). In relation to a lock-out, the relevant employees include all those who are directly interested in the dispute, which may be a wide category of persons (*Fisher v York Trailer Co Ltd* [1979] ICR 834). An employee is not a relevant employee for the purpose of a strike unless he was taking part in the action; mere passivity may not be enough (*McCormick v Horsepower Ltd* [1981] IRLR 217). Participation in a strike cannot be assumed e.g. by virtue of a statement by a shop steward (*Dixon v Wilson Walton Engineering Ltd* [1979] ICR 438), but motives for staying away from work may be irrelevant (*Coates v Modern Methods & Materials Ltd* [1982] IRLR 318).

See REASON FOR DISMISSAL – TAKING PART IN A STRIKE.

Relevant transfer (Transfer of Undertakings (Protection of Employment) Regs 1981). A transfer of physical assets without the goodwill of a business is not a relevant transfer within the meaning of reg. 3 of the Regulations (*Robert Seligman Corpn v Baker* [1983] ICR 770).

Remuneration (EPCA, Sch. 14, Part II). This should be looked at from a common sense point of view, e.g. basic weekly wage plus commission (*Weevsmay Ltd v Kings* [1977] ICR 244), bonuses, if there is a contractual entitlement (*Mole Mining Ltd v Jenkins* [1972] ICR 282), a proportion of an annual bonus (*J. & S. Bickley Ltd v Washer* [1977] ICR 435), but not an *ex gratia* bonus (*Hobbs Padgett & Co Ltd v Stannard*, unreported), expenses, in so far as they constitute a profit in the employee's hands (*S. & U. Stores v Wilkes* [1974] IRLR 283), but not payments in kind, e.g. free car, petrol and maintenance (*British Transport Hotels Ltd v Ministry of Labour* [1966] 2 ITR 165). Payments made by a third party, e.g. tips, are not part of remuneration (*Palmanor Ltd v Cedron* [1978] IRLR 303). The amount of the remuneration is determined by the calculation date; thus, a subsequent wage award which applies retrospectively is not to be included in the calculation (*Leyland Vehicles Ltd v Reston* [1981] IRLR 19).

See WEEK'S PAY.

Repudiatory conduct. If an employee, by his conduct, effectively repudiates the contract, it is open to the employer to accept the repudiation, and dismiss the employee (*Terinex Ltd v D'Angelo* [1981] ICR 12). This, in law, is a dismissal, which the employer may then seek to justify as being fair in accordance with the usual principles (*London Transport Executive v Clarke* [1981] ICR 355).

See ACTED REASONABLY.

Requirement or condition (SDA, s. 1 (1) (b); RRA, s. 1 (1) (b)). These words do not have separate or distinct meanings, but were used to extend the ambit of the concept intended by Parliament. Consequently, they should not be narrowly construed, and can include a qualification or a disqualification for a benefit or detriment (*Clarke v Ely (IMI) Kynock Ltd* [1982] IRLR 482). However, taking into account a number of factors in order to assess personal qualities is not applying a requirement or condition (*Perera v Civil Service Commission* [1983] ICR 428). A nebulous promotion procedure may consist of a requirement or condition (*Watches of Switzerland Ltd v Savell* [1983] IRLR 141), but a lack of promotion opportunity because women are in a 'dead end' job does not imply a requirement or condition (*Francis v British Airways Engineering Overhaul Ltd* [1982] IRLR 10). If the requirement or condition, though discriminatory, is of a kind permitted by the Act, there is no remedy available to an aggrieved person (*McGregor Wallcoverings Ltd v Turton* [1978] ICR 541).

An obligation that an employee be required to work full-time (as opposed to part-time) was held to be a requirement or condition in *Home Office v Holmes* [1984] IRLR 299, and it is a question of fact in each case whether the requirement or condition can be justified.

See SEX DISCRIMINATION ACT 1975; RACE RELATIONS ACT 1976; JUSTIFIABLE.

Requirements of that business (EPCA, s. 81 (2) (b)). A dismissal on the grounds of economy, with a redistribution of the employee's work among other employees, can be a redundancy (*Delanair Ltd v Mead* [1976] ICR 522). The test is not whether the work has ceased or diminished, but whether the requirements of the business for employees to carry out that work has ceased or diminished (*Higgs Hill Ltd v Singh* [1976] ICR 193). Thus if a fixed term contract is not renewed because there is no work for the employee to do, there is a dismissal on the ground of redundancy (*Notts County Council v Lee* [1980] ICR 641).

See REDUNDANCY.

Resignation. A resignation may be a unilateral act (*Devon County Council v Cook* [1977] IRLR 188) or a consensual agreement to end the employment (*Harvey v Yankee Traveller Restaurant* [1976] IRLR 35). In either event it cannot constitute a dismissal unless it amounts to a constructive dismissal (*qv*). If an employee uses words which are clear and unambiguous, and which clearly indicate a present intention to resign (*Sothern v Frank Charlesly & Co* [1981] IRLR 278) there can be no doubt as to what was intended, but in other circumstances, the question may be, what would a reasonable employer understand by the words used, and what was the intention of the parties (*Tanner v Keen Ltd* [1978] IRLR 110)?

To threaten an employee with dismissal unless he resigns is a dismissal, not a resignation (*Haseltine Lake & Co v Dowler* [1981] IRLR 25) but a threat that a disciplinary hearing will be held which may result in dismissal is not a dismissal (*Martin v MBS Fasteners (Glynwed) Distributions Ltd* [1983] IRLR 198). To threaten to call in the police unless the employee resigns is a dismissal (*Allders International Ltd v Parkins* [1981] IRLR 68), as is a forced early retirement (*Penprase v Mander Bros Ltd* [1973] IRLR 167).

An employee who resigns because he has been induced to do so by a satisfactory financial settlement has resigned, and cannot claim that he has been dismissed (*Sheffield v Oxford Controls Ltd* [1979] IRLR 133). Whether an employee has resigned or not is a question of fact for the industrial tribunal to determine, and is not a point of law (*Martin v MBS Fasteners (Glynwed) Distributions Ltd,* supra).

See CONSTRUCTIVE DISMISSAL.

Restrictive covenant. This is a promise by an employee that after leaving his employment he will not damage the employer's interests by seeking employment with a rival firm, or by soliciting customers, or disclosing trade secrets, etc. Such an agreement is *prime facie* void as being in restraint of trade, but it will be valid if it can be shown to be reasonable (*Esso Petroleum Ltd v Harpers Garage (Stourport) Ltd* [1968] AC 269). To ascertain the reasonableness of the covenant, regard may be had to the position held by the employee (*Mason v Provident*

Clothing & Supply Co Ltd [1913] AC 724) the interests sought to be protected (customers, trade secrets, etc.), but not competition *per se*, (*Bowler v Ludgrove* [1921] 1 Ch 642) the length of time the restriction operates (*Herbert Morris Ltd v Saxelby* [1916] 1 AC 688) the area covered by the restriction (*Fitch v Dewes* [1921] 2 AC 158) etc. If the covenant is too wide, or covers matters which the employer has no legitimate interest to protect, it will be void, unless there are separate covenants which can be severed (*Littlewoods Organisation Ltd v Harris* [1978] 1 All ER 1026).

See EX-EMPLOYEE.

Review by the Industrial Tribunal (Industrial Tribunal (Rules of Procedure) Regulations 1980). A review may be sought on the following grounds:

(a) the decision was wrongly made as a result of an error by the tribunal staff;

(b) a party did not receive notice of the proceedings;

(c) the decision was made in the absence of a party entitled to be heard;

(d) new evidence has become available the existence of which could not have been reasonably foreseen;

(e) the interests of justice require a review.

An application for a review may be made at the hearing, or within 14 days from the date the decision was sent to the parties (though the time limit can be extended). The application must state the grounds upon which the review is sought and the grounds upon which it is contended that the decision of which he seeks a review as wrong (*Drakard & Sons Ltd v Wilton* [1977] ICR 642). A review can correct major or minor errors in the previous proceedings (*Trimble v Supertravel Ltd* [1982] ICR 440), or enable the industrial tribunal to vary or revoke its previous decision, even to the extent of reversing a previous finding of fairness or unfairness, provided they have sufficient evidence before them on which to make such a decision (*Stonehill Furniture Ltd v Phillipo* [1983] ICR 556). Facts discovered after the industrial tribunal hearing can be used to support an application for review, e.g. for the purpose of reducing the compensation award (*Ladup Ltd v Barnes* [1982] ICR 107). If there was evidence which was known to the parties at the time of the original hearing, the fact that they did not introduce it at that time is not a ground for review (*Flint v Eastern Electricity Board* [1975] ICR 359). However, if a party fails to attend a hearing because he has been misled (e.g. by the conciliation officer (*qv*)) the industrial tribunal should permit that party to explain the circumstances before denying a review (*Drakard & Sons Ltd v Wilton, supra*). Although the Regulations provide for five grounds upon which a review may be sought, most of the applicatons appear to be made on the fifth ground, namely that the interests of justice require a review (*Aged Housing Association v Vidler* [1977] IRLR 104).

Revoke or vary (Industrial Tribunals (Rules of Procedure Regs. r. 10)). On an application for review, an industrial tribunal may vary a decision, even to the extent of coming to the opposite conclusion. The words 'vary' and 'variation' are not limited to a minor alteration in the decision, and thus an industrial tribunal may substitute the 'correct' order without ordering a rehearing. As an alternative, the industrial tribunal may revoke the previous order and order a rehearing (*Stonehill Furniture Ltd v Phillippo* [1983] ICR 556).

See REVIEW BY THE INDUSTRIAL TRIBUNAL.

Right to return to work (EPCA, ss. 33, 45, 46). A woman who has been absent from work because of pregnancy or confinement is entitled to return to work any time up to 29 weeks from the actual week of confinement (but note the restriction on employing women within four weeks of childbirth, see Factories Act 1961, Sch. 5, Public Health Act 1936, s. 205). To obtain this right, she must (a) have been continuously employed for two years prior to the eleventh week prior to the expected week of confinement, (b) she must be employed on that week, but not necessarily working, (c) she must inform her employer in writing at least 21 days before her absence begins (or as soon as is reasonably practicable) that she will be absent from work because of pregnancy, that she intends to return to work with him, and the expected date of confinement. She must also produce, if requested to do so by her employer, a certificate from a registered medical practitioner or certified midwife stating the expected date of confinement. Seven weeks after the actual week of confinement the employer may write to her asking her to reconfirm, in writing, that she still intends to return to work, and if she fails to do so within 14 days, she will lose her rights.

The woman exercises her right to return to work by giving three week's notice in writing that she intends to return. This notice must expire not later than the end of the 29 weeks from the actual week of confinement, but she is entitled to have an extention of four weeks beyond that date if she produces a medical certificate indicating that she is suffering from disease or bodily or mental disablement. She is also entitled to an extension if she is prevented from returning to work because of an interruption (whether due to industrial action or otherwise) which makes it unreasonable to expect her to return on the notified date of return, and she may return as soon as is reasonably practicable thereafter. The employer, for his part, may postpone the actual day of return for a period of up to four weeks.

If the woman follows the correct procedures, she is entitled to

129

return to work on terms and conditions not less favourable than those which would have been applicable to her had she not been absent. If it is not practicable to permit her to return to work because of redundancy she is entitled to be offered suitable alternative employment were there is a suitable vacancy. If the employer does not permit her to return to work, this will constitute a dismissal with effect from the notified date of return. However, if she worked for an employer who employed five or fewer employees (including any employees employed by an associated employer (*qv*)) and it was not reasonably practicable to allow her to return to work, there is no dismissal. With regard to other employers, if it was not reasonably practicable to allow her to return to work for reason other than redundancy, and suitable and appropriate employment was offered, and she accepts or unreasonably refuses that offer (*qv*) she will not be regarded as having been dismissed (s. 56A).

A failure to comply with the procedure laid down in s. 33 before she goes away on maternity leave (*Lavery v Plessey Telecommunications Ltd* [1982] IRLR 180) or the procedure laid down in s. 46 in the exercise of her right to return to work (*Kolfor Plant Hire Ltd v Wright* [1982] IRLR 311) will disentitle her to exercise her rights under these sections.

If a woman has contractual as well as statutory rights, she may take advantage of whichever is the more favourable (*Bovey v Board of Governors of the Hospital for Sick Children* [1978] IRLR 241). Moreover, a woman who is a full-time employee, and who wishes to return to employment on a part-time basis, may be able to claim that she has been unlawfully discriminated against if this request is refused (*Home Office v Holmes* [1984] IRLR 299). But even though she has not followed the correct procedure, if a contract of employment subsists throughout her absence, a failure to permit her to return to work can amount to a dismissal in law (*Lucas v Norton of London Ltd* [1984] IRLR 86).

Right to work. This phrase is sometimes used in an emotive sense as meaning that the state has a duty to ensure that jobs are available for all those who wish to avail themselves for work, but such legal right does not exist in British law. More recently, it can imply a right to work without a trade union card (*Langston v AUEW* [1974] ICR 180), or, perhaps more important, the right of an employee to require that an employer provides him with work. Earlier cases had suggested that provided an employer pays wages or other remuneration, there is no obligation to provide the employee with actual work (*Turner v Sawdon & Co* [1901] 2 KB 653), although it is recognised that a right to work may exist where the work is essential to maintain the employee's reputation (*Herbert Clayton & Jack Waller Ltd v Oliver* [1930] AC 209), or to keep up his skills (*Langston*'s case, supra). However, regard must nowadays be had to the contract of employment, and whether there is an implied term that there is an obligation on the employer to provide the employee with work to do (*Bosworth v Angus Jowett & Co Ltd* [1977] IRLR 374). If there is such an obligation, and the employer fails to provide the work, the employee may be able to resign and treat the breach by the employer as a constructive dismissal (*qv*) and claim unfair dismissal or redundancy payment (*Breach v Epsylon Industries Ltd* [1976] IRLR 180).

S

Safety committee (HSWA, s. 2 (7)). When at least two safety representatives so request, the employer shall establish a safety committee, to keep under review the measures taken to ensure the health and safety at work of employees. In setting up this committee, the employer shall consult with the safety representatives who made the request, and with the representatives of any recognised trade union whose members work at any workplace in respect of which the committee is intended to function. The employer shall post a notice stating the composition of the committee, and the committee shall be established within three months from the request being made (see the Safety Representatives and Safety Committees Regulations 1977 and the Code of Practice issued by HSC, together with the Guidance Notes).

See HEALTH AND SAFETY AT WORK ETC. ACT 1974.

Safety policy (HSWA, s. 2 (3)). Every employer shall prepare and as often as may be appropriate revise a written statement of his general policy with respect to health and safety at work of his employees, and the organisation and arrangements in force for carrying out that policy, and bring the statement (and any revision) to the notice of all employees. The only exception to this duty is an employer who carries on an undertaking in which for the time being he employs less than five employees (Employers' Health and Safety Policy Statements (Exceptions) Regulations 1975. In *Osborne v Bill Taylor of Huyton Ltd* [1982] IRLR 17 the employers operated 31 betting shops, and these were held to be 'an undertaking' for the purposes of the Act, and although each shop employed fewer than five employees, since there was central control, all the shops represented a single undertaking.

See HEALTH AND SAFETY AT WORK ETC. ACT 1974.

Safety representatives (HSWA, s. 2 (4)). A recognised trade union may appoint safety representatives from among the employees, who shall represent the employees in consultation with the employer with a view to the making and maintenance of arrangements to co-operate effectively in promoting and developing measures to ensure the health and safety at work of the employees, and in checking the effectiveness of such measures. There is no obstacle to the appointment of safety representatives in non-union situations, but these will lack the statutory backing. Other functions of safety representatives are laid down in the Safety Representatives and Safety Committees

Regulations 1977, and reference should also be made to the Code of Practice on Safety Representatives issued by HSC, and the accompanying Guidance Notes.

See HEALTH AND SAFETY AT WORK ETC. ACT 1974; TIME OFF WORK FOR SAFETY REPRESENTATIVES.

Secondary action (EA 1980, s. 17). Section 13 (1) of TULRA does not prevent an act from being actionable if a person induces a breach of any contract or interferes with a contract which is not a contract of employment, and which is not the permitted secondary action. Secondary action is permitted when (1) the purpose is to prevent or disrupt the supply of goods or services during the trade dispute between the employer who is a party to the dispute and another employer whose employees are taking the action, and the secondary action was likely to achieve that purpose or (2) the secondary action involves employees of an associated employer of the employer in dispute or employees of their suppliers or customers if the purpose of the action is directly to prevent or disrupt the supply during the dispute of goods or services to or from the associated employer and the supplier or customer, which, but for the dispute, would have been supplied by or to the employer in dispute, and the action was likely to achieve that purpose, or (3) secondary action which consists of lawful picketing carried out by an employee of the employer in dispute or a trade union official (see *Merkur Island Shipping Corpn v Laughton* [1983] ICR 490).

See TRADE UNION IMMUNITIES; PICKETING.

Secondment. Where an employee is 'loaned' temporarily from a general employer to a temporary employer, the employers may, by contract, lay down their respective legal liabilities in the event of any question arising of vicarious liability for the acts of the employee (*Arthur White Ltd v Tarmac Civil Engineering Ltd* [1967] 3 All ER 586). In the absence of any such agreement, it is a question of law as to which employer is responsible (*Mersey Docks and Harbour Board v Coggins & Griffith* [1947] AC 1). There may be a difference when a complicated piece of equipment is loaned together with the employee and when an unskilled worker is transferred. In the latter case, it is easier to infer the transfer of the liabilities from the general to the temporary employer (*Garrard v Southby & Co* [1952] 2 QB 174). But although the employers, as between themselves, can determine their legal responsibilities, this cannot affect the contractual relationship between the general employer and the employee, unless there has been some specific agreement on this. Consequently, it will be the general employer, not the temporary employer, who is the employer for the purpose of unfair dismissal and redundancy payment rights (*Cross v Redpath Dorman Long Ltd* [1978] ICR 730).

Secret ballots before industrial action (Trade Union Act, s. 10). Section 13 (1) of TULRA shall not be a defence to an action in tort against a trade union on the grounds that there is an inducement to break a contract of employment or to interfere with its performance, or there is an inducement to break a commercial contract, if the act is done without the support of a ballot. The trade union must ballot all those who are taking industrial action, there must be a majority in favour of the action, and the authorisation or endorsement of the industrial action must take place after the ballot and within four weeks thereof. The ballot must be conducted in accordance with the provisions of s. 11 of the Trade Union Act 1984.

Secret ballots for trade union elections (Trade Union Act 1984, ss. 1–9). Every person who is a voting member of the principal executive committee of a trade union must be elected by a secret ballot at least every five years. If a person is a member of that committee by virtue of holding an office (e.g. general secretary) the ballot provisions apply to him, and any term in a contract of employment to the contrary shall be disregarded. If a person is not re-elected to the committee, he may continue in office for a period (not exceeding six months) as may be reasonably necessary to give effect to the result of the election. The voting in the election must be in accordance with the provisions of s. 2 of the Act.

See TRADE UNION.

Segregation. *See* CONGREGATION.

Selection for redundancy. If there is an agreed procedure or customary arrangement (*qv*) that selection for redundancy shall be on the basis of last in first out (*qv*) it is continuous service which counts, not cumulative overall service (*Dorrell and Ardis v Engineering Developments Ltd* [1975] IRLR 234). If jobs are interchangeable between departments the proper selection system should be made on the basis of employees of the description to be made redundant, not on a departmental basis (*Woolcocks v Wailes Dove Bitumastic* [1977] 12 ITR 420). In the absence of any agreement or customary arrangement, the employer may select on the basis of an effective evaluation system, based on abilities, experience, the needs of the firm to retain a balanced workforce, disciplinary records, lateness and absenteeism, etc. (*Paine and Moore v Grundy (Teddington) Ltd* [1981] IRLR 267). Long service, however, should be an important feature of any such system (*Selby v Plessy & Co Ltd* [1972] IRLR 36).

When redundancies are being considered, it is good industrial relations practice to follow the guidelines laid down in *Williams v Compair Maxam Ltd* [1982] ICR 156, namely (a) the employers should give as much warning as possible to enable trade unions and employees to seek alternative solutions or alternative employment (b) they will consult with the trade unions to agree acceptable criteria which should then be followed (c) the criteria for selection should not depend on the opinion of the person making the selection, but should be capable of objective assessment (d) the employers will consider any representations made, and (e) alternative employment will be considered. These principles are guidelines, not rules of law. They must not be treated as a shopping list, and will need to be applied with great care in respect of small firms (*Meikle v McPhail* [1983] IRLR 351) and with non-union firms (*Simpson & Son (Motors) v Reid* [1983] IRLR 401).

See REDUNDANCY; REASON FOR THE DISMISSAL – UNFAIR SELECTION FOR REDUNDANCY.

Self employed. The parties to a contract are entitled to make whatever arrangements they wish, but they cannot evade legal responsibilities by putting a 'label' to the relationship which does not reflect the true situation (*Massey v Crown Life Insurance Co Ltd* [1978] ICR 590). Unless there is some inconsistency, or a practice develops which is different from that stated in the contract, effect should be given to the intentions of the parties where possible (*BSM 1257 Ltd v Secretary of State for Social Services* [1978] ICR 894).

See CONTRACT OF EMPLOYMENT; EMPLOYEE.

Self-certification. A doctor is no longer required to issue a medical note unless the absence from work has lasted for more than seven days. However, the introduction of Statutory Sick Pay enables employees who are off work sick to obtain statutory sick pay after an absence from work of more than three days (less, if the linking provisions apply). Consequently, employees are normally required to complete a self-certification note, outlining the reason for their absence, which should be submitted to the appropriate foreman or manager, counter-signed, and used for records purposes. There is no reason why the self-certification note cannot be used for absences other than sickness.

See SICK NOTE; STATUTORY SICK PAY.

Sex Discrimination Act 1975. The Sex Discrimination Act makes it unlawful to discriminate against a person on grounds of sex or marital status. Discrimination is defined as treating a person less favourably (*qv*), and may be direct (*qv*) or indirect (*qv*). The Act applies to discrimination against men as well as women. It is also unlawful to victimise a person because he has brought any proceedings under the Act or the Equal Pay Act 1970, or given evidence in any proceedings, or done anything in relation to the discriminator or made allegations of discrimination or contravention, but this does not apply if those allegations were not made in good faith.

In employment, it is unlawful to discriminate (a) in the arrangements one makes for determining who shall be employed (b) in the terms on which employment is offered (c) by refusing employment (d) in the way a person is afforded access to benefits or facilities, or to promotion or training, or (e) by dismissing a person, or subjecting him to any other detriment.

The Act does not apply to employment for the purpose of a private household, or where the number of employees does not exceed five, or to provisions in relation to death or retirement. No account is to be taken of special treatment afforded to women in connection with pregnancy or childbirth, and it is permissible to discriminate if sex is a genuine occupational qualification (*qv*) for the job, or it is necessary in order to comply with an Act passed before the Sex Discrimination Act (*Page v Freight Hire Transport Ltd* [1981] ICR 299).

The Act created the Equal Opportunities Commission. who may carry out investigations, issue non-discrimination notices, and give assistance to persons, but the major enforcement lies in the hands of individuals who are affected. Actions must be commenced in the industrial tribunal within 3 months of the alleged discriminatory act, unless an extension of time is granted (*Hutchinson v Westwood TV Ltd* [1977] IRLR 69).

She continues to be employed (EPCA, s. 33 (3) (a)). The fact that 'she' stops work before the 11th week prior to the expected week of confinement is irrelevant, as long as 'she' is still 'employed' in the legal sense (*Satchwell Sunvic Ltd v Secretary of State for Employment* [1978] IRLR 235). The fact that the employer returns the employee's P45 is not conclusive that the employment has terminated (*Secretary of State for Employment v Doulton Sanitaryware* [1981] ICR 477). On the other hand, if the employee resigns prior to the 11th week, the employment has ceased, and no maternity pay is payable, consequently the employer, if he pays it, is not entitled to the rebate (*Williams & Co Ltd v Secretary of State for Employment* [1978] IRLR 235).

See RIGHT TO RETURN TO WORK; MATERNITY PAY.

Shop steward. In the absence of express authority, whether a shop steward has implied authority to take industrial action will depend on the evidence as to the union's policy (*General Aviation Services Ltd v T&GW* [1976] IRLR 244). However, he is regarded as a skilled adviser for the purpose of unfair dismissal legislation, so that if he fails to advise that there is a statutory time limit of three months within which a claim has to be presented, a claim made outside that time limit will be out of time (*Syed v Ford Motor Co Ltd* [1979] IRLR 335).

See OFFICIAL.

Short time (EPCA, s. 87 (2)). *See* LAY-OFF – SHORT TIME.

Sick note. An employer is entitled to look behind a sick note if there is a suspicion that it is not genuine (*Hutchinson v Enfield Rolling Mills Ltd* [1981] IRLR 318).

See REASON FOR THE DISMISSAL – ILL HEALTH.

Sick pay. There is no presumption of an implied term in a contract of employment that sick pay will be payable. Whether it is payable will depend on all the facts and circumstances, including the way the contract has operated since it was made (*Mears v Safeguard Security Ltd* [1982] IRLR 183). If the contract does provide for sick pay, there is an implied term that this shall be for a reasonable period of time, which can be ascertained by looking at what normally applies in the industry, or by reference to the nearest relevant national agreement (*Howman & Son v Blyth* [1983] IRLR 139).

See STATUTORY SICK PAY.

Sit-in. Employees have permission to be on the employers' premises and to work there, but once that permission has been revoked, their presence on the premises constitutes a trespass. In *Galt v Philp* [1984] IRLR 156 a 'work-in' was held to constitute 'watching and besetting' for the purpose of the Conspiracy and Protection of Property Act 1875, s. 7.

See PICKETING.

Sixteen hours or more (EPCA, Sch. 13, para. 4). The number of hours to be counted are the contractual hours. Thus voluntary overtime is excluded (*ITT Components Ltd v Kolah* [1977] IRLR 53), as are hours when an employee is not required by contract to be working (*Lake v Essex County Council* [1979] IRLR 241). Nor is it possible to average the number of hours worked over a period of time (*Opie v John Gubbins (Insurance Brokers) Ltd* [1978] IRLR 540).

See CONTINUOUS EMPLOYMENT.

Social Security and Housing Benefits Act 1982. This Act requires employers to pay statutory sick pay to employees, provided the qualifying conditions are met. The first requirement is that there must be a period of incapacity for work, which means four successive days. The second requirement is that the days in question fall within a period of entitlement, and the third requirement is that the days in question are qualifying days. The maximum entitlement is eight weeks in any tax year. The employer pays the statutory sick pay, and recovers the amount from payments due to the DHSS or tax office. Statutory sick pay is deemed remuneration for the purpose of income tax and national insurance.

See STATUTORY SICK PAY.

Spare time employment. An employee who works in his spare time for another employer may be fairly dismissed if it can be shown that he is causing great harm to the main employer's business (*Nova Plastics Ltd v Froggatt* [1982] IRLR 146) either by way of working for competitors or working for oneself in competition with the employer (*Rowe v Radio Rentals Ltd* [1982] IRLR 177). But the test, as always, is the reasonableness of the employer's action (*Frame v McKean & Graham Ltd* [1974] IRLR 179). Thus if the employee's spare time employment does not cause harm to the employer's business, and in no way interferes with the employee's ability to carry out his work, an employer should not seek to restrict the activity, or dismiss the employee for carrying on the activity.

Special award (EPCA, s. 75A). If an employee is unfairly dismissed because of his trade union membership or non-membership, and no order for reinstatement or re-engagement is made, the industrial tribunal will make a special award, which will be 104 weeks pay, subject to a minimum of (currently) £10,500, and a maximum of £21,000. If the industrial tribunal makes an order for reinstatement or re-engagement, then, unless the employer shows that it was not practicable to comply with the order, the special award shall be 156 weeks pay, with a minimum of (currently) £15,750, and no maximum. The special award may be reduced (a) proportionately, when the employee is over the age of 64 (man) or 59 (woman) by one-twelfth for each month over that age, until it ceases altogether at the age of 65 or 60; (b) where the industrial tribunal considers that it would be just and equitable to reduce the award because of the employee's conduct before the dismissal; (c) where the employee has unreasonably prevented an order for reinstatement or re-engagement from being complied with.

See COMPENSATORY AWARD.

Special circumstances (EPA, s. 101 (2)). The onus is on the employer to show that there are special circumstances in the individual case which rendered it not reasonably practicable to consult within the statutory time limits. He must then show that consultation began at the earliest opportunity (*Amalgamated Society of Boilermakers etc. v George Wimpey Ltd* [1977] IRLR 95). Insolvency, *per se* is not a special circumstance, if it brought about as a result of a steadily deteriorating financial situation (*Clarke's of Hove Ltd v Bakers Union* [1978] ICR 1076), although a sudden action of a bank in stopping credit and the appointment of a receiver could be (*USDAW v Leancut Bacon Ltd* [1981] IRLR 295). To be special, the circumstances have to be out of the ordinary or uncommon, such as the unexpected loss of a key order (*AUEW v Cooper Plastics* [1976] IDS Brief 90), or the unexpected failure to obtain renewal of an important contract (*NUPE v General Cleaning Contractors* [1976] IRLR 362). Ignorance of the statutory requirements (even if induced by a Government department) is not a special circumstance (*Secretary of State for Employment v Helitron Ltd* [1980] ICR 523), nor is a genuine belief that the employer does not recognise the union for collective bargaining purposes (*Joshua Wilson Ltd v USDAW* [1978] ICR 614).

See CONSULTATION ON REDUNDANCIES.

Special treatment to women (EqPA, S. 6 (1) (b)). 'Special treatment' means specially favourable treatment, not favourable or unfavourable treatment. The parallel provision in s. 2 (2) of the Sex Discrimination Act 1975 applies to specially favourable treatment which is accorded to women in connection with pregnancy and childbirth, because that section is dealing with discrimination against men, and unfavourable treatment of women could not constitute discrimination against men. Section 6(1) of the Equal Pay Act 1970 should be likewise construed (*Coyne v Export Credits Guarantee Department* [1981] IRLR 51).

Spent convictions. Although the Rehabilitation of Offenders Act 1974 contains no redress if a person is refused employment because of a conviction which is spent within the meaning of the Act, a failure to disclose a spent conviction is not a proper ground for dismissing a person from any office, occupation or employment (*Property Guards Ltd v Kershaw* [1982] IRLR 175) and it will be unfair to dismiss on this ground (*Hendry v Scottish Liberal Club* [1977] IRLR 5). However, an employer is not bound to follow the social policy behind the Act and disregard convictions which are not spent within the meaning of the Act (*Torr v British Railways Board* [1977] ICR 784).

See REHABILITATION OF OFFENDERS ACT 1974.

Staff employee. An employee who is paid on a weekly or monthly basis is generally regarded as being a member of the staff. His remuneration, in the absence of any contractual term to the contrary, is not dependent on the number of hours worked, and consequently he is not entitled to be paid overtime (*Cole v Midlands Display Ltd* [1973] IRLR 62).

Starts work (EPCA, s. 151 (3)). This refers to the date the contract of employment begins, and is not to be interpreted literally as the date on which the employee actually commences work. Thus, if the day on which the employee is due to start work happens to be a holiday or other non-working day, he still starts work on that day for the purpose of calculating his period of continuous employment (*Salvation Army v Dewsbury* [1984] IRLR 222).

See CONTINUOUS EMPLOYMENT.

Statutory Joint Industrial Council (SJIC). An SJIC is a Wages Council (*qv*) without any independent members. Its powers and functions are the same as Wages Councils but, if there is a failure to agree, the services of ACAS may be utilised to resolve the matter by conciliation, failing which, compulsory arbitration must be resorted to, with the arbitration award final and binding. It was intended that SJICs would replace Wages Councils and ultimately lead to the abolition of State involvement machinery altogether, but this development has not happened, and to date no SJICs have been created.

Statutory sick pay (Social Security and Housing Benefits Act 1982). In respect of an employee who has been off work for four or more days through sickness or injury, and employer shall pay

Statutory sick pay for a period of up to 8 weeks. The amount thus paid is recouped by the employer by deducting the money from the national insurance returns, or income tax returns. Thus the administrative burden of paying sick pay is shifted from the State to the employer. The amount of sick pay payable is dependent on the employee's earnings, and the money paid is deemed remuneration, so that national insurance and income tax, where appropriate, should be deducted. Statutory sick pay is payable immediately the employee commences employment, and part-timers are covered by the scheme, as long as they have reached the appropriate earnings level. Married women who pay the reduced national insurance contribution are covered by the scheme. After eight weeks absence, State Sickness Benefit is payable, where appropriate.

Further details of the scheme can be obtained from local offices of the DHSS.

See SICK PAY; SELF–CERTIFICATION.

Strike. 'A strike is a concerted stoppage of work by men done with a view to improving their wages or conditions, or giving vent to a grievance or making a protest about something or other, or supporting or sympathising with other workmen in such endeavour.' per Lord Denning in *Tramp Shipping Ltd v Greenwich Marine* [1975] ICR 261). For a definition for the purpose of Sch. 13 (unless the context requires otherwise) see para. 24 (1) to the Schedule.

See REASON FOR THE DISMISSAL – TAKING PART IN A STRIKE; OTHER INDUSTRIAL ACTION.

Suitable alternative employment (EPCA, s. 85 (5)). If the employer makes an offer (whether in writing or not) before the end of the employment to renew the contract or re-engage the employee under a new contract, so that the renewal or re-engagement takes effect immediately or within four weeks, and the provisions of the new contract as to capacity, place of employment and other terms and conditions would not differ from the previous contract, or, if they do differ, the offer constitutes an offer of suitable employment in relation to the employee, and the employee unreasonably refuses that offer, he shall not be entitled to a redundancy payment.

The industrial tribunal must consider, in an objective sense, whether the offer is suitable, and this is a question of fact. Employment is suitable if it is the same as the previous employment, not if it is substantially different, even though at the same salary (*Taylor v Kent County Council* [1969] 2 All ER 1080). The offer of new employment which involves loss of status is not suitable employment (*Harris v Turner & Sons (Joiners) Ltd* [1973] ICR 31), although if this is only a minor matter, the employment may be suitable (*Kane v Raine & Co Ltd* [1974] ICR 300). However, it is permissible for the industrial tribunal to take into account loss of financial benefits (*Davis Transport Ltd v Chatterway* [1972] ICR 267), loss of functions (*Harris v Turner & Sons (Joiners) Ltd*, supra), and the reployment of a skilled worker in a less skilled job (*Standard Telephone & Cable Ltd v Yates* [1981] IRLR 21). If the offer is of regular employment, the duration of that employment does not affect its suitability (*Morgan Crucible Ltd v Street* [1972] ICR 110). An offer to work on a distant site has been held not to be suitable (*Wilson-Undy v Instrument and Control Ltd* [1976] ICR 508). The employer must prove that an offer was made (*Simpson v Dickinson* [1972] ICR 474), and the industrial tribunal will decide as a fact whether it was suitable (*Taylor v Kent County Council*, supra). If the industrial tribunal decide that the offer was suitable, they will then go on to consider whether the employee unreasonably refused that offer.

See REDUNDANCY; UNREASONABLY REFUSES THAT OFFER.

Summary dismissal. This is instant dismissal, without any notice being given. Summary dismissal may be carried out if there is an act of gross misconduct, which is conduct so serious that it amounts to a fundamental breach of contract by the employee. This will obviously depend on the facts of each case, but account must be taken of current *mores* of society, and many of the earlier cases on this topic must be treated with reserve, if not disdain (*Wilson v Racher* [1974] IRLR 114).

See LAWFUL DISMISSAL; FAIR DISMISSAL; WRONGFUL DISMISSAL; GROSS MISCONDUCT.

Suspension. The employer's power to suspend an employee as a disciplinary sanction can only be based on a term in the contract (or relevant disciplinary procedure (*qv*)) to this effect, although it would not be difficult to imply such a term (*Pirie & Hunter v Crawford* IDS Brief 155). A precautionary suspension, for the purpose of carrying out an investigation is not a dismissal (*Jones v British Rail Hovercraft Ltd* [1974] IRLR 279), nor is a punitive suspension, unless it is out of all proportion to the offence (*BBC v Beckett* [1983] IRLR 43).

A temporary suspension from work for matters unconnected with discipline is not possible unless there is a contractual term which allows this, in which case it may amount to a dismissal for reason of redundancy (*McKenzie Ltd v Smith* [1976] IRLR 345).

See DISCIPLINARY PROCEDURE; LAYOFF.

Suspension on medical grounds (EPCA, s. 19). An employee who is suspended from work on medical grounds in consequence of any requirement imposed under the under-mentioned enactments, or a recommendation contained in a Code of Practice issued by HSC, shall be entitled to a week's pay (*qv*) for a period of 26 weeks. To qualify for the right, the employee must have been employed for more than one month prior to the suspension, or not be employed under a contract for a fixed term of three months or less, or under a contract which was not expected to last for more than three months. The employee is not entitled to pay if he is unable to work because of any disease or bodily or mental disablement. Nor is he entitled to pay if the employer offers him suitable alternative employment (whether or not it is work which under his contract he is employed to perform) and he unreasonably refuses that offer, or he does not comply with reasonable requirements of his employer with a view to ensuring that his services are available.

The relevant statutory provisons which may lead to suspension on medical grounds are as follows:

(1) India Rubber Regulations 1922,
(2) Chemical Works Regulations 1922,
(3) Ionising Radiations (Unsealed Radioactive Substances) Regulations 1968,
(4) Ionising Radiations (Sealed Sources) Regulations 1969,
(5) Radioactive Substances (Road Transport Workers) (Great Britain) Regulations 1970–75,
(6) Control of Lead at Work Regulations 1980.

T

Takes part in a strike (EPCA, s. 92 (1)). If, during the obligatory period (*qv*) of the employer's notice i.e. the lawful notice which the employer must give to terminate the employment, (see s. 85 (5)), or if the employee has given notice under s. 88 (1) (lay-off or short time (*qv*), and see s. 87), the employee then goes on strike, and is consequently dismissed, he is still entitled to be considered for a redundancy payment, despite the provisions of s. 82 (2). However, if the employee takes part in a strike, and is then dismissed for reason of redundancy, no redundancy payment is payable (*Simmons v Hoover Ltd* [1977] 1 All ER 775).

Taking part in a strike (EPCA, s. 62 (1) (b)). *See* REASON FOR THE DISMISSAL — TAKING PART IN A STRIKE.

Temporary cessation of work (EPCA, Sch. 13, para. 9 (1) (b)). Whether there has been a temporary cessation of work is a question of fact and degree for the industrial tribunal to determine (*Ford v Warwickshire County Council* [1983] ICR 273). The matter should be looked at as a historian, looking backward, rather than as a journalist, recording a chronicle of present or future events (*Fitzgerald v Hall Russell & Co Ltd* [1970] AC 984). The industrial tribunal should have regard to the total period of employment, and the length of the break in that employment (*Bentley Engineering Ltd v Crown* [1976] ICR 225). The fact that during the break the employee has taken another job is not, by itself, conclusive of the cessation being permanent (*Thompson v Bristol Channel Ship Repairers Ltd* [1969] 4ITR 262). Thus, if an employee is dismissed for reason of redundancy, and is re-engaged at a later date, there is a fair presumption that his absence during the intervening period was temporary (*Fitzgerald v Hall Russell & Co Ltd*, supra), although if an employee is dismissed for misconduct, or resigns voluntarily, and is then re-engaged at a later date, his absence in the intervening period cannot be due to a temporary cessation of work *Wessex National Ltd v Long* [1978] ITR 413).

The Schedule applies to successive fixed term contracts in the same way it applies to contracts of an indefinite duration. One must look at the length of the contract, and the length of the intervals between the contracts. Thus seasonal contracts will only result in continuous employment if the length of the interval between them is short in comparison with the length of the season during which the employee is employed (*Ford v Warwickshire County Council*, supra). The Industrial Tribunal does not have to look behind the temporary cessation of work and consider what caused that temporary cessation (*University of Aston v Malik* [1984] ICR 492 at 497).

See WORK.

Temporary employee. There is no legal definition of a temporary employee. As long as a person works for more than 16 hours per week for more than one year (or two years in the case of a 'small' employer) or works between 8 and 16 hours per week for more than five years, he has all the rights of the employment protection legislation. If a person is appointed on a temporary basis in order to replace a woman who has gone on maternity leave of absence, or as a temporary replacement for someone who has been suspended on medical grounds, then, provided the person has been notified in writing that the appointment will be terminated when the original employee returns to work, the dismissal of the replacement will be for some other substantial reason (*qv*), but without prejudice to the rule that the employer must still act reasonably (*qv*).

Terms and conditions of employment. This phrase does not appear to have been the subject of a statutory definition, though it has been discussed in connection with its use in TULRA, s. 29 (1), which defines a trade dispute e.g. *BBC v Hearn* [1977] ICR 685, where it was stated that the phrase includes the totality of the provisions of employment, i.e. not only those expressly agreed, but also those which might be reasonably understood. There does not appear to have been any authoritative decision on the distinction between 'terms' and 'conditions'. It is submitted that the former are those matters which are contractually agreed, and which therefore can only be changed by mutual agreement, whereas the latter are those matters which are laid down unilaterally by the employer (e.g. disciplinary procedure, works rules etc.), and which can be changed on giving reasonable notice.

Three months beginning with (EPCA, s. 67 (2)). The date of the effective date of termination (*qv*) is to be included in the calculation (*Hammond v Haigh Castle & Co Ltd* [1973] 2 All ER 289). A month means calendar month.

See EFFECTIVE DATE OF TERMINATION.

Time off to look for work (EPCA, s. 31). An employee who has been given notice of dismissal for reason of redundancy, and who has been employed for more than two years, is entitled to be allowed reasonable time off work (with pay) to look for new employment or make arrangements for re-training. The sanction for a failure of the employer to permit an employee to exercise this right is an award of two day's pay by an industrial tribunal.

There is no requirement that the employee should produce a list of appointments which he may have made, for the right to have time off is for the purpose of looking for work (*Dutton v Hawker Siddeley Aviation Ltd* [1978] ICR 1057).

Time off work for ante-natal care (EPCA, s. 31A (1)). A woman who is pregnant, and who has been advised to receive ante-natal care is entitled not to be unreasonably refused time off work, with pay, to enable her to keep the appointment. She must produce (if requested) a certificate stating that she is pregnant, and an appointment card (but not for the first appointment). A failure to allow her to have time off for this purpose, or a failure to pay her for the time off, may be the subject of a complaint by her to the industrial tribunal.

If the employer permits a woman to have time off, this would indicate that he thinks it is reasonable for her to have the time off, and hence she must be paid. However, there may be circumstances when it may be reasonable for her to make arrangements for ante-natal care in her own time, and hence it would not be unreasonable to refuse her the time off during working hours (*Gregory v Tudsbury Ltd* [1982] IRLR 67).

Time off work for public duties (EPCA, s. 29). Every employee is entitled to have time off work (not necessarily with pay) for the purpose of taking part in the following public duties

(a) justice of the peace,
(b) member of a local authority,
(c) member of a statutory tribunal,
(d) member of a Health Authority,
(e) governor of an educational establishment maintained by a local authority,
(f) member of a water authority.

The amount of time off, the occasions on which, and any conditions subject to which, time off shall be taken are those that are reasonable in all the circumstances, having regard in particular to how much time off the employee has had under the headings of trade union duties and activities, how much time off is needed to perform the public duty in question, and the circumstances of the employer's business and the effect of the employee's absence on the running of that business.

The statutory requirement is for the employer to give the employee time off work. It does not mean that the employee's duties shall be re-arranged so that he can use his own spare time (*Radcliffe v Dorset County Council* [1978] IRLR 191). On a complaint under s. 30, the industrial tribunal's powers do not include the making of recommendations or conditions as to the way time off shall be granted (*Corner v Bucks County Council* [1978] IRLR 320).

Time off work for safety representatives (Safety Representative and Safety Committee) Regulations 1977. An employee who is a safety representative (*qv*) is entitled to have time off work, with pay, for the purpose of carrying out his duties as a safety representative, and to go on a training course (see Code of Practice issued by HSC).

There is no statutory requirement that the training course for safety representatives shall be approved by the TUC or a trade union (*White v Pressed Steel Fisher Ltd* [1980] IRLR 176). But if, when a safety representative is on a training course, he would have been laid off and paid a guarantee payment, he is nonetheless entitled to his normal pay during the period of the training course, for he is entitled to be paid not for what he has lost, but for the work he would have ordinarily been doing (*Diamond v Courtland Textiles Ltd* [1979] IRLR 449).

See HEALTH AND SAFETY AT WORK ETC. ACT 1974.

Time off work for trade union duties (EPCA, s. 27). An employee who is an official (*qv*) of an independent trade union is entitled to have time off work, with pay, to enable him to carry out those duties which are concerned with industrial relations between his employer and his employees, and to go on an approved training course. The amount of time off, the occasions on which, and any conditions subject to which time off shall be taken shall be that which is reasonable, having regard to the Code of Practice (*qv*) issued by ACAS.

The employee is entitled to be paid as if he had worked for the whole of the time he has taken off. Consequently, he is entitled to the remuneration he would have received had he been working his normal contract (*McCormack v Shell Chemicals UK Ltd* [1979] IRLR 40) but he is not entitled to be paid for the overtime he would have worked, unless he was contractually bound to work overtime (*Davies and Alderton v Head Wrighton Teesdale Ltd* [1979] IRLR 170).

The employee is entitled to have time off with pay to enable him to be better prepared for his trade union duties, or to make him a better representative. Thus he is entitled to go on relevant training courses even though the knowledge gained would not have immediate usefulness, as he may be able to make representation for changes (*Young v Carr Fasteners Ltd* [1979] IRLR 420). The mere exchange of information among trade union officials does not qualify as a trade union duty, but if the purpose of the meeting is to discuss matters generally, the industrial tribunal can examine the items to be discussed, and if part of the meeting falls within the ambit of trade union duties, that part may be considered for payment (*RHP Bearings Ltd v Brookes* [1979] IRLR 452). The reasonableness of the amount of time off is a matter for the industrial tribunal to determine (*Thomas Scott & Sons (Bakers) Ltd v Allen* [1983] IRLR 329).

The right to remuneration at the statutory rate only applies when time off is granted under the section; if it is granted under the employers' own internal machinery, the right to remuneration does not arise (*Ashley v Ministry of Defence* [1984] ICR 298).

Tips. *See* WAGES.

To induce (RRA, s. 31; SDA, s. 40). To induce means to persuade or prevail upon a person to bring about the desired result (*CRE v Imperial Society of Teachers of Dancing* [1983] ICR 473).

   See RACE RELATIONS ACT 1976; SEX DISCRIMINATION ACT 1975.

Trade dispute (TULRA, s. 29). A trade dispute means any dispute between workers and their employers which relates wholly or mainly to one of the following:

(a) terms and conditions of employment, or physical conditions in which workers are required to work;

(b) engagement or non-engagement, or termination or suspension of one or more workers;

(c) allocation of work or the duties of employment of one or more workers;

(d) matters of discipline;

(e) membership or non-membership of a trade union;

(f) facilities for officials of trade unions;

(g) machinery for negotiation or consultation, or other procedures, including recognition by employers of the right of a trade union to represent workers in any such negotiation or consultation or in carrying out such procedures.

A trade dispute may exist between workers and the Crown even though the Crown is not the employer, if the dispute relates to matters which have been referred for consideration to a joint body on which a Minister is represented, or refers to matters which cannot be settled without the Minister exercising a power conferred on him by an enactment. A trade dispute exists even though it relates to matters outside the United Kingdom so long as the persons who take action in the United Kingdom would be affected by the outcome of the dispute.

There must be clear evidence that a trade dispute is in existence – a mere 'grumble', which has not yet crystalised into a trade dispute is not sufficient (*Conway v Wade* [1909] AC 506). It is not necessary that there should have been a confrontation between the parties (*Health Computing Ltd v Meek* [1980] IRLR 437), or that inflexible positions have not been taken (*Beetham v Trinidad Cement* [1960] AC 132). Whether or not a trade dispute exists is an objective matter, to be determined by the courts on the evidence, not on whether one party thought that there was a trade dispute in existence (*NWL Ltd v Nelson and Laughton* [1979] IRLR 478). A trade dispute must concern one or more of the matters listed in s. 29 (1), but the dispute must be between the workers and their own employer. The latter, however, cannot escape from the dispute by a change in the legal identity, for the court will lift the veil of incorporation, and look at the reality of the situation (*Examite Ltd v Whittaker* [1977] IRLR 312).

NB: the statutory definition of 'trade dispute' contained in EPA

s. 126A is that which was used in TULRA *before* the latter was amended by the Employment Act 1982. The reason is to ensure that for the purpose of conciliation under s. 2 of EPA the 'old' definition applies. Hence, ACAS have a wider brief to conciliate than they would otherwise have under the modern, more restricted, definition of 'trade dispute'.

Trade Union (TULRA, s. 28). A trade union is an organisation (whether permanent or temporary) which either (a) consists wholly or mainly of workers of one or more description and whose principle purposes include the regulation of relations between workers and employers or employers' associations, or (b) consists wholly or mainly of (i) constituent or affiliated organisations which have these purposes, or (ii) representatives of such constituent or affiliated organisations, and in either case whose principle purposes include the regulation of relations between workers and employers or employers' associations, or include the regulation of relations between the constituent or affiliated organisations.

An organisation which wishes to become a trade union must apply to the Certification Officer (*qv*) to be included on the list of trade unions. The application must be accompanied by the appropriate fee, with a copy of its rules, list of officers, address of head office, and name. An organisation which is refused such a listing, or which is removed from the list, may appeal to the Employment Appeal Tribunal against the decision of the Certification Officer, on a question of law or fact. A trade union which is on the list has all the immunities conferred by s. 13 (1) of TULRA (as amended) in respect of actions in tort for acts committed in furtherance or contemplation of a trade dispute (*qv*), but none of the advantages of certification until it obtains a certificate of independence (*qv*). Every trade union must keep a register of members (Trade Union Act 1984, s. 4).

See MEMBERSHIP OF A TRADE UNION; TRADE UNION IMMUNITIES; SECRET BALLOTS FOR TRADE UNION ELECTIONS.

Trade Union Act 1984. This Act requires trade unions to hold secret ballots for members of the principal executive committee of the union, secret ballots to be held before industrial action, and secret ballots on the setting up or continuance of a political fund. It also requires that employers shall not deduct anything from an employee's emoluments if he has been notified that the employee does not wish to contribute to a union's political fund.

See SECRET BALLOTS FOR TRADE UNION ELECTIONS; SECRET BALLOTS BEFORE INDUSTRIAL ACTION; POLITICAL FUND; CHECK–OFF AGREEMENT.

Trade union activities. *See* ACTIVITIES OF AN INDEPENDENT TRADE UNION.

Trade Union and Labour Relations Act 1974 (TULRA). This Act, which repealed the Industrial Relations Act 1971, has itself been the subject of considerable amendment and repeal. The main provisions which are still in force concern the status of trade unions and employers' associations, the truncated s. 13, which gives certain immunities to trade unions for acts done in furtherance or contemplation of a trade dispute, provision relating to peaceful picketing, and the non-enforceability of collective agreements.

Trade union immunities (TULRA, s. 13 (1)). An act done in furtherance or contemplation (*qv*) of a trade dispute (*qv*) shall not be actionable in tort on the ground only (a) that it induces another person to break a contract or interferes or induces another person to interfere with its performance, or (b) that it consists of his threatening that a contract will be broken or its performance interfered with, or that he will induce another person to break a contract or to interfere with its performance. This is the major immunity available in trade disputes, and protects any person (trade union, official, shop steward, employers' association, etc.) from the tort of inducing a breach of contract (or threatening to do so) and interference with commercial contracts. However, the immunity does not apply to secondary action (*qv*) which is not lawful by virtue of the provisions of s. 17 of the Employment Act 1980, or in respect of picketing (*qv*) which is not lawful under the provisions of s. 15 of TULRA (as amended) or if a ballot has not been held under the Trade Union Act 1984, s. 10, or in respect of inducing union/non-union labour only contracts (*qv*) or inducing trade union recognition requirements (*qv*) under the provision of the Employment Act 1982, ss. 11–13.

Section 13 (4) of TULRA provides an immunity from the common law tort of civil conspiracy as long as the act would not be actionable if done by an individual.

If a trade union is not immune from action by virtue of s. 13 (1), there are financial limits on the amount of damages which can be awarded against the union, depending on its size. If the membership is less than 5,000, the limit is £10,000, between 5,000 and 24,999, the limit is £50,000, between 25,000 and 99,999, the limit is £125,000, and if it has 100,000 or more members, the limit is £250,000 (Employment Act 1982, s. 16).

Trade union recognition requirement (EA 1982, s. 13). Any term or condition in a contract for the supply of goods or services shall be void in so far as it purports to require any party to the contract to recognise one or more trade unions, or to negotiate or consult with any official of a trade union. Section 13 of TULRA shall not be a defence if a person induces or attempts to induce another person to

149

incorporate into a contract a term which would be void as above.

See UNION/NON-UNION LABOUR ONLY CONTRACTS; TRADE UNION IMMUNITIES.

Transfer of Undertakings (Protection of Employment) Regulations 1981. These Regulations are designed to protect certain employment rights when there is a relevant transfer of an undertaking (within the meaning of the Regulations) from one person to another. Generally, a transfer does not operate so as to terminate the contracts of employment of persons employed by the transferor, and these take effect as if made with the transferee. A dismissal before or after a transfer may be an unfair dismissal, unless justified on economic, technical or organisational grounds. Rights under a collective agreement are also transferred (but not in respect of occupational pension schemes), and trade union recognition rights are also transferred. There are provisions relating to informing and consulting with trade union representatives on the implications of the transfer, and measures which will be taken, and the effect of 'hiving down' agreements made by liquidators or receivers.

The Regulations are designed to implement the 'Acquired Rights' Directive (77/187).

See CONSULTATION ON TRANSFERS.

Transferred from one person to another (EPCA, Sch. 13, para. 17). *See* CHANGE IN THE OWNERSHIP OF THE BUSINESS.

Transferred redundancy. This arises when an employee, who has been made redundant, is transferred to another job, and the holder of that job is therefore dismissed for reason of redundancy (*Gimber & Sons Ltd v Spurrett* [1967] 2 ITR 308). In effect, the redundancy is transferred from one person to another, and the person who has been displaced is dismissed for reason of redundancy (*Elliott Turbomachinery Ltd v Bates* [1981] ICR 218).

See REASON FOR THE DISMISSAL; REDUNDANCY.

Treaty of Rome. This Treaty, which created the European Community, affects British employment law in a number of ways. One of the objects is to achieve harmonisation on a number of issues, and in particular in matters relating to 'employment, labour law and working conditions, basic and advanced vocational training, social security, protection against occupational accidents and diseases, occupational hygiene, the law of trade unions, and collective bargaining between workers and employers' (Article 118). There are several ways the impact of the EC can be felt on British law. Firstly, the Articles of the Treaty are directly applicable. In practice, two Articles are relevant; Article 119 states that the Member States of the EC shall ensure that men and women receive equal pay for equal work (see *Defrenne v Sabena* [1976] ICR 547), and Article 48, which guarantees the freedom of workers to move within the Community and not to suffer discrimination as regards employment, remuneration and other conditions of work and employment (see *Van Duyn v Home Office (No. 2)* [1975] Ch. 358).

Second, there are Regulations made by the Council of Ministers or the European Commission which are again directly applicable and binding in their entirety. However, no Regulation relating to employment law has yet been made.

Third, there are Directives issued by the Council of Ministers or European Commission, which are binding as to the result to be achieved, but leave national authorities the choice of form and method. There is some authority for the view that a Directive has a binding effect on a State (see *Van Duyn v Home Office*, supra), but it appears that it cannot be enforced against an individual within that State (see *Hugh Jones v St John's College Cambridge* [1979] ICR 848).

Fourth, there are EC Decisions, which are binding upon the person to whom they are addressed, and recommendations and opinions, which have no binding force.

See DIRECTIVE.

Trial period (EPCA, s. 84). If an employee is dismissed for reason of redundancy, and his contract is renewed, or he is re-engaged under a new contract, he will not be regarded as having been dismissed. If the new contract differs, as to capacity, place or work, or other terms and conditions, from the old contract, he will be entitled to a trial period of four weeks, or such longer period as may be agreed for the purpose of retraining. In the latter case, the agreement must be between the employer and the employee or his representatives before the employee starts work under the new contract, must be in writing, must specify the date of the end of the trial period, and must specify the terms and conditions which will apply at the end of that period. If, during the trial period, the employer or employee terminate the contract, the employee will be regarded as having been dismissed for reason of redundancy.

The statutory trial period is for four weeks. Any longer period, agreed between the parties, is only for the purpose of retraining (*Meek v Allen Rubber Co Ltd* [1980] IRLR 21). But if the employer repudiates the contract, by making a unilateral change in the contract so that the employee is entitled to claim constructive dismissal (*qv*), the employee has a reasonable period within which to consider whether or not to accept the repudiation. This is not the statutory trial period (*Air Canada v Lee* [1978] ICR 202). If he decides to accept the new contractual situation, he has a further four weeks within which to make up his mind, before losing the right to treat himself as being dismissed (*Turvey v Cheyney & Son Ltd* [1979] IRLR 105).

Truck Act 1831. It is unlawful to pay a manual worker (*qv*) wages in anything other than current coin of the realm, and any agreement to the contrary is void and illegal. Certain deductions are permissible (e.g. for the value of tools purchased by the employee), but these must not exceed the true value, and must be authorised by an agreement in writing. Statutory deductions (income tax, national insurance) may be made, as well as a deduction in favour of a third party (e.g. a trade union subscription see *Williams v Butlers Ltd* [1975] ICR 208), again if written authorisation is given. In *Brooker v Charrington Oils Ltd* [1981] IRLR 147 it was held that payment by a post office giro-cheque did not violate the Truck Act, for the employee could go to the Post Office and collect the money, it being argued that the Act does not state where the coin of the realm has to be paid. The decision, however, is one of a county court, and is of interest, but has no value as a precedent.

By the Payment of Wages Act 1960 a manual worker may give a written request that his wages be paid by cheque or by postal or money order, and payment may be made in this manner (but not by cheque) if the employee is away or absent from his usual place of work. A written statement must be given, detailing gross wages and all deductions.

See FINES; DEDUCTIONS; PAYMENT OF WAGES ACT 1960.

U

Undergo training (EPCA, s. 27 (1) (b)). The training must be relevant to the trade union duties (*Menzies v Smith & McLaurin Ltd* [1980] IRLR 180). If the employer does not know the purpose of the training, he may not act unreasonably in refusing to give permission for time off (*Ministry of Defence v Crook and Irving* [1982] IRLR 488).

See TIME OFF WORK FOR TRADE UNION DUTIES.

Undertaking (Employers Health and Safety Policy Statement (Exception) Regulations 1975). An undertaking is one business, even though it is carried on from different premises (*Osborne v Bill Taylor Ltd* [1982] ICR 168).

Unfair dismissal. *See* DISMISSAL; REASON FOR THE DISMISSAL; ACTED REASONABLY.

Union membership agreement (TULRA, s. 30 (1)). A union membership agreement (UMA) is an agreement or arrangement made by an independent trade union (*qv*) and an employer (or employers' association) which relates to an identifiable class and has the effect in practice of requiring employees of that class to become a member of the trade union or another specified trade union. For the 'practice' to exist it is not necessary that there should be a 100% membership (*Taylor v Co-operative Retail Services Ltd* [1982] IRLR 354). In respect of UMAs entered into prior to August 1980, there must have been a ballot in which at least 80% of those entitled to vote, or 85% of those actually voting, have voted in favour. In respect of agreements entered into after that date, at least 80% of those entitled to vote must have voted in favour. If an employee is dismissed for not joining a trade union as required by the UMA, his dismissal will not be fair if the ballot was not held within five years of his dismissal.

See REASON FOR THE DISMISSAL – NON-MEMBERSHIP OF A TRADE UNION.

Union/non-union labour only contracts (EA 1982, s. 12). Any term in a contract shall be void in so far as it purports to require that the whole or part of the work shall be performed only by persons who are members or non-members of trade unions or any particular trade union. It is a tort of breach of statutory duty if, on grounds of union membership or non-membership, a person (a) fails to include a particular person's name on a list of approved suppliers of goods or services (b) terminates a contract for the supply of goods or services (c) excludes a person from tendering for the supply of goods or services (d) fails to permit a person to submit a tender, or (e) otherwise determines not to enter into a contract for the supply of goods or services. If any person uses pressure to induce another to incorporate into a contract a term which would be void as provided above, s. 13 of TULRA will not be a defence. If any person induces another to break a duty as provided above, again, s. 13 of TULRA will not provide a defence.

See TRADE UNION RECOGNITION REQUIREMENT; TRADE UNION IMMUNITIES.

Unreasonable conduct (EAT Rules 1980, r. 27). If proceedings are unnecessary, improper or vexatious, or there is unreasonable delay or other unreasonable conduct, the EAT may make an order of costs against the offending party. To launch an appeal against a decision of the industrial tribunal which has little prospect of success, and then to abandon it, could be unreasonable conduct (*J. & H. Smith Ltd v Smith* [1974] ICR 156), as is an appeal concerned purely with a point of fact, not law, which also cannot hope to succeed (*Dacres v Walls Meat Co Ltd* [1976] IRLR 20). To abandon an appeal just before the hearing, or not to turn up at the hearing, can also amount to unreasonable conduct (*Croyden v Greenham (Plant Hire) Ltd* [1978] ICR 415). To delay a hearing for a long time may amount to unreasonable delay (*Dacres v Walls Meat Co Ltd*, supra).

See APPEAL TO THE EMPLOYMENT APPEAL TRIBUNAL.

Unreasonably refuses that offer (EPCA, s. 82 (5)). To determine whether or not there was an unreasonable refusal of an offer of alternative employment (*qv*) it is permissible to take into account personal considerations affecting the employee (*Paton Calvert & Co Ltd v Westerside* [1979] IRLR 364), but not personal fads (*Fuller v Stephanie Bowman* [1977] IRLR 87). These factors may include loss of status or income (*Archibold v Rossleigh Commercial Ltd* [1975] IRLR 231), the lateness of the offer made (*Thos Wragg Ltd v Wood* [1976] ICR 313), the viability of the company which may bring fears of future redundancies (*Pilkington v Pickstone* [1966] 1 ITR 363) and so on.

See SUITABLE ALTERNATIVE EMPLOYMENT.

V

Variation of the contract. If there is an express term in a contract of employment which permits a variation in the terms or conditions, then this will be binding on the employee, and the change does not constitute a breach of contract by the employer (*Bex v Securicor Transport Ltd* [1972] IRLR 68). In the absence of such term, a variation amounts to a dismissal, though whether the dismissal is fair or unfair has to be determined in accordance with the usual principles. The test may be, what are the advantages to the employer of the proposed changes, and was it reasonable for him to terminate the old contract and offer a new one (*Chubb Fire Security Ltd v Harper* [1983] IRLR 311)?

If the variation is not accepted by the employee, but he continues to work in accordance with its terms, there must come a point in time when he will be deemed to have accepted it (*McNamara v National Coal Board* [1972] IRLR 69). If the employee accepts the change, the contract is varied, not terminated (*Grant v Shell Repairing Ltd* [1975] IRLR 150).

Consultation with an appropriate trade union is only one of the factors to consider in determining whether the employer acts reasonably (*qv*) in seeking to dismiss an employee who refuses to go along with a proposed variation. Other factors include (a) has the change been imposed unilaterally (b) has it been properly handled by a patient understanding of the employee's opposition (c) is the re-organisation sensible and in the interests of the firm and employees generally (d) have the employee's views been taken into account, and (e) is it possible to make an exception in the case of an individual, and not to force him into a collective arrangement (*Martin v Automobile Proprietary Ltd* [1979] IRLR 64)?

Vexatious or frivolous (Industrial Tribunals (Rules of Procedure) Regulations 1980). Vexatious implies doing something over and above that which is necessary for the disposal of the proceedings, and suggests the existence of some improper motive or a desire to cause embarrassment to the other party (*Marler Ltd v Robertson* [1974] ICR 72). Thus to pursue a second application without exhausting the legal remedies available on the first application (e.g. review or appeal) may be vexatious (*Acrow (Engineers) Ltd v Hathaway* [1981] ICR 510). Frivolous is to pursue a case in the knowledge that it is bound to fail, but to pursue it as 'a try on' (*Prajapati v Richard Thomas & Baldwin Ltd* [1966] ITR 564), in full knowledge that there is no substance in the claim (*Carr v Alan-Bradley Electronics Ltd* [1980] IRLR 263). To have an appeal rejected on the ground that there is no arguable point of law, and then to pursue a further appeal may be said to be frivolous (*Neefjes v Crystal Products Ltd* [1974] IRLR 63).

See UNREASONABLE CONDUCT; COSTS; FRIVOLOUS.

Victimised (RRA, s. 2 (1)). A person is victimised if he is treated less favourably than others are treated in like circumstances. Thus, if others would be treated in the same way, he cannot claim he has been victimised (*Kirby v Manpower Services Commission* [1980] IRLR 229).

See RACE RELATIONS ACT 1976.

Void (EPCA, s. 140). Any agreement shall be void in so far as it purports to preclude a person from bringing a complaint (*Council of Engineering Institutions v Maddison* [1977] ICR 30) or bringing any proceedings before an industrial tribunal (*Naqvi v Stephen Jewellers Ltd* [1978] ICR 631). An agreement made with a trade union which enabled a redundant employee to be redeployed is void in so far as it deprives him of his right to a trial period or to reject the offer of alternative employment (*qv*) (*Tocher v General Motors Scotland Ltd* [1981] IRLR 55). If an industrial tribunal makes a consent order which allows a complaint to be withdrawn on the basis of an agreement between the parties to settle the complaint, that order will be binding on them, and no further proceedings may be brought (*Times Newspaper Ltd v Fitt* [1981] ICR 637).

See CONCILIATION OFFICER.

Voluntary redundancy. Where an employee 'volunteers' to be made redundant, he is still dismissed for reason of redundancy, and hence is entitled to a redundancy payment (*Burton Allton & Johnson Ltd v Peck* [1975] IRLR 87).

See CONSENSUAL TERMINATION.

W

Wages (EPCA, s. 8 (a)). Tips, received from customers, are not wages, and therefore do not have to be included in the itemised pay statement (*Cofone v Spaghetti House Ltd* [1980] ICR 155).

Wages Councils Act 1979. In a number of industries, where trade union organisation is weak, Wages Councils have been set up to provide a framework for fixing wages and other terms and conditions of employment, which are then given statutory force. Currently, there are 42 Wages Councils in existence, and also the Agricultural Wages Board for England and Scotland. If the Secretary of State for Employment considers that there is no effective machinery for regulating wages in a particular industry, he may establish a Wages Council which will consist of an equal number of representatives of employers and employees, with the addition of not more than three independent members. The Council may make Orders concerning pay, holidays and other terms and conditions of employment, which then become the minimum terms and conditions for those employees covered by the order as an implied term of the contract. An aggrieved employee who claims that these terms and conditions are not met has a civil remedy against his employer in the county court, and additionally the Wages Inspectorate may institute criminal proceedings against the employer who defaults on the statutory obligations.

Currently, the Wages Councils are in operation in Great Britain for the following industries:

Aerated Waters (England and Wales)
Aerated Waters (Scotland)
Boot and Shoe Repairing
Button Manufacturing
Coffin Furniture and Cerement Making
Corset
Cotton Waste Reclamation
Dressmaking and Women's Light Clothing (England and Wales)
Dressmaking and Women's Light Clothing (Scotland)
Flax and Hemp
Fur
General Waste Material Reclamation
Hairdressing Undertakings
Hat, Cap and Millinery

> Lace Finishing
> Laundry
> Licensed Non-residential Establishment
> Licensed Residential Establishment and Licensed Restaurant
> Linen and Cotton Handkerchief and Household Goods and Linen Piece Goods
> Made-up Textiles
> Ostrich and Fancy Feather and Artificial Flower
> Perambulator and Invalid Carriage
> Pin, Hook and Eye and Snap Fastener
> Ready-made and Wholesale Bespoke Tailoring
> Retail Bespoke Tailoring (England and Wales)
> Retail Bespoke Tailoring (Scotland)
> Retail Bookselling and Stationery Trades
> Retail Bread and Flour Confectionery Trade (England and Wales)
> Retail Bread and Flour Confectionery Trade (Scotland)
> Retail Drapery, Outfitting and Footwear Trades
> Retail Food Trades (England and Wales)
> Retail Food Trades (Scotland)
> Retail Furnishing and Allied Trades
> Retail Newsagency, Tobacco and Confectionery Trades (England and Wales)
> Retail Newsagency, Tobacco and Confectionery Trades (Scotland)
> Rope, Twine and Net
> Rubber Proofed Garment Making Industry
> Sack and Bag
> Shirtmaking
> Toy Manufacturing
> Unlicensed Place of Refreshment
> Wholesale Mantle and Costume
> See STATUTORY JOINT INDUSTRIAL COUNCIL.

Want of prosecution (Industrial Tribunal (Rules of Procedure) Regulations 1980). Before an industrial tribunal can strike out an application for want of prosecution, an opportunity must be given to the applicant to show cause why such an order should not be made (*Kelly v Ingesoll-Rand Co Ltd* [1982] ICR 476).

Warning of impending dismissal. A dismissal can only take place if there is a specified or ascertainable date on which the contract will cease. Consequently, a warning that the employment will come to an end at some future but unascertained date is not a dismissal (*Haseltine Lake & Co v Dowler* [1981] ICR 222).

> See DISMISSAL.

Warnings. There is no rule of law that a warning should be given in every case before dismissal (*Hopper v Feedex Ltd* [1974] IRLR 99) for warnings are matters of substance, not procedure (*Dunning & Co (Shopfitters) Ltd v Jacomb* [1973] ICR 448). Thus, if an employee is so incompetent that a warning is unlikely to result in an improvement, no warning need be given (*Littlewood Stores Ltd v Egenti* [1976] ICR 516). Warnings need to be looked at as part of the whole picture (*Newall Insulation Ltd v Blakeman* [1976] ICR 543). Nor should an industrial tribunal sit in judgement on whether a final warning was justified. Sufficient that it was given in good faith and that there were *prime facie* grounds (*Stein v Associated Dairies* [1982] IRLR 447).

If it is alleged that a warning was given not with a view to improving an employee's conduct, but with the object of disheartening him, this could constitute a constructive dismissal (*qv*). Consequently, the industrial tribunal should investigate such allegations fully (*Walker v Josiah Wedgewood* [1978] IRLR 105). If it can be suggested that a warning was manifestly inappropriate, the industrial tribunal may take that factor into account (*Stein v Associated Dairies*, supra).

The procedural aspects of prior warnings should not cloud the main issue of whether or not the employer acted reasonably (*qv*) in treating the reason as a sufficient reason for dismissal (*Brown v Hall Advertising Ltd* [1978] IRLR 246).

Watching and besetting (Conspiracy and Protection of Property Act 1875, s. 7). *See* SIT-IN; PICKETING.

Week (EPCA, s. 49 (6)). Although a week normally ends with the usual pay day (or on a Saturday, see s. 153 (1)), this definition does not apply to the provisions relating to the giving of notice. Thus it would appear that notice may be given on any particular day within a week, and expire with the corresponding day in subsequent weeks. This appears also to be the situation if an employee is given a month's notice by virtue of his contract, unless the contract specifies that notice must be given at a particular time in the month.

Week's pay (EPCA, Sch. 14, Part II). A week's pay is the amount payable under the contract of employment, not the amount received by the employee. Thus, for redundancy payment purposes, the week's pay is the gross week's pay (*Secretary of State for Employment v John Woodrow & Sons (Builders) Ltd* [1983] ICR 582).

See REMUNERATION.

What particulars (EPCA, s. 11 (1)). The industrial tribunal must first ascertain whether a term has been agreed orally (or by necessary implication), or whether the term should be implied. The term may then be included in the written statement (*qv*). If particulars are given, but are incorrect, the industrial tribunal may alter them (*Mears v Safecar Security Ltd* [1982] IRLR 183).

Without reasonable justification (SDA, s. 65 (3)). If there is a delay before a recommendation can be implemented, the employer does not fail to comply without reasonable justification (*Nelson v Tyne & Wear Passenger Transport Executive* [1978] ICR 1183).

See SEX DISCRIMINATION ACT 1975.

Witness order. Before exercising their discretion to issue a witness order, the industrial tribunal should be satisfied (a) that the witness could give relevant evidence, and (b) it is necessary to issue the order because the witness would refuse to attend voluntarily (*Dada v Metal Box Co Ltd* [1974] ICR 559). A witness order may require the witness to bring with him documents (*Wilson v HGS Ltd* [1976] ITR 43).

Work (EPCA, Sch. 13, para. 9). Work means 'paid work' (*University of Aston v Malik* [1984] ICR 492).

See TEMPORARY CESSATION OF WORK.

Work of a particular kind (EPCA, s. 81 (2) (b)). This refers to the particular kind of work which the employee is required to do, with reference to skills, aptitude, knowledge etc. (*Amos v Max-Arc Ltd* [1973] ICR 46). It is the nature of the work, not the nature of the employee (*Kleboe v Ayr County Council* [1971] 7 ITR 201) which is relevant, although personal attributes may be relevant if they reflect on the employee's skill (*Wren v Wiltshire County Council* [1969] 4 ITR 251). A re-organisatuion which results in a reduction of overtime or a change in working hours (*Lesney Products Ltd v Nolan* [1977] ICR 235), or a change in the tasks performed, or the total hours worked, is not a redundancy unless there is a reduction in the number of employees needed to do that work (*Johnson v Notts Police Authority* [1974] ICR 170). But if a re-organisation leads to the creation of a new post which is different from that previously performed, an employee who has to be dismissed because he cannot perform that new job is dismissed because the requirements of the employer for work which was of a particular kind has ceased or diminished (*Robinson v British Island Airways* [1978] ICR 304). The work of a particular kind is the work the employee was doing at the time of the redundancy, and the fact that his contract enables the employer to do other work is not relevant (*Cowan v Haden Ltd* [1983] ICR 1).

See REDUNDANCY; REQUIREMENTS OF THAT BUSINESS; CEASED OR DIMINISHED.

Work permit. See FOREIGN EMPLOYEES.

Work rated as equivalent (EqPA 1970, s. 1 (5)). See JOB EVALUATION STUDY.

Work to rule. See OTHER INDUSTRIAL ACTION.

Worker (TULRA, s. 30). A worker can be a self-employed person (*Broadbent v Crisp* [1974] ICR 248), but not, apparently, authors and writers (*Writers Guild v BBC* [1974] ICR 234).

Workers' co-operative. If a workers' co-operative is registered as a limited company, it has a legal personality separate and distinct from its members, and is capable of employing and dismissing its workforce. Consequently, a dismissed member may bring a claim for unfair dismissal. If it is not so registered, it may still have some form of legal personality, or have members who are capable of giving and being given instructions, and the whole body could employ and dismiss (*Drym Fabricators Ltd v Johnson* [1981] ICR 274).

Working hours (EPCA, s. 58 (2)). These are the hours when the employee is actually being required to work. The fact that the employee is on the employer's premises, and being paid whilst being there, but not actually working, e.g. during a tea break, and seeks to carry on trade union activities, does not mean that those activities are being carried on during working hours (*Zucker v Astrid Jewels Ltd* [1978] ICR 1088).

See ACTIVITIES OF AN INDEPENDENT TRADE UNION; APPROPRIATE TIME.

Workless day (EPCA, s. 12). A workless day is the whole of a day in which the employee would be required to work in accordance with his contract of employment, and on which he is not provided with work by his employer by reason of (a) a diminution in the requirements of the employer's business for work of a kind which the employee is employed to do, or (b) any other occurrence affecting the normal working of the employer's business in relation to work of the kind which the employee is employed to do.

If an employer has an arrangement that employees may work during the holiday period, but fails to provide such work, the holiday period does not consist of workless days, for they are not days when the employee is normally required to work (*York v Colledge Hosiery Co Ltd* [1978] IRLR 53). If the employee's contract has been altered so that the number of working days in the week is reduced, there is no right to guarantee pay in respect of the days no longer worked (*Clemens v Peter Richards Ltd* [1978] IRLR 332).

See GUARANTEE PAY; OCCURRENCE.

Works rules. These are non-contractual unilateral instructions laid down by the employer (*Secretary of State for Employment v ASLEF* [1972] ICR 19) although they may have contractual force if they are incorporated into the individual contract of employment (*Dal v Orr* [1980] IRLR 413). The rules must be promulgated (*Rigden-Murphy v Securicor Ltd* [1976] IRLR 106) reasonable (*Richards v Bulpitt & Sons Ltd* [1975] IRLR 134) and enforced consistently, otherwise a discretion sets in which may be difficult to justify (*Frame v McLean & Graham Ltd* [1974] IRLR 179). If the violation of a particular rule will lead to summary dismissal (*qv*), this fact should be spelt out clearly, but there is no principle which requires that a breach of a rule will inevitably lead to a dismissal (*Elliott Bros v Colverd* [1979] IRLR 92).

The fact that a dismissal is mandatory under the works rule in question does not necessarily mean that it will always be fair to dismiss, for the test is whether the employer has acted reasonably (*qv*). Thus, a trivial or minor breach of the rules is not necessarily a fair reason for dismissal (*Ladbroke Racing Ltd v Arnott* [1979] IRLR 192).

Written statement (EPCA, s. 1 (1)). Within 13 weeks from the commencement of employment, every employee is entitled to receive a written statement containing the following information:

(a) the names of the parties,

(b) date when the employment began,

(c) date when continuous employment began (taking into account any employment with a previous employer),

(d) the scale or rate of remuneration, or method of calculating the remuneration,

(e) the intervals at which remuneration is paid,

(f) any terms and conditions relating to hours of work,

(g) any terms and conditions relating to entitlement to holidays (including public holidays) and holiday pay and accrued holiday pay, sick pay and pension schemes,

(h) the length of notice the employee must give and is entitled to receive,

(i) the title of the job which the employee is employed to do,

(j) whether a contracting out certificate is in force in respect of the State Pension Scheme.

It is sufficient if the employer refers the employee to some document which he has a reasonable opportunity of reading in the course of his employment or is made reasonably accessible to him in some other way.

The statement should also contain a note

(a) specifying any disciplinary rules applicable to the employee (or referring to a document which specifies such rules,

(b) specifying by name or by description the person to whom he can apply if he feels dissatisfied with any disciplinary decision,

(c) explain the steps for such an application or referring to a document which explains the procedure.

The written statement given under s. 1 is not the contract betweeen the parties (*Robertson v British Gas Corpn* [1983] IRLR 302) although its terms may be strong *prima facie* evidence of what are the terms of the contract. Even if an employee signs it, he is merely acknowledging its receipt, not its accuracy (*System Floors (UK) Ltd v Daniels* [1982] ICR 54). Nor does the fact that the employee does not object to a unilateral variation of terms and conditions which are contained in the written statement imply that he consents to that change, particularly if they are not intended to take effect immediately (*Jones v Associated Tunnelling Co Ltd* [1981] IRLR 477).

The employer must give some document which either informs the employee of the terms and conditions of employment or refers to a document which contains those terms (*Green v Moyses Stevens Ltd* [1974] IRLR 274). If he fails to do so, or if a statement is given which is not accurate, an application may be made to an industrial tribunal for a determination as to what particulars ought to be so included, but this does not empower the industrial tribunal to re-write the contract (*CITB v Leighton* [1978] IRLR 60).

Written statement of reasons for dismissal (EPCA, s. 53). If an employee is dismissed with or without notice, or if a fixed term contract expires without being renewed, he is entitled to be given, on request, within 14 days, a written statement giving particulars of the reason for his dismissal. This right applies to employees who have been continuously employed for a period of six months or more, but note that the provisions of s. 55 (5) may operate to 'pull him past the post' (*see* MINIMUM PERIODS OF NOTICE). A complaint may be made to an industrial tribunal that the employer has unreasonably refused to provide such a statement, or that the particulars in such a statement are inadequate or untrue, and if the complaint is well-founded, the industrial tribunal may make a declaration as to what were the reasons for the dismissal, and shall award the employee two weeks pay (not subject to the statutory limits). The complaint must be presented within the statutory time limit of three months.

The employer must provide the statement within 14 days of the request (*Keen v Dymo Ltd* [1977] IRLR 118) but if he can produce a convincing explanation why it was provided outside that period, it may be that he did not unreasonably refuse to provide the statement (*Lowson v Percy Main etc. Social Club Ltd* [1979] IRLR 227). The statement must disclose the reasons for the dismissal in such a way that anyone reading it will know without reference to any other document the reason why the applicant was dismissed (*Horsley Smith & Sherry Ltd v Dutton* [1977] IRLR 172). Thus, a reply which refers to an earlier document does not satisfy the requirements of s. 53 (*Gilham v Kent County Council* [1983] IRLR 353). But there is no unreasonable refusal to provide the statement if the employer believes that the employee was not dismissed (*Broomsgove v Eagle Alexander Ltd* [1981] IRLR 127).

The written statement of the reasons for dismissal is admissible in industrial tribunal proceedings.

Wrongful dismissal. An employee who is dismissed without notice, or with less notice than he is entitled by virtue of his contract or by statute (whichever is the greater period) may bring an action for wrongful dismissal. The remedy is only available in the High Court or county court, not in an industrial tribunal (*Treganowan v Robert Knee & Co Ltd* [1975] ICR 405). The question as to whether the dismissal was wrongful has no direct bearing on whether the dismissal was fair or unfair.

See SUMMARY DISMISSAL.

Y

Youth Training Scheme. This scheme is operated by the Manpower Services Commission to provide a year's training and planned work experience for school-leavers. Mode 'A' of the scheme places them with public or private employers, while Mode 'B' places them with community projects or training workshops.

It is generally thought that there is no contractual relationship between the trainee and the employer, and certainly no contract of employment arises (*Daley v Allied Suppliers Ltd* [1983] ICR 90). Consequently, the trainee has none of the employment protection rights generally, and the period of training does not count towards continuity of employment should the trainee be subsequently taken on in employment. The scheme itself does provide for some rights, e.g. full allowance for four week's sickness, the right to join a trade union, reasonable time off work to attend for interviews. Additionally, by the Health and Safety (Youth Training Scheme) Regulations 1983 the definition of 'work' and 'at work' is extended to include those on training schemes, and thus the protection conferred by the Health and Safety at Work etc. Act 1974 is extended to cover youth trainees.